AF553461

New Dimensions in Indian Banking Sector

by

Dr. Asha Kadam-Pendhari

First Published 2019

ISBN 978-93-87537-15-6

Published by:
CRESCENT PUBLISHING CORPORATION
4806/24, Mathur Lane,
Ansari Road, Darya Ganj,
New Delhi - 110 002
Ph.: 011 - 23244131
Mob.:+ 91 - 9711991838, 9999021668
E-mail:crescentbook@gmail.com
Website:www.crescentpublishingcorp.weebly.com

Preface

Banking of all the nations has traditionally built on the branch banking model of that nation. The unparalleled speed of technological changes over the last two decades has changed the way of banking into E-banking which has been done over centuries. Technology has offered tremendous opportunities to banks to cover geographical, commercial and demographic barriers and to deliver products and services at virtually zero marginal cost combined with boundless reach.

The success of a bank is now determined by its ability to deliver innovative products and services and to prove remote access in a technologically advanced way that meets the changing needs of the customers. We now have a variety of delivery channels from ATMs and the Internet banking to Mobile banking which are collectively termed as E-banking i.e. Electronic banking.

However this has carried risks as well as benefits. Some of the traditional risks associated with banking activities such as strategic risks, operational risks, legal risks and reputational risks etc. All these banking risks have been modified and heightened for banks providing e-banking services. This has influenced the overall risk profile of banking sector. Now it has become more critical for banks to have flexible and responsive operating processes, as well as sound and robust risk management systems that recognize, address and manage all the above risks in a prudent manner according to the basic characteristics and challenges of e-banking services.

Risk management is not a new concept or challenge for banks. Banks have traditionally adopted risk mitigation measures, but the focus has generally been on financial risks such as credit, market, interest rates and liquidity. Non-financial risks such as strategic, operational, compliance and reputational risks have received only as swift treatment, more as a need to meet legal and regulatory requirements.

This book has pioneering efforts to provide a conceptual framework for the management of risks in an e-banking environment, supplemented by an overview of sound practices based on international standards and guidelines on risk management.

I would like to express my gratitude to the almighty and my master for being graceful without which this study would not have been completed.

To ***Dr. V.G.Mamde***, my guide, for his constant support, ***Shri Govindraoji Holkar***, Secretary, NVP Mandal's Arts, Commerce & Science College, Lasalgaon

I am thankful to my husband ***Shri Prabhakar Pendhari***, and all my parents, my spouse (Jidnyasa and Omkar) and all my colleagues whose patience and love helped me sail through the good and bad times and reach ultimate completion.

Lastly, I would like to give my heartfelt thanks to the Cresent Publication, New Delhi for their valuable support in the realization of my dream by publishing this book.

Dr. Asha Kadam-Pendhari

Contents

Chapter 1 Introduction and Research Methodology

Chapter 2 Review of Literature

Chapter 3 Socio-Economic Profile of Study Area

Chapter 4 E-Banking services: A Theoretical Framework

Chapter 5 Business Analysis of Banks

Chapter 6 Management of Customer Services with E-Banking

Chapter 7 Findings and Recommendations

List of Tables

List of Graphs

Introduction and Research Methodology

1.1 Introduction

Cooperation is one of the most important pillars in the development of the nation and the progress of nation is impossible without the cooperation. But after introduction of NER it becomes difficult to cooperative sector banks to survive in banking sector without the support of information and communication technology. ICT is the bye-product of IT sector but due its features of speed, accuracy, efficiency, cost reduction and competitive advancements, it is essential for all types of banks to adopt it and to provide techno-based self-enabled services to its customers. Private sector banks are leading in the business strategy with the help of technology that they are profit oriented but today it is necessity of all banks to adopt this technology as a business strategy. Cooperative sector banks are service oriented and also have greater impact of management that resulted into slow adoption and development of banks; thus the researcher tried to show the present scenario of cooperative banking.

The researcher classified this chapter between two parts: first is of Introduction and second is of Research Methodology. The first part of Introduction started with Co-operative movement resulted in establishment and development of Co-operative Banks, and ends with new avenues in banking sector. The second part of this chapter included to Research Methodology which included problem statement of the research work with objectives of the research study, hypotheses of the study, justification of study, scope of the study and limitations of the study, research samples, sampling methods, statistical methods, etc. In this research the researcher focused on working terms of banking technologies that customers independently use for banking transactions without any interaction with bank employees and present scenario of E-banking services in co-operative banks in Nashik district.

1.2 Emergence of Co-operative Movement

In England, Robert Owen (1771-1858) has given an idea of 'self-help through mutual help' to control the exploitation of the society. During the industrial revolution, this idea had given direction to the persons belongs from the class of exploitation. From that period, there has been always struggle for fairness, justice, freedom and equality. In 1844, 'The Rochdale Equitable Pioneers Society' was registered and established for world-wide self-help movement. These societies were competed effectively with economically more powerful money-lenders and traders.

The origin of cooperative movement was raised due to situation of crisis, exploitation and sufferings. According to Rochdale Pioneers, 'social and economic progress is impossible without cooperation[1]'. On this basis Robo bank (Netherland) and D.G. Bank (Germany) were established. Today there is no any country which is not covered with cooperative sector and there was no area of economic activity where co-operative principles have not yet registered a mark.

1.2.1 Cooperative Movement in India

Cooperative movement in India is one of the largest movements in the world that it has been in existence for over a century and which has made tremendous progress in every aspects of the Indian economy. According to many critics, 'the movement is an utter failure and should be scrapped and the movement has done nothing to abolish poverty of the rural masses nor has to contribute to increase agricultural production, to establish better marketing conditions, better living, etc'. It has to reduce and to eliminate the rapacious money-lender from the rural area. The utter insignificance of the co-operative movement was indicated by the fact that in 1954 (exactly after 50 years of its existence) the co-operative institutions supplied just 3 % of the farmers. The All-India Rural Credit Survey Committee (1954) stated: "Co-operation has failed, but co-operation must succeed." Since then, Government and the Reserve bank have taken active interest and thus the cooperative movement has made great progress. The progress in the last four decades is much more than the progress which was achieved in the first 50 years of its emergence[2].

1.2.2 Co-operative Movement in Maharashtra

In Maharashtra, cooperative sector become an important weapon for solving various problems of farmers, such as lack of availability of credit for small farmers, heavy burden of money lenders, inability to repay debts due to crop loss, high rate of interest charged by the money lenders, rising cost of cultivation, etc[3]. All the above mentioned causes are resulted in poor performance of the agricultural sector, decreasing standard of living of farmers, affects on social and economic development of state and nation and finally also affects economic growth of the nation. Central and State Government, both have identified the importance of the cooperative sector for development of rural areas, empowerment of people and for implementation of poverty alleviation programme. Maharashtra has good political, historical, social and cultural heritage. In Western Maharashtra, the leader from Pune, Mumbai and Ahmednagar districts initiated social reforms. As a result, the first Pravara Sugar Cooperative Factory limited is established in 1949, and is also working successfully[4].

1.3 Cooperative Banking and Commercial Banking

Since 1954, the co-operative credit societies are meeting increasingly the requirements of farmers. More than 60 percent of the credit needs of farmers were met by the cooperative societies. The monopoly of the money lenders, landlords were broken in the villages. Today cooperative sector covered 100 % villages and 75 % rural households and functioning over 545 thousand cooperatives at various levels[5]. Thus cooperative banks have been recognized as an effective tool for the economic development and for improvement in the socio-economic condition of the nation.

Table 1.1

Classification Between Cooperative Banks and Commercial Banks

Cooperative banks	Commercial banks
A) Registration	
These banks are registered under the Cooperative Societies Act. Their main regulator is the State Government or Central Government if the working is in more than one State.	These banks are registered under the Banking Regulation Act/Companies Act and are regulated by RBI.
B) Management	
The organizational structure and management set up is based on cooperative principles.	The organizational structure and management set up is based on RBI.
C) Size of Banks	
The size of assets/liabilities of these banks is much smaller than commercial banks.	The size of assets/liabilities of these banks is larger than cooperative banks.
D) Principle of Banks	
These banks are operating on 'no profit no loss' principle of cooperation and it is mandatory to transfer 25 % profit to Reserves and Surplus a/c	These banks are operating with 'profit motive' and it is mandatory to balance their profit objective with 40 % of their net bank credit.

E) Financing Pattern	
Rural cooperative banks are financing to agriculturists and Urban cooperative banks are financing to tiny units, artisans and small size of trade and commerce.	These banks are financing to PSL i.e. agriculture, SSI, small business units, exporters, individual housing, education and for GoI sponsored schemes.

Objectives of Co-operative Banks

The cooperative banks has been moved towards rural areas for overcoming the problems and providing the capital required through short term and long term borrowings at a reasonable rate of interest. Due to these efforts of co-operative banks made an attempt to bring about unorganized and organized parts of the Indian financial system.[6] According to Dr. Mathur (1975), Co-operation is as a form of organization, where in persons, voluntarily associate together as a human beings on a basis of equality for the promotion of the economy with their own interest. According to this, the objectives of Cooperative banks are as follows[7]:

1. The cooperative banking sector is the first government sponsored, supported and subsidized financial agency in India.
2. The main theme is serving on the basis of 'no profit and no loss.'
3. The cooperative banks have a three tier linkage structure and straight line integration, i.e. RCBs (working in villages and in rural areas), DCCBs (working on district level) and SCBs (working at state level as a mediator between DCCB and RBI).
4. The borrowings are made from RBI, NABARD and other APEX Institutions.
5. They are subject to monitory policy control and earlier their regulations were controlled by RBI, but now their control has been mostly deregulated.

1.4 Regulatory Framework of Cooperative Banking

Under the guidance of Dr. Kavthekar V.L., mutual aid society was formed in Baroda State in 1889. Madras government took initiatives at first and deputed Sir Fredrick Nicholson in 1892. His reports were published in 1895 and 1897 which focused on starting of Rural Credit Cooperative Banks[8].

1.4.1 Cooperative Act, 1904

Cooperative Credit Societies act was passed in 1904 by Imperial Legislative Council. Before that cooperative societies were registered under the Cooperative Societies Act of 1860 or Indian Companies Act 1882. The act of 1904 was provided for the constitution and control of the Cooperative Credit Societies and special stress given for the development of rural areas. The main objective of this act was to encourage thrift, self-help and cooperation amongst agriculturists, artisans and persons of limited means.

1.4.2 Cooperative Act, 1912

A faster rapid growth in terms of number and activities of the cooperative societies were observed between 1906 and 1911. The act of 1904 was found insufficient to face the expanding activities because there was no provision for Central and non-credit societies. Thus new act was passed in 1912 to cover the defects of the act of 1904. This act supplemented to the act of 1904 by granting legal status to productive and distributive societies and to different forms of Central organizations. This act also differentiates rural and urban societies. As a result, the number of societies, their membership and the amount of working capital increased steadily and various new types of societies were registered i.e. marketing societies, producing societies, central banks etc.

1.4.3 Reform Act, 1919

In October 1914, the Maclagan Committee was appointed to assess the progress of the cooperative movement and the committee submitted its report in 1915. This committee noted warning on hurried expansion of the movement and recommended that the proper care should be taken for the formation of a society. It focused the moral side of the movement, emphasizing the need of audit and supervision of the cooperative departments.

According to these recommendations, Constitutional Reforms Act was passed in 1919 under the charge of a Minister in each province and much remarkable progress was achieved by several provinces as per their suitability. Some provincial governments passed their own act to facilitate multi-sided developments.

1.4.4 Banking Companies Regulation Act, 1949

After introducing this act, Cooperative Banks were managed and governed by the State Government under the provision of respective Cooperative Societies Act and Banking Companies Regulation Act, 1949. This act come into force for Cooperative Societies from March 1966 but the powers regarding establishment, incorporation and management of banks continued in the Registrar of Cooperative Societies and the Banking Companies Regulation act 1949 vested the RBI with various statutory powers and supervision over the cooperative banks. With this cooperative banks particularly UCB were organized under dual control of RBI and respective State Government.

This Banking Companies Regulation Act, 1949 has been amended in 1983 (Bank Laws Amendment Act) and in 1991 (Banking Regulation Amendment Act). Banking Regulatory Act 1949 empowers the RBI to regulate and supervise the banking related matters[9]. The applicability of banking laws to cooperative banks resulted in duality of control between the RBI and Registrar of Cooperative Societies/Central Registrar of Cooperative Societies.

Table 1.2

Establishment of Cooperative Societies Act in different States of India

State/Area	Name of Cooperative Society	Year of Act
Bombay	Cooperative Societies Act	1925
Madras	Cooperative Societies Act	1932
Bihar	Cooperative Societies Act	1935
Orissa	Cooperative Societies Act	1935
West Bengal	Cooperative Societies Act	1940
Tripura	Cooperative Societies Act	1948
Punjab	Cooperative Societies Act	1953
Himachal Pradesh	Cooperative Societies Act	1956
Jammu & Kashmir	Cooperative Societies Act	1956

1.5 Structure of Cooperative Banking

Co-operation is a state level subject thus each state has its separate 'Co-operative Societies Act', as Maharashtra State Co-operative Societies Act, 1961, regulating the working of the co-operative movement in Maharashtra. Mainly development of agriculture and allied sectors is the motto of cooperative credit structure in Maharashtra State Economy[10].

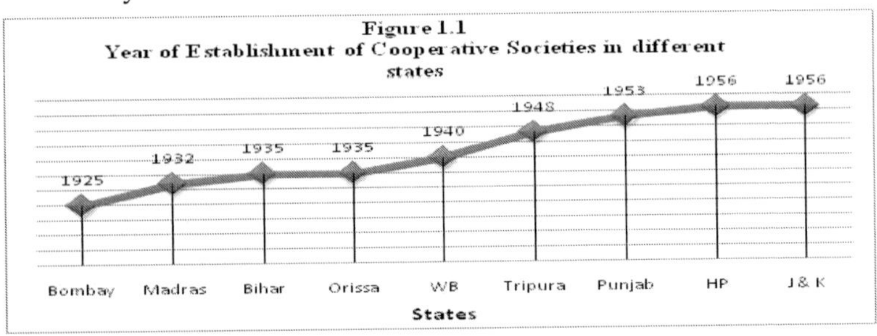

Figure 1.1
Year of Establishment of Cooperative Societies in different states

Figure 1.2

Co-operative Credit Structure

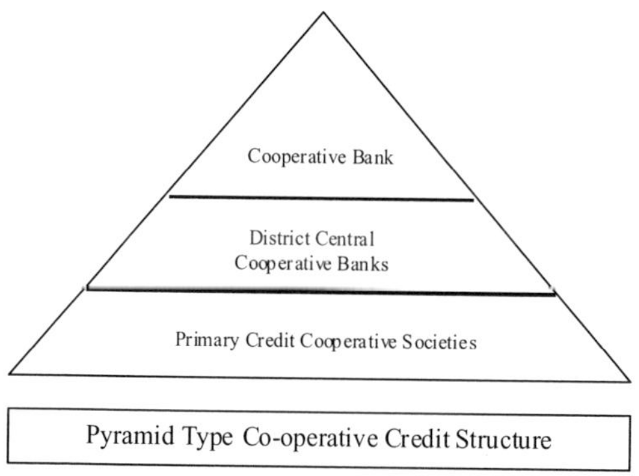

Pyramid Type Co-operative Credit Structure

Figure 1.2 indicates the structure of Cooperative Credit Societies with its working areas and it is realized that;

Cooperative credit society's form the base on which the entire structure of the cooperative credit organization is based. The cooperative credit structure in India consists of two parts; one part which is engaged in short and medium term credit and the other in long-term credit[11]. From the pyramid structure diagram given below, it is seen that the cooperative credit societies have a sound structure in the credit sector. In India, there are three tier structures of Cooperative Credit Societies and Cooperative banks[12];

a. Apex Bank at state level which is serving to the entire state.

b. District Central Cooperative banks- district level.

c. The Primary Agricultural Cooperative Credit Societies- village level

1.5.1 Apex/State Cooperative Banks:

The Apex Bank or State Cooperative Bank of each state is linked with RBI which provides financial assistance to cooperative credit structure. It finances, controls and regulates the working of DCCBs in each state. The State Cooperative Banks are helping the cooperative credit movement, promoting other cooperative ventures and extending the principles of cooperation. All apex banks have been given the statues of a 'Scheduled Bank'. It acts as a link between DCCBs and RBI from which State Cooperative Banks get finance.

The main feature of State Cooperative Banks are to serve as the balancing center in the state, organize provision of credit for credit worthy farmers, carry out banking business and leads the cooperative movement as a leader of the cooperatives in the state. The main source of working capital is the share capital, reserve funds, deposits from members, borrowing from the RBI. For healthy performance of the banks it is necessary to keep minimum level of percentage of over dues of loans. Therefore, growth rate showed that the progress achieved during the period is fluctuated.

1.5.2 District Central Co-operative Banks:

District Central Co-operative Banks are known as linkage between Apex bank and primary societies. These are federations of primary credit societies in a specified area, normally spreads all over a district. The membership of these banks is given to individuals and the societies. These individuals provide finance and management. Board of Directors is elected for particular period for working and for looking after the management and supervision. The central co-operative banks raise the necessary funds from share capital, deposits from public and borrowing from the State Cooperative bank. The Central banks provide financial assistance for short-term period and for medium term period as loans to the primary societies. The Co-operative Societies Act of 1912 was made immediate result that central cooperative banks are increased in huge quantity in the whole nation. The major objective of central co-operative bank has been to provide advance loans to the primary co-operative societies in time of need so that they can fulfill the requirements of farmers. Central Co-operative banks are working as balancing centre in the district as a central financing agency, carry out banking business and organize and sanction credit to primary co-operative societies, monitor and control implementation of policies.

1.5.3 Urban Co-operative Banks

During the year 1912, there were very few cooperative banks working in the country, such as Non-Agricultural Credit Societies, Urban Co-operative Banks, Employees Credit Societies and other societies. But till the year 1912 (The cooperative societies act has passed), the progress of cooperative sector was not satisfactory. But after then they made good progress. Even after the First World-War, their progress did not slowed down. In the period of depression, the urban credit movement was not much affected. Because the incomes of banks in urban areas were comparatively more than rural areas, and it was found that they were commanding larger resources and better management. During the Second World-War these organizations made further progress. Their membership and income increased and they were able to secure good deposits. Thus they have surplus resources with them which were invested in Govt. securities.

During this period, these units in certain states also worked as Government agencies for the distribution of controlled commodities. Such co-operatives have made rapid progress since independence. "Urban Credit Societies and Banks are the most popular examples of the progress of co-operative movement in India, and they also recover the drawbacks of banking sector in the absence of joint stock banking facilities provided in smaller towns. They also capture valuable place among the agencies by providing credit needs of people living in urban areas. They provide advances and loans mostly to small traders, artisans and salary earned on personal security as well as against gold, silver and produce".

In short, at the top of the pyramid Apex/state Cooperative Bank is working at state level and Primary Credit

Cooperative societies are working at bottom level and in between District Central Cooperative banks are working. In village when any member needs financial assistance, he has to apply at society. If the society has no funds for disposal of loan, it applies at District Central Co-operative Bank and if the DCCB has no funds, it applies at the Apex/ State Bank. Thus it is seen that all are linked with one another and functioning effectively. It means the strength of the chain depends upon the strength of each of the linked units.

Figure 1.3

Structure of Co-operative Credit Institutions (as on 31st March 2009)13

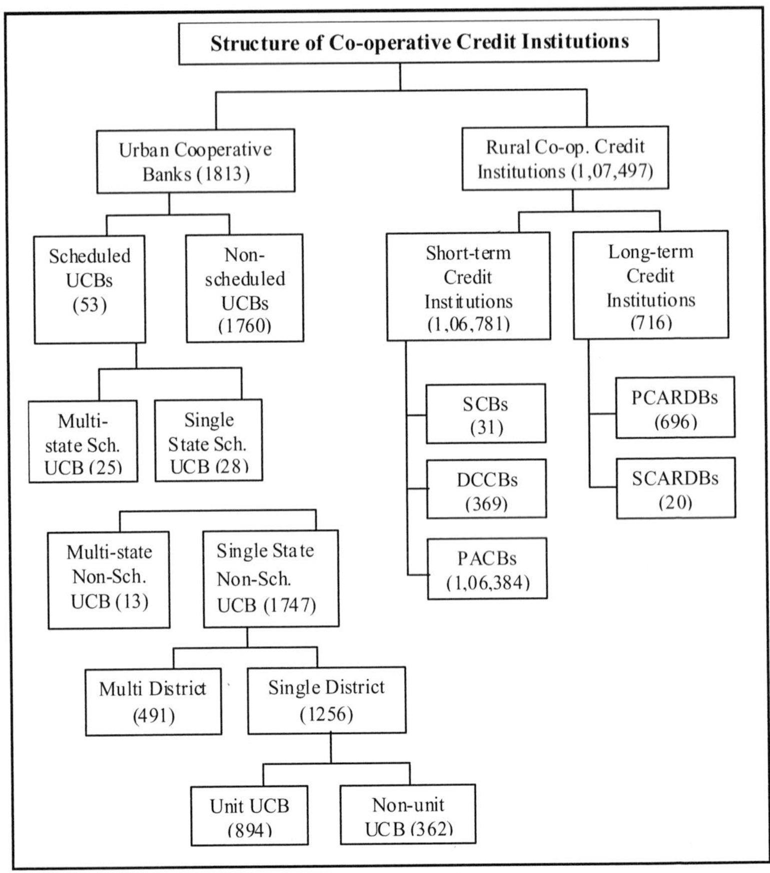

1.6 Management of Cooperative Banking

The management structure of the cooperative banks composed as under[14]

A. General Body consisting of general members.

B. The elected Board of Directors.

C. The Chairman of the Board

A. General Body consisting of general members: The supreme authority of cooperative banks vested in the general body which makes the bye-laws of the bank, elects the board of directors, and takes all decisions by majority of votes. It consists of all those shareholders who are eligible to vote at the general meeting of the society. This general body is the medium through which the members may control over the management of bank. General meeting is a platform where anyone can express their views and share their thoughts with discussion and criticism.

B. The elected Board of Directors: The management of Cooperative banks vests into board of directors who is elected by general body consisting of all members. Boards of Directors are representatives of the members, discharge the responsibilities entrusted to them. Members exercise control upon the board and in turn the later exercise control on behalf of the members over the management consisting of executive officials and paid staff. The directors are appointed in the general meeting of the members. The tenure of the board of directors are varies from state to state such as; Electing for each year, once in three years or each year by rotating one third of the members of the board.

C. The Chairman of the Board: Chairman of the cooperative banks is an individual office bearer has a special importance and placement in the organization. He regulates the discussions in the meetings of the Board of directors and controls the deliberations in a manner facilitating arriving at decisions. He is the leader of Board of directors and always in touch with the management. The Chairman presides over all the meetings of the board and also over the AGM and SGM. In case of equality of votes in the Board meeting, the chairman is authorized to exercise his 'Casting vote'.

1.7 Development of Cooperative Banking

After 63 years of independence, it is realized that the growth of the Indian economy is very slow. As a solution and for rapid economic development, it is necessary to accept a mixed economy as an economic system for the balanced growth of public and private sector together with a major role for cooperative societies to contribute for the progress of the Indian economy. In globalised era, it becomes necessary for developing countries like India to devote greater attention towards rural development. After the introduction of NER and adoption of NEP, fundamental changes have taken place. The major objectives of NEP are to impart a new element of dynamism to agriculture, trade and industry, to encourage foreign investment and technologies for making Indian products competitive in the international market to improve the performance of public undertaking and to influence cooperative sector[15].

The success of co-operative banks depends upon the activities performed in the fields of production, finance, marketing, distribution, construction, etc. Co-operatives are mainly organized and administered by those persons who have better qualification and the necessary experience needed for job. Due to the absence or experience and better qualification, many co-operative units are failed and the development through co-operation remains closed[16]. With efficient management, proper educational qualification of workers and training is also important than the resources and business experiences. The co-operative society is a democratic body and thus each member of this society is equally important.

1.7.1 Major events in the history of Cooperative banks in various Five Year Plans

After India attained Independence on 15th August, 1947, cooperatives assumed a great significance in poverty removal and faster socio-economic growth. With the advent of the planning process, cooperatives became an integral part of the Five Year Plans. As a result, they emerged as a distinct segment in our national economy. Before launching a Five Year Plan, it was specifically stated that the success of the Plan would be judged, among other things, by the extent it was implemented through cooperative organizations[17].

Following table 1.3 shows Government initiatives and the major events in the history of cooperative societies in different five year plans.

Table 1.3

Major events in the History of Cooperative Sector

First Plan	Recommended for training of personnel's and setting up of Co-operative Marketing Societies
Second Plan	Laid down proposals for extending co-operative activities with special emphasis on the warehousing at the State and Central level.
Third Plan	Brought new areas under Co operative societies and established cooperative training College at Pune and many regional centers to train the workers for the fields of sugarcane, cotton, spinning, milk
Fourth Plan	Introduced new programmed for high yielding crops by organizing different credit societies to serve these programmers
Fifth Plan	Special provisions for improvement of Central Banks and also recommended for establishment of Farmer's Service Societies

Sixth Plan	Introduced a point programme for co-operative societies and aimed at transforming the primary village societies to multipurpose societies; a. To reconstruct the policies for economic development of nation. b. To extend co-operative activities in various fields of food processing, poultry farming, dairy farming, fishery, etc. c. To give necessary training and guidance for developing skills in the efficient personnel's.
Seventh Plan	Focused on growth and expansion of co operative societies to ensure public participation to achieve its main objectives of social justice, employment and poverty alleviation.
Eighth plan	For the emergence of national federations of cooperative societies needed a comprehensive Central legislation to consolidate and governing the laws. The Multi-State Cooperative Societies Act, 1984 was enacted by Parliament under Entry No. 44 of the Union List of the Constitution of India. The All-India Rural Credit Survey Committee Report, 1954 recommended an integrated approach and emphasized the need for viable credit cooperative societies by expanding their area of operation, encouraging rural savings and diversifying business. The Committee also recommended for Government participation in the share capital of the cooperatives.
Ninth plan	Cooperative has been operating in the economic areas such as credit, production, processing, marketing, input distribution,

	housing, dairying and textiles. In some of the areas of their activities like dairying, urban banking and housing, sugar and handlooms, the cooperatives have achieved success to an extent but there are larger areas where they have not been so successful.
Tenth plan	Cooperative banks has been worked in banking sector preferentially with the shifting of commercial banks to hi-tech borrowers and big accounts on cost considerations in the present era of liberalization, the only avenue available for rural people is the cooperative. Only 9.9% (518) Co-operative banks have to meet their credit requirements. So cooperatives will have to concentrate their attention at cost reduction and diversification of their activities. The primary level cooperative credit institutions at village level should be made healthy for effective delivery of credit. To achieve these objectives, the cooperative banks functioning in the rural areas have to be revitalized and their financial health has to be improved.[18]
Eleventh plan	Cooperative banks focus on the inclusive growth of cooperative sector through concentrating on the non-farm sector activities with special reference to generation of employment and alternative sources of income. The cooperative banks have to keep the parameters of deposits and advanced provided for various economic activities and programs. New areas of demand for advances shall be explored, so that sustainability in the level of flow of credit can be maintained. This sector

	performs the vital functions of enabling productivity and income growth in the economy as a whole, and has an equally important part to play in making this growth more inclusive. The sector has to be enabled to attain an increasing level of sophistication so as to meet the requirements of globalization.[19]

Twelfth Plan (Maharashtra) Strategies of Cooperative Development

This projected level of credit appears feasible in view of the Eleventh Plan achievement. Many issues continue to confront agricultural credit, particularly in the area of financial inclusion necessary for ensuring inclusive growth. On these issues, the working group has pointed to the need for more objective assessment of credit requirements for direct and indirect financing of agriculture and also to redefine the priority lending sectors. It has suggested updating of banking services with priority to intensive use of ICT applications to track the flow of credit and transmission losses, with reference to financial inclusion. Some ongoing and emerging changes appear to hold promise of triggering off better financial inclusion for banking activities[20];

1. The CB Platform provides seamless connectivity with the telecom infrastructure and brings a new architecture to access financial services.
2. The CB model, together with mobile phones, can along with post offices provide significant last mile connectivity.
3. Mandating payments through advanced channels are helping to reach financial services to those so far not reached such as wages under the National Rural Employment Guarantee Act, pension dues, etc.

4. The enormous economies of scale generated by SHG Federations (each of 150–200 SHGs) is enabling banks to give larger loans for housing and health facilities for their members. A variety of insurance services are also being made available, including life, health, livestock and weather insurance.
5. The UID project of the GoI with biometric identity may facilitate easier opening of bank accounts, although this has yet to happen.

1.7.2 Challenges faced by Cooperative Banks in India[21]:

1. The challenges regarding laws need the proper application of the acts of 1966 of co-operative banks but not effectively implemented.
2. The political parties interfere in cooperative bank laws changes.
3. The loan recovery is not proper adequate by cooperative bank laws systems.
4. These banks are mainly depends upon capital of Government than the contribution of shareholders.
5. The workers participation in the working is much lesser than expected.
6. It is seen that dual control of RBI and Registrar of Cooperatives societies is creating a lot of confusion in the working of Scheduled Co-operative Banks.
7. The NPA of the co-operative banks are higher than commercial banks.
8. Cooperative banks are facing infrastructural weakness and structural laws.
9. Cooperative banks have limited ability to mobilize resources.
10. These banks incurred high cost of transactions.
11. The SCBs are not able to formulate their respective policy for investment of their surplus resources due to certain restrictions.

12. Prior approval of RBI is mandatory for opening of new branches of SCBs. The SCBs are required to submit the proposal for opening of new branches through NABARD whose recommendations are mandatory.

1.8 Importance of Cooperative Banking

The cooperative banking system forms an integral part of the Indian financial system. It includes UCBs (single-tier structure-primary cooperative banks) and RCBs (two or three tier structure). [22] Both the bank units are playing vital role by helping to the units which have weaknesses, lack of sound corporate governance, unethical lending, high level of NPA and inability to operate in a liberalized environment are either liquidated or merged with other banks. These banks operate mainly for the development of rural area.

Cooperative banks are chiefly responsible for breaking the monopoly of money lenders in providing credit to agriculturists. Cooperative banks have extensive branch network and reach out to people in remote areas. They have traditionally played an important role in creating banking habits among the lower and middle income groups and in strengthening the rural credit delivery system

1.9 New Dimensions in Banking Sector

E-banking is a concept which enables everyone to conduct business with a bank from the comfort of home or office. E-banking does not involve any physical exchange of money, but it's all done electronically, from one account to another, using the internet. E-banking is playing vital role in the development of banks and in financial inclusion of banking sector. Due to which various industries have entered in banking sector for providing financial support. E-banking is the major cause of the rapid growth of private sector banks in India. Banks are one of the oldest financial intermediaries in financial system. They play an important role in mobilizing deposits and disbursement of credit to various sectors of the economy. The economic reforms initiated by GoI in early 1990s have brought a sea change in operational environment in banking sector. The features of this change are;

1. Increasing sophistication of capital markets.
2. Emergence of global investments.
3. Industry consolidation.
4. Heightened focus on customer relationships.
5. Proliferations of new players entering in the market.

After introduction of NER in banking sector, various banks have established i.e. private sector banks, foreign banks, multi-national banks, etc. Entry of new banks resulted in a paradigm shift in the ways of banking in India. With the rapid growth in banking sector; customers' hierarchy is also increased[23]. The growing competition, growing expectations led to increased awareness amongst banks on the role and importance of technology in banking. Most of the Private sector banks are providing electronic services, which helps them to attract the customers. But in the competition of these banks, co-operative banks are developing very slowly which is resulting in minimizing the number of customers. Many customers have closed their accounts and withdraw their deposits from co-operative banks due to lack of e-banking services. Customers want reliable and flexible services from banks, so they often search for substitute to their need. Today e-banking is the popular substitute for the customers which fulfill the needs of customers by offering online shopping, online payments and many services useful for cost and time savings and for quick transactions.

1.9.1 Impact of Globalization on banking sector:

Indian financial market is presently undergoing dynamic transformation with many new financial products and delivery systems. Banks are one of the oldest financial intermediaries in financial systems. The Indian banking industry has to re-orient its strategy towards marketing to accommodate the changes and challenges that are taking place in the present globalised scenario. The growing competition, growing expectations led to increase the awareness amongst banks[24]. The arrival of foreign and private banks with their superior state of art technology based services pushed Indian banks to follow suit by using technologies so as to meet the competition and retain their customer base. During the year 2003-04, banking sector witnessed strong growth in deposits and advances and in consumer finance. This growth is coupled with growth in number of new financial products offered to meet different consumer requirements, which are according to their particular needs. Now banks are emphasizing on the customer retail marketing known as mass-marketing[25]. Individual customers typically use banks for basic services such as savings and current accounts, mortgages, loans, debit/credit cards, depository services, fixed deposits and investment advisory services, etc.

Due to globalization, new generation of private sector banks and many foreign banks have entered in the market with recent innovative and techno-based useful products. Due to forced competition, PSB are also becoming more technology savvy and customer oriented. As an impact of LPG, RBI permit new banking licenses for economic reforms in banking sector and many banks are from corporate sectors increased huge competition among banking sectors. Banks are motivating customers to open new accounts in their banks and to increase number of account holders (customers). Banks have target of largest account holders and to motivate to each & every mature once to open an account and to carry financial transactions through banks.

New Bank Licensing Committee chairmen Nachiket More defined that RBI is working for controlling drawbacks and removing technical problems on national level[26]. RBI also permits incenses for opening their branches in rural and village and in tribal areas. RBI is also trying to adopt new policies for improving customer services and for increasing the financial transactions smoothly and safely with the help of banks. India has achieved tremendous success in the progress of technology. Today technology is the third largest technical manpower in the world which helps to manage modern industrial economy[27]. Areas like revenue growth market share, increased customers' satisfaction, are concern for innovations. The sources of innovations are customers, employers, consultants, business partners and competitors.

1.9.2 E-banking: A competitive strategy of banks

E-banking is the buy product from ICT which created new markets and opportunities for the banking sector in India and in this banking environment managing and satisfying the customers has become the key issue for various players in the industry. Thus the IT has emerged as a strategic resource for banks. Usage of technology by banks is due to the challenge of competition, rising consumer expectations and shrinking margins of banks which leads in reducing the transaction cost and enhancement of productivity, efficiency and costumer convenience, saving time, having operational frequency and no time binding. Indian banking industry has formed suitable grounds to apply technological innovation because banking activities are easily digitalized and automated[28].

The banking environment all over the world is undergoing a great transformation. Only cards are provided to customers having PIN and POP and these cards are applicable in any electronic operational machine which helps in successful completion of business services. These cards are known as plastic money. The banks which are not providing e-banking services and are not fulfilling the needs of customers may lose their customers[29]. In Maharashtra particularly in Nashik district, many co-operative banks are carrying traditional banking system and are not providing these services that they are losing their customers. Two banks have also closed their banking business and one bank is in the process of merging itself in Cosmos Cooperative Bank. These banks are running slowly only due to the policies announced by that BOD. It is also realize that very a few co-operative banks are providing these services slowly.

1.9.3 Service Centered Economy

Growing importance of services sector is the main feature of Indian Economic Development. In India the growth of service sector is more than the development of Agriculture and Industries. In GDP of India the share of service sector is more than other sectors and it is also involved in the state level development. Service sector have nearby 60 per cent share in the GDP of the country. Services sector has created more employment opportunities and more income sources from the decade 1990 and it also developing with the growing rate of 9 per cent per annum.[30] According to the budget of 11th Five year plan, GDP has increase at 8 to 9 per cent. According to Shankar Acharya, The development of service sector is impossible without the development of agricultural and Industrial sector in India. Today after globalization highest growth rate in the economy since last decade is performance in the manufacturing and service sector and mainly in finance, insurance real estate.

1.9.4 Types of E-banking services

Following figure 1.4 shows the various types of e-banking services[31];

Figure 1.4

E-banking services →
- ATMs (Automated Teller Machine)
- Debit Cards
- Credit Cards
- Phone Banking
- Mobile Banking
- Internet Banking
- RTGS/EFT
- Online Payment of Bills

1.9.5 Services: Operations, Delivery and Quality

After globalization, banks have introduced various techno-based services to its customers and customers are also using these services with high frequency. Due to the introduction of these services banks have to pay only 1/6th cost per transactions with compared to other non-techno based bank units. According to International Internet Banking Report, E-banking transactions need expenditure around sterling 1.07 to 0.27. As well as it need less time for completing the transactions. The overall performance and productivity has spiraled upwards with major attention given for improvement of customer services[32]. The banks are becoming competitive and technology driven. An outcome of these factors has been an expansion of their product range coupled with improvements in product operations, product delivery and product quality.

With the recent developments of ICT, majority of banking operations have been computerized by most of the banks. The process is still on for extension and upgradation of computerization by banks in India. E-banking provides a bouquet of new channels, contributed to speed, accuracy and confidentiality of customers' transactions while enhancing customers' convenience. Internal housekeeping is done accurately and much faster through programmed packages/software at the branch and also at centralized platforms involving several branches of a region or zone[33]. The basic universal principles of banking which typically characterize banks are the principles of intermediation, liquidity, profitability, solvency and trust. Due to this banking is spread in universal under a single roof of IT. With the help of security and other qualities numbers of customers are increasing. Today E-banking is key factor for development of banking sector and national economy.

A. Benefits to Customers

1. After introduction of above e-services, banks are also introducing new banking channels such as Home Banking, Quick Banking, etc.

2. Enhancing customer convenience through initiatives such as 'anytime and anywhere banking and 24*7*365 days banking'.
3. Making routine banking transactions speedier, safe and secure.
4. Achieving integrated banking services through inter-connectivity of branches.
5. Making banker-customer communication fast and neat and providing information service 24*7*365 days basis via call centers.
6. Carrying out non-banking services for the customers, e.g. payment of electricity/telephone/gas bills, insurance premium and receipt if pension/interest/dividends etc.

B: Benefits to Banks

In modern age, banking services are playing an important role in the Indian Economy and Nashik District is also captured by Banks for rendering various services to its customers. Banking services are divided into two parts-first is services rendered by public sector banks and second is services rendered by private sector banks. But all the banking services are concerned with product, place, distribution, pricing and promotion decisions in the changing socio-economic and business environment. In India all these services are rendered according to users of services, behavior of user, user's psychology etc.

Changing financial policies brings various risks and opportunities in banking sector for bank management and regulatory and supervisory authorities. It includes cross-border transactions, lower transaction costs and the greater ease of banking activities, and from the reliance on techno-regulatory risks. Internet allows services to be provided from anywhere in the world, there is a danger position that banks will try to avoid regulation and supervision. Why regulators are necessary? They can require even banks that provide their services from a remote location through the internet to be licensed[34]. Licensing would be particularly appropriate where supervision is weak and cooperation between a virtual bank and the home supervisor is not adequate. Determining when a bank's electronic services trigger the need for a license can be difficult, but indicators showing where banking services originate and where they are provided can help. Regulators need to establish guidelines to clarify the gray areas between these cases.

1.10 Importance of E-banking services

As an impact of globalization, banks have introduced various techno-based services to its customers and customers are also using various services as per their need and satisfied their wants through branches which are providing e-banking services. Today use of technological services is the basic need in the globalised era and customers are also agree to pay fees for such VAS[35]. With the use of less cost service system, bank employees may concentrate on various other transactions and other functions of banks and customers may fulfill their need with these services in the nearest located ATMs centers as well as with their own techno-based instruments.

i. Integrated Internal Accounting System: Today book-keeping in banks has made automatically, fast, accurate, and in less time. Staff can use their time in marketing and such other work after the banking hours.

ii. MIS: MIS meant for the middle and top management; have improved due to data classification and retrieval, integrated accounting system, communication and conferencing system and inter-connectivity of branches.

iii. Cross selling of various financial products has been made easy due to data mining and electronic marketing channels.

Users of services: The line of services or product planning and development, offering of the services, the pricing strategies, interest/cost charged for servicing are resulted in the promotion of services and changing psychology of actual and potential users[36]. Today customers prefer refined service and claim for an increased rate of interest for channelizing their savings. Industrial users demand for credit facilities on liberal terms and conditions.

Figure 1.5

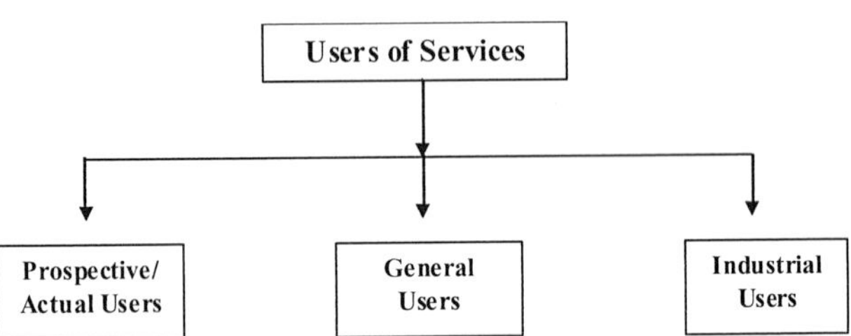

Prospective/actual users are those types of users which are presently not utilizing the services of banks but are to be expected more for future. Such expectations are promoted due to growing rate of literacy, environmental conditions, governmental regulations, sophistication in communication, innovation in education and various related factors govern for the promotion of banking services. In past, there have been greater changes in the needs and requirements of all the groups of users, during the decades 1970s and 1980s.

1.11 Financial Inclusion

The objective of financial inclusion is to provide access to financial services and timely and adequate credit to vulnerable groups such as weaker sections and low income groups at affordable cost. Bank has introduced smart card banking through business correspondents as per the guidelines of RBI for providing banking facilities in un-banked villages. During the year, bank has issued smart cards and transactions undertaken in the smart card terminal is nearby 60 to 70 percent[37].

Financial inclusion is generally defined as the availability of banking services at an affordable cost to disadvantaged and low-income groups. According to the Rangarajan Committee (2008), "Financial may be defined as the process of enduring access to financial services and timely and adequate credit where needed by vulnerable groups such as weaker sections and low income groups at an affordable cost[38]". In India the basic tool of financial inclusion is having a saving or current account with a bank. The scope of financial inclusion includes services like opening of bank accounts, immediate credit facilities, insurance facilities, financial advisory services etc. Financial inclusion through cooperative banks can be a viable option for inclusive growth in India. By being local in nature and intricately interwoven with the local community, cooperative banks for financial inclusion. Labor costs of cooperative banks are considerably less than that of commercial banks and generally operating costs are also minimal. It is evident that cooperative banks have feasible options for inclusive growth through rural development, creating opportunities for employment, income generation.

India needs more banks and innovative banking to displace moneylenders who occupy the unbanked vacuum. More banks will mean more competition, driving banks to rural areas. The new index of financial inclusion, released by CRISIL, shows that BIMARU states and even industrialized ones like Gujarat and Maharashtra fare poorly in financial inclusion. Against a national average of 40.1, Gujarat's score was 38.6 and Maharashtra 37.5 which faring better[39]. RBI reckons that financial inclusion can be achieved only through expansion of branch networks to rural areas. A new bank must have at least 25 per cent of its branches in rural areas. Instead, The RBI must allow innovative forms of banking, especially mobile banking that is well-placed to leverage on the electronic infrastructure being put in place by the unique identity project. It is easier for the cooperative banks to crack the psychological barrier and to create trust among its target community by improving quality of e-banking services that proves in increasing financial inclusion.

1.12 Research Methodology

For customer satisfaction and efficiency in banking transactions, banks are providing various types of e-banking services in an effective manner with the features of time saving, cost reducing and 24*7 facilities, etc. These services are benefited to the banks and to the customers[40]. But while using these services customers are facing various types of problems and it is a challenge for the bank employees to provide effective services and to solve the problems of customers by giving satisfied solutions in quick manner. "In banking sector, it is impossible to compete with other banks when the customers of banks are not satisfied and the satisfaction level of customers is not better". The satisfaction level of customer should have to increase and banks have to adopt and to provide the recent technologies in effective manner.[41] Many banks have established special cell and appointed a special officer for solving the problems of customers (if any while using e-banking services), but still a few customers are regretting to these services due to fear about security and privacy issue of transactions, theft and misuse of cards, absence of proper knowledge and proper information for using these services, etc.

The researcher aimed at studying the evolution and application of e-banking services, the problems faced by customers (in using e-banking services) and bank employees (in providing e-banking services) for effectiveness of e-banking services, response and perception of customers as well as bank employees at electronic banking services, and impact of these services over on the development and business of cooperative banks to suggest proper ways and means for effective use of these services and for development in the banking sector.

1.12.1 Statement of the Problem

The title of the proposed research work is, a study of "E-Banking Services provided by Co-operative Banks in Nashik District"

In Maharashtra, Cooperative Banking Act was passed in 1960, established with service motive and therefore, historically those were not profit maxi-misers. In rural finance in particular, these banks held monopoly. But After adoption of New Economic Policy (NEP) in 1991, modern customer services were initially introduced in private sector under the pressure of global competition, to which the nationalized banks also followed. Cooperative Banks are facing keen competition with Public and Private Sector Banks including Foreign Banks that are technologically advanced. Cooperative banks are very slow in adopting new technology. Management of cooperative banks rests in the hands of rural leadership that takes time to adjust with modern technology. This is the reason, why the growth of Cooperative banks has slowed down in the NEP era.

The Public and Private Banks are offering a variety of E-Banking services. Now, by the initiative of the government and SCBs of the states are encouraging Cooperative banks to adopt modern technology in banking[43]. A few Co-operative Banks have adopted this technology and introduced new customer services including E- Banking, whose progress is likely to be different from those who have not yet modernized.

The researcher has done her research work mainly with E-banking services with the technological and developmental attitude. A very few research work has been done on E-banking services having customers' attitude. The researcher has focused at Co-operative banking sector which is known as backbone for rural development. But today adoption of NEP increased competition in banking sector which also increased competition amongst banking sector. A very few banks from Co-operative sector have adopted e-banking technology and large number of banks are adopting these services slowly and is also in developing process. Thus the researcher has selected this topic to study various problems shown as objectives of the study.

1.12.2 Significance of the study

Co-operative Banks are service oriented and also trying to fulfill the financial needs of customers. Today, 'E-Banking' is the latest customer service that plays an important role in providing most needed services to the customers. These value-added services (VAS) are time saving and profit maximizing. In absence of these services, Cooperative Banks may lose their customers to their competitors; Public and Private Sector and Foreign Banks also.

Many customers have less knowledge about using the techno-based services of banks so it becomes necessary to know how far the customers know about these services. Many customers are facing problems or are afraid for loss of cards or misuse of cards, so they are not using the services. Many customers are using the services but are also facing the problems due to Inadequate Installation of Technology and in some areas (particularly in rural areas) there is absence of e-services. Employees of many cooperative banks are also facing the problems in adopting and providing the techno-based services, 24 hours security to the ATM centers. Customers are facing the problems due to light fluctuating and machine operating while withdrawing cash. According to C.Rangarajan, customers as well as bank employees face the problems of managerial, operational/technological, socio-cultural, etc.

This study has enlightened the prospects and problems in adopting e-banking technology in cooperative banks in Nashik District. The study is significant from the point of view of cooperative bankers, who have learnt the benefits; they could derive in enhancing their business through providing neo customer services. The new researchers will find other services that may make the progress path of cooperative banks as a topic for their research. The policy makers may find some measures through this study that will strengthen the cooperative banks in the state as well as in the nation.

1.12.3 Objectives of the study

This study is undertaken with the purpose of attaining following objectives:

1. To study the evolution and application of E- Banking services in Cooperative Banks.
2. To identify the response of customers and perception of bank employees at e-banking services.
3. To study the difficulties (if any) faced by customers and bank employees regarding e-banking services.
4. To know the impact of e-banking technology over on the development (with business) of Cooperative Banks.
5. To suggest various ways and means to improve these services and for development of cooperative banks in the context of e-banking.

1.12.4 Statements of Hypotheses:

Researcher has tested following statements of hypotheses through the study:

1. H_1: "E-banking Services in Co-operative banks:
   a) E-banking services in cooperative banks are slowly developing.
   b) E-banking services in cooperative banks are slowly accepted by customers and by bank employees."
2. H_2: E-banking services have positive impact in the development of cooperative banks.
3. H_2: "Customers in need of E- Banking Service prefer Public or Private sector banks rather than co-operative Banks."

1.12.5 Working Definition of Technical terms used

The E- Banking is a Computerized Technique used by Banks for fulfilling their transactions under Centralized Common Technology Platform (CCTP). All technological services are also provided with the help of E- Banking technology. It helps in faster and easier financial transactions independently. The use of technology is beneficial to the service providers i.e. standardize service delivery, reduce labor costs, and expands the options for provisioning of services. This study is restricted to the technology based e-banking services such as: ATMs, Debit/Credit Cards, Phone Banking, Mobile Banking, Internet Banking, RTGS/ EFT, Online Bill Payments, etc.

1.12.6 Scope of the study

The scope of the study is to observe, to define and to analyze the aspect of e-banking services, attitude of bank employees and customers towards e-banking services provided by co-operative banks in Nashik district. An attempt has made to focus on the customers' perception and perspective of cooperative banks. This study also highlighted the causes that why co-operative banks are adopting these services slowly and developing slowly. The study involved only those co-operative banks which have adopted e-banking technology and working in Nashik District.

1.12.7 Limitations of the study

The study is limited only for those cooperative banks which are providing technology based e-banking services such as ATM, Debit/Credit cards, Phone banking, Mobile Banking, Internet Banking, RTGS/EFT, Online payment of bills, and no any other e-banking services are considered in this study.

The study is based on 20 per cent (13) co-operative banks which are providing e-banking services through their branch which are located in Nashik District. The branch units are selected as per the seniority of adoption of e-banking technology and when maximum branches have adopted this technology in same period, in this situation the branches which are providing maximum types of e-banking services to its customers are selected for the study.

The respondents are bank employees and bank customers only from co-operative bank using e-banking services.

1.13 Methodology

The research is related with E-banking facilities provided by co-operative banks. This service is of recent origin and a by-product of IT application to Banking Sector. After introduction of New Economic Reform 1991, various banks have adopted this technology very fast to modernized customer services including E- Banking Services. However, a very few co-operative banks are providing E- Banking Services to their customers. Main thrust of study is on primary as well as secondary data.

1.13.1 Sample selection

Sample selection is the major part of the research work. Purposive sampling method has been used for selection of banks and Simple random sampling method has been used for the selection of customers. The type of research is exploratory used for identification of actual problems of customers (in using these services and/or neglecting these services) and of bank employees (in providing efficient/ qualitative services). This method helped to researcher in identifying the causes of the problems for neglecting e-banking services and the problems faced by customers while using these services. The main objective of this method is to provide baseline for the acceptance of e-banking services by the customers. It focused on the situation by viewing different alternatives and find out the fresh thoughts. The main aim of using this method for research work is to identify vague problems and to suggest proper solutions on such problems.

(1) Selection of Banks

The researcher has selected 20 per cent (13 out of 64) cooperative banks from the total number of cooperative banks which have adopted e-banking technology as per the seniority of adoption of e-banking technology and also located in Nashik District. When maximum branches have adopted this technology in same period, in this situation the branches which are providing maximum types of e-banking services are preferred for the study. For this purpose the researcher has conducted primary investigation of cooperative banks regarding automation in branches.

(2) Selection of customers

According to Marshall (1996), 'selection of appropriate sampling method and of sample size depends upon the objectives of the study'. 10 per cent sample size from the total number of customers' (which are suing e-banking services) is selected to draw the conclusions. This sample size is quite sufficient for the research work because it is not possible to the researcher to interview with maximum customers (more than 10 percent or all customers) and it is also difficult to the researcher to draw conclusion with less than 10 percent sample size. Phone banking service is provided to all the customers who have current and saving account in the bank thus the numbers of account holders are available easily from the branches of cooperative banks. As per 10 per cent sampling, 9916 are the sample customers to whom the researcher has issued structural questionnaires, but only 7858 questionnaires are received back in which only 6885 are completely filled up and thus the researcher has used only 6885 questionnaires for this study.

Table 1.4
Sample Design

Sr. No	Particulars	Total Numbers	Sample
1	Co-operative Banks in Nashik District.	64 banks	20 per cent (13 Banks)
2	Customers (e-banking users) from Cooperative banks (Current + Saving Account-holders)99155		10 per cent (9916)
	Number of Respondents		6885

1.13.2 Sources of data collection

Researcher has made pilot study to the final distribution of questionnaires to the targeted group. The purpose of this study is to evaluate clarity and appropriateness of the questions contained in the questionnaires.

Primary data has collected from the bank employees of 13 sample banks by using structured questionnaire and interview technique and oral discussion with them on phone, as necessary.

Secondary data has collected from RBI reports on small banks and magazines, annual reports of banks, printed cards and pamphlets, news-papers, journals and various websites.

1.13.3 Statistical tools used

Various statistical tools like percentage, average/mean, mode, index has applied for research work.

Chapter Scheme

1. Introduction and Research Methodology
2. Review of Literature
3. Socio-economic Profile of Study area
4. E- Banking Services: A Theoretical Framework
5. Business Analysis of Sample Banks.
6. Management of Customer Services with E-Banking.
7. Findings and Recommendations.

   Bibliography

   Appendix-

   Questionnaire

References

1. Mathur B.S., (2005), 'Co-operation in India', Sahitya Bhavan, Agra, Pp-73
2. Gokhale S.D. (2009), 'Problems & Prospectus of Rural Development in Maharashtra', Shrividya Prakashan, Pune, Pp-46-48
3. Govilkar Vinayak, 'Rural Development', An article in Daily Lokmat, dated Oct., 2013, Pp-6
4. Sangale B.R., Sangale G.T., Kayandepatil, Pawar N.C., 'Indian Banking System', Chaitanya Publication, Nagpur, Pp-6.16-6.22
5. Kunjukunju Benson, 'Commercial Banks in India: Growth, Challenges & Strategies', First Edition2 008, New Century Publications, New Delhi, Pp-184-89
6. Yashwantha Dongre (2011), 'Rural reconstruction through co-operative resurgence', Editorial: G.V.Joshi, P.A.Rego, Sinam M., Banking for rural development in India, Bangalore University, Published by Macdonald & Evans, Pp-147-156
7. Editorial, 'Co-operative banking in India,' The Economic Times, 24th March, 2011 Pp-6
8. Agrawal Meenu, 'Regional Rural Banks in India', First Edition 2009, New Century Publications, New Delhi
9. www.cooperativebank.com
10. Ibid, Pp-173
11. Bhagwati, Jagdish (1993), 'Banking for Rural Development', Clarendon Press, Oxford Publication
12. Ibid, Pp-218
13. Datta, Sundaram (2012), 63rd Edition, 'Indian Economy', S.Chand Publication, New Delhi, Pp-593-597
14. www.cooperative_banking.com
15. Thakur Vishwas, (Chairman-Vishwas Cooperative Bank limited, Nashik), an article, 'Dynamic changes in banking sector', in Daily Deshdoot, supplement of Banking Special, dated 20th Feb., 2015, Pp-1
16. Ibid, Pp-6
17. Tripathy S.N. (2000), 'Cooperative: Growth and New Dimensions', Discovery Publishing House, New Delhi
18. www.spc.tn.gov.in/tenthplan
19. www.planningcommission.nic.in
20. State Planning Commission, 12th Plan Vol. II Pp-11
21. Ibid, Pp-93
22. Seetaraman S.P., Mohanan N., (1986), 'Framework for studying Cooperative Organisation', Oxford & IB Publishing Company, New Delhi
23. Trehan, Ruchi, Soni Niti & Sharma Arti, 'Indian Banking moving

towards better Tomorrow', Editorial, R.K.Uppal, Innovations in Banking, Mahamaya Publications, page-48

24. Jalan, Bimal, (1992), 'Indian Economy: Problems and Prospectus', Penguin Books India (P) Ltd, New Delhi

25. Basel Committee on Banking Supervision, (2010), 'Principles for enhancing Corporate Governance', Basel: Bank of International Settlements.

26. The Economic Times, 'Technology, Not Coercion for Banks', 27th June 2013, Pp-10

27. Dwiwedi Shyam Mohan & Mishra Hridya Narayan, Ranjana Patel, 'Service Sector in India: Growth Potential', Service Sector in India- Editorial, Adhyayan Publications, Pune, Pp-46-51

28. Kulwant Singh Pathania and Mamta Sharma, 'Adoption of Banking Technologies', Indian Journal of Commerce, July-Sept., 2010, Vol. 63, Number. 3.

29. Daily Sandyanand, Nashik District ,Maharashtra: 16/04/2014

30. Editorial, 'Risk/Opportunities in E-banking services', IRJCM, ISSN-2277-5838, Vol-1, No-1, Feb., 2014, Pp-110-113

31. Pragati for NET/SET, Paper 2 & 3, 'E-banking', Pragati Publications, Pune, Pp-7.51

32. A. Karunaiathal, 'Performance of Private Sector Banks in Erode District', Banking, Micro Finance and SHGs (Self Help Groups) in India, New Century Publication, First Edition, July 2009, New Delhi.

33. Ashwinikumar Bhalla, 'Financial services,' editorial: R.K. Uppal, Indian Banking Industry in 2020, Mahamaya Publishing house,Pp-266-276

34. Pravinkumar Tayal & Sugan C. Jain, 'Financial Reporting of Banking Companies in India- an Evolutionary stage', Editorial- Dangwal R.C.& Kashmir Singh, New trends in Finance, , Page no. 255

35. Rabindra Kumar Mishra, (2013) 'New Avenues in Banking sector', Economic Development in India, AVON publication, New Delhi, 1st Edition,: Pp-60

36. www.projectshub.com, Dasgupta, Feb., 2012, 'Future of E-banking in India', An Article

37. PooniaM.S., 'Development Banking in India', Pratiksha publication, Jaipur

38. Rangarajan C., 'Know Your Banking,' RBI press, Mumbai, Pp-14-15

39. M. Narendra, MD, BOI, Chennai, Chairmen's speech, on 8/06/2013, published in The Economic times on 1st July, 2014

40. Kundi and Shah, 2009, 'Indian Banking in Globalised Era', Indian banking moving towards better tomorrow, Editorial, R.K.Uppal ,Pp-5

41. Iyer V.R., BOI, Chairperson's speech, '17th Annual General Meeting of shareholders at Mumbai', 29th June 2013, published in The Economic times on 1st July, 2013

42. Swami .R., Gupta B.L., 'Rural Development & Cooperation in India', Indus Valley Publications, New Delhi, Pp-17-21

43. The Economic Times, Editorial,27th June 2013, Page 10

Review of Literature

The views of various contributors helps in identifying the need of e-banking technology in globalised era, its importance in banking sector and actual Indian banking scenario. As this the events of actual problems encountered by customers and bank employees in using this technology, solutions on the problems and development of banking sector from the literature including those from establishment of banking sector and adoption of e-banking technology. It especially focuses on various aspect of e-banking services provided to its customers. This chapter shall review the works already done in the same area so far to the extent researcher could have access to it. The reviews start with introduction of e-banking services in developed nations and in India and ends with the benefits and problems of these services with working groups or committees appointed by RBI for the development of e-banking services in India. Mainly these reviews of literatures are divided into following parts.

A) Introduction to E-banking services

B) E-banking services: Adoption and Development

C) Financial Inclusion/Crisis

D) Impact of E-banking

E) Opportunities and Challenges

F) Competitive Strategy

G) Benefits and Problems

H) Working Groups/Committees

A. Introduction to E-banking services

Bhatt (1988)[1] has examined behaviour of banks and bank employees in is research regarding adoption of new technology in banking sector. He found that adoption of new technology is influenced by sex, age, marital status, degree of exposure to internet banking and the characteristics of banks. It also resulted that social norms dominate to the adoption of banking technology.

Kohok M. A. (1993)[2] defined the origin of credit cards and its development on National and international level. He has also defined the purpose and procedure of using the credit cards with its advantages to the Banks, Customers and Merchants. Various banking instruments mainly ATM and Credit Cards are used for making purchases and sales transactions on international level.

Jhingan M.L. (2008)[3] examined the organizational setup of the cooperative banking system in India which is based on the credit needs of agriculturists. It consists of three tiers for the short-term and medium-term credit. But the main purpose of all these cooperative banks is to provide services to needy it meant to develop the spirit of mutual help and cooperation among their members, besides their credit and other needs.

Ahluwalia Rupali (2008)[4] highlighted that LPG is making the Indian banks competitive, profitable and vibrant. Financial sector reforms were introduced by Narsimhan committee with some recommendation of 1991 and 1998; this phase witnessed the liberal entry of private and foreign banks having operational freedom to the banks, deregulation of the interest rates, reduction in the statutory reserve requirements, etc. These changes brought development in the Indian banking industry and profitability became the core business of the banking sector.

S. Ganesan (2009)[5] defined that e-banking is a generic term which includes internet banking, phone banking, mobile banking etc. It is a process of delivery of banking services and products through electronic channels such as telephone, internet, mobile etc. The concept and scope of e-banking is still developing i.e. quick banking, home banking etc. E-banking facilitates an effective payment and accounting system enhancing the speed of delivery of banking services. E-banking has improved efficiency and convenience but still it has to face several challenges to the regulators and supervisors.

R.K. Uppal (2009)[6] defined that Finland was the first country in the world to have taken lead in e-banking and in India; ICICI is the leading bank which have taken initiative for the progress of e-banking technology under the brand name of 'Infinity'. As other countries India also does not have any specific regulatory laws for the adoption and development e-banking technology. But RBI has issued guidelines to banks to recognize the risks arising from electronic modes and to devise control mechanisms that are needed to mitigate the risks such as IT environmental risks, operational risks, product risks, etc.

According to Maheshwari and Govindrajan (2009)[7] poor performance of public sector banks during the 18th century provided necessary platform to the banking sector to operate on the basis of operational flexibility and functional anatomy which resulted into efficiency, productivity and profitability in banks. Advancement of IT has become one of the important pillars of banking revolution which created lot of opportunities for banking business in India and also invited many challenges for the bankers.

R. Bhaskaran (2011)[8] has given detailed information about utility of new technologies for its careful use which are used by the banks for development purpose. Banking functions are classified as traditional functions and modern functions. Modern functions of banks encompass a wide range of financial services to meet the customers' varied requirements under 'one umbrella' e.g. cross-border banking, merchant banking, credit card business, factoring, leasing and insurance. Some of these services are rendered by Banks in India.

Padhye, Kishor C, Mishra, Rakesh Roshan (2011)[9] viewed that as per the Section 5B of Banking Regulation Act, 1949; banks are working for the purpose of lending or investments of deposits/ money from the public, repayable on demand/ otherwise withdraw able by Cheques, draft, and order or otherwise. Banks have target of largest account holders and to motivate to each and every mature once to open an account and to carry financial transactions through banks.

Editorial (2011)[10] noted that Private sector banks have established since in 1991. On 11th Aug., 2010 RBI recommended for feedback of experts. Banks are economic representative used for security of money, thus it should be needed to give attention for the licensing of banks. According to RBI regulation 25% branches should be in rural area where banking facilities are not available.

Govilkar Vinayak (2011)[11] defined that there are two separate wings of the co-operative credit structure in India, first wing provides short term loans and medium term loans and second wing provides long term loans. There have been three tier systems with the state co-operative banks at the Apex, at the central co-operative banks working at district level and primary credit society working at the village level. Today share of co-operative banks has increased 17 times and it covers 65% areas from total villages of India.

Rabindrakumar Mishra (2013)[12] observed that RRB was started in 1975 to cater the need of rural banking in India. The basic purpose of RRB was to have such banks which have roots in rural areas. RRBs have so far been able to achieve the main objectives of helping the weaker section in the rural areas. Nearly 90% of the loan of RRBs was provided to the weaker section. But they have not been able to replace co-operative credit society but have supplemented it.

B. E-banking Services: Adoption and Development

S.S. Sisodia (1995)[13] has defined that cooperative banks are promoted by honest, hard working and dedicated groups of people. These banks can do well for economic development of its members and the society. Relatively large number of its members and high degree of population has a strong base for development of cooperative banks and for adoption of IT.

Aggarwal (2002)[14] defined five key areas in banking where technology has contributed preferentially for product development, market infrastructure, risk control and market research. India has an extensive banking network, covering rural and urban areas of banks. The numbers of PSBs are comparatively more than other banks which are working at rural and urban areas and also providing technological services to their customers. Private sector banks are choose by citizens living in urban areas where technology penetration is high and cooperative banks are selected in rural areas, but PSBs are preferred in rural as well as in urban areas.

Acharya & Shankar (2002)[15] evaluated that the banking system in developed countries is more advanced compared to the banking system of developing countries and under-developed countries. With the introduction of e-banking services in developed nations, developing nations like India have also adopted these services.

Avadhani V.A. (2008)[16] studied that the rates of management skills, ideas, innovation accompanied by sufficient net worth are the key points of success in the financial world of highly competitive and global environment. Each service activity needs a different type of market strategy to meet the challenges of globalization. They need dynamic management team modified value systems suitable to requirements of customers and market thrust to meet the challenge of competitors. Today customers are demanding and they want to deal with people who are empathetic, knowledge, responsive, communicative and professionalized.

According to S. Sanmuga Pria (2009)[17] GoI and RBI have taken several initiatives for the development of e-banking in India. RBI has made considerable progress in consolidating existing payment and settlement system and in upgrading technology for establishment of efficient, integrated and secure system functioning in real-time environment. GoI passed the IT act 2000 which provides legal recognition to electronic transactions and other means of e-commerce.

Shrinivas Joshi (2009)[18] opined that automation in banking sector becomes most important factor for the development of banking sector and for sustainable development of banks for being facing global competition. Today PSBs, Private sector banks, foreign banks and a very few cooperative banks have adopted modern technology for providing e-banking services to their customers. Banks are using this technology due to the features of accuracy, time savings, cost reducing and high speed transactions.

Puja Arora (2009)[19] RBI issued specific guidelines for evolving of e-banking technology. It covers various issues of framework of technology, security standards, legal and regulatory issues. Virtual banks which have no offices and doing functions only on-line are not permitted for offering e-banking services in India. Only the banks which are permitted to offer e-banking services must be registered under the banking regulatory act 1949 and should have physical presence in India. Each bank units have to report RBI regarding development and failure of security systems and procedures in e-banking.

Nayak Keyur (2009)[20] examined that today banks need to use retail as a growth trigger which requires product development and differentiations, innovations and business process. E-banking is able to lead growth of the banking industry in future would depend upon the capacity building of banks to meet the challenges and make use of the opportunities profitably. The kind of technology used and the efficiency of operations would provide sufficient competitive edge for success in retail banking business.

According to Nigamananda Biswas (2010)[21] IT has made tremendous changes in the computer processing. Automated

Bio-metric system becomes available during the last few years. It helps to recognize human bio-metrics. Canara Bank (1906) has become one of the India's leading banks and has launched first ATM machine in 2007 and obtain ISO Certification. But Dena Banks launched BATMs in Nov., 2006. Then other banks have started introducing BATMs as it seems to be an effective way of preventing PIN theft as well as helps to control occurring frauds and is also a channel to expand banks in rural and illiterate masses.

Gian Kaur (2011)[22] noticed that till the end of March 2004, there were total 90 scheduled commercial banks in India of which 27 were PSB (19 nationalized banks + 8 belonging to the SBI group), 30 Private sector banks (21 old + 9 New private sector Banks) and 33 foreign banks. All these banks had network of 53061 branches in which 46984 branches of PSB followed by 5860 Pvt. Banks and only 217 foreign banks. Thus most banking business in India is dominated by PSB. Banks have competitive edge in the market oriented system. But co-operative banks are service oriented and thus these banks have comparatively less share in the competition of banks.

Dongre Yashwantha, (2011)[23] opined that Co-operatives are institutions that have been tried but failed to satisfy their customers. However close look revealed that co-operative movement was not tried in the way it should have been. Hence it is needed to re-introduce the co-operative structures in a refined and restructured manner. During the past two decades co-operative banks play a central role in achieving and sustaining overall development. Thus co-operative being one of the major civil society institutions naturally got a boost during this period.

Rajeshwari H (2011)[24] analyzed that improvement in saving habits of customers is essential for the purpose of development of banks. After nationalization of banks in 1969, banks experienced a tremendous growth by gaining the confidence of the customers. Banks are playing significant role in the development of economy. Today the banks are a single unit providing loans to public and industries at lowest rate. After globalization many private banks have entered in the banking sector. Now we have more than 308 banks in India with more than 68000 branches.

Gupta, O.P., Nagpal Poonam (2011)[25] evaluated that use of IT and Internet both have had major impact on overall stability and efficiency of banking system of India. With the introduction of technology, there has been a significant change in the operating system of banks. The technologies have processed in shorter period of time. ATMs provide easy access to cash. But it is not clear that whether the customers of banks are fully satisfied with the services provided by banks.

Dutta-Sundaram, (2012)[26] opined that with the rapid advancement in various information delivery systems, IT refers to the entire media and devices used to transmit and process information for use of various target groups in the society. IT is known as 4th factor of production. In the knowledge economy IT is recent origin but it is spreading fast in India.

Deshpande V.S (2013)[27] focused on the success of development program which is based on inputs and outputs of that program and any program must focus on the life style of the people. Many Public sector banks and private sector banks have tried to formulate development pattern which would indicate technological improvement in banking sector. The expansion of banking units is necessary for central process of development. The concept of development in banking sector is consisting with economic, social, biological, psychological and technological dimensions.

According to Padhy C., Mishra Rakesh Roshan, (2013)[28] eligibility for autonomy in banking sector should be in the areas of pursue new line of business, make suitable acquisition, close/merge unviable branches, open overseas offices, set up subsidiaries, prescribe qualification standards and modalities of recruitment to various categories, undertake visit to foreign countries to interact with investors/ depositors and other stakeholders, lay down policy of accountability and responsibility of bank officials.

Govilkar, Vinayak (2013)[29] defined that Jawaharlal Nehru had a strong faith in the cooperative movement. While opening an international seminar on cooperative leadership in South-East Asia he had said "But my outlook at present is not the outlook of spreading the cooperative movement gradually, progressively, as it has done. My outlook is to convulse India with the Cooperative Movement or rather with cooperation to make it, broadly speaking, the basic activity of India, in every village as well as elsewhere; and finally, indeed, to make the cooperative approach the common thinking of India. Therefore, the whole future of India really depends on the success of this approach of ours to these vast numbers, hundreds of millions of people".

As per the views of Iyer V.R. (2013)[30] SMS based grievance redressal system" is being brought to the notice of the Zonal head on real-time basis, provide facility of balance enquiry for saving bank account and overdraft account through SMS using "missed call" facility free of cost to the customers, online acceptance of PPF subscription in PPF account maintained with bank, online acceptance of donation for Prime Minister national relief fund, linking of Adhar number and account number on the basis of customer ID which will enable direct cash transfers of subsidies into the banks account of the beneficiaries under government's various welfare schemes.

C. Financial Inclusion/Crisis

An article of Jack Ewing (1992)[31] viewed that universal banking model is under attack by regulators as the industry faces new pressures. Regulators are controlling all big banks with measures, under particular scrutiny because of a perception considered grossly unfair by bank management that it is too thinly cushioned against losses if there were another financial crisis. The regulatory pressure comes in addition to a host of other challenges, including a long list of official investigations and lawsuits, most linked to investment banking that are likely to be a burden on bank profits and its reputation.

An article published in The Economic Times (2007)[32] indicated that the new index of financial inclusion, released by Crisil, shows that Bimaru states and even industrialized ones like Gujarat and Maharashtra fare poorly in financial inclusion. Against a national average of 40.1, Gujarat's score was 38.6 and Maharashtra 37.5 which faring better. RBI defined that financial inclusion can be achieved only through expansion of branch networks to rural areas. A new bank must have at least 25% of its branches in rural areas. Instead, The RBI must allow innovative forms of banking, especially mobile banking with unique identity project. This can be achieved by a joint venture between a public sector bank and a telecom operator.

According to Dangwal R.C, Singh Kashmira (2007)[33] banks are working as engines of economic growth and social transformation. Indian financial market is in developing stage and the banking companies are most important source of finance for majority of firms. Banks are main depository of the savings of the people. The globalization of the market economy has exposed the Indian financial sector in general and the banking sector in particular to challenges from global financial giants.

Chetia Dilip Kumar (2008)[34] reported that a well developed and efficient banking system is most essential for Economic Development of the nation. Banks can motivate people towards savings and earnings. Banks can fulfill financial requirements of people for development of Agriculture and Industries through expansion of banking facilities.

Ritu Goyal and Rajinder Kaur (2008)[35] noticed that maximum numbers of Private Sector Banks are following aggressive practices for customers and also recommended that various New Banks are established in Private Sector with minimum startup capital and other liberal requirements for increasing competition to lead to higher productivity and efficiency in the Banking system.

Ram Mohan T.T. (2010)[36] focused on India's Banking system which has been less affected by ongoing crisis than banking system in US and Europe. The Indian Banking system has greater shape in the advanced economy. RBI defined that entry of New Private Sector Banks lists a number of issues in the next round of licensing of such banks. The better performance is given by ICICI Banks, HDFC Banks and UTI (Axis) Banks which are promoted by financial institutions.

Syal Ginni, Gulati Sonu (2011)[37] observed that financial education is playing an important role in changing financial landscape of the country which has presented with new opportunities for future collective growth. The major problems in the delivery of financial services are the lack of basic knowledge and lack of awareness of the products and services available from banks. Various difficulties addressing in use of such services affect to common man.

Gandatra Navdeep Kumar & Rama (2011)[38] opined that Indian financial markets are increasingly converging with global markets. As a result Indian Financial sectors are also ready for global best practices. New banks are setting the pattern of change in the banking sector. Today 80% market area is coming under increasing pressure of new generation. PSBs must concentrate on upgrading their technology and becoming more customer-friendly by improving efficiency and stability.

Kumar Navdeep (2011)[39] highlighted on the journey of Indian banking system which is classified into three phases: a) from 1786 to 1969 B) Nationalization of banks and upto 1991 and C) New phase of NER after 1991. The government establishes board of financial supervision in RBI for giving sufficient financial strength and to enable them to gain access to capital markets. In 1993, RBI also permitted private entry into the banking sector with the assumption that the new banks were well capitalized and technologically advanced.

In the views of Mishra Rabindrakumar (2013)[40] India has achieved tremendous success in the technology. Today technology is the third largest technical manpower in the world which helps to manage modern industrial economy.

Economic survey (2013-14)[41] defined a well-structured and efficient network of international financial institutions; helps top boost economic growth. These institutions provide credit to all sections of the society and infrastructure projects at reasonable rate. After liberalization, international financial institutions transformed the conservative financial sector to a dynamic one. Banking institutions are prime financial institutions in India. Other financial institutions like joint stock companies, insurance companies, mutual funds, etc. are also playing significant role in providing finances. Among scheduled commercial banks, national banks including SBI and its associates are engaged in credit delivery in rural areas.

D. Impact of E-banking

John h. dunning, Elsevier, (1999)[42] defined that globalization has been attracting widespread attention over the past few years. The impact of globalization has been uneven across regions, countries and sectors. It improves international competitiveness and productivity among the banking units which harnesses the welfare maximizing beneficial effects. Without innovation improvement cannot be done, thus the experts have to shift low technology content into high technology for development into a drag on growth and welfare. As per the experience of USA, internal productivity improvements can even substitute for international competitiveness.

Herbst (2001)[43] opined that innovations have taken place in the last decade of the 20th century in banking sector with crucial implication of technology in business and finance which helps to remove traditional, paper-based transactions by using electronic network transactions which include primarily Internet-based electronic stock exchange, e-banking, e-cash services and smart cards ATMs which replace traditional bank operations into click banking. It is to note that the impact of IT has been significant in the banking and financial services industry.

Bhasin T.M. (2001)[44] analyzed the impact of IT on banking sector. It has transformed the repetitive and overlapping systems and procedures into simple single key pressing technology resulting in speed, accuracy and efficiency of conducting business and enabling them to enter into the new activities. The banking industry has itself prepared and is strongly emerging to play a major supplementary role in nurturing e-commerce applications which is still in the infancy stage in India.

Reddy Y.V. (2006)[45] defined that IT is changing drastically the way in which people live and particularly banks offer their products and services, focusing on factors behind the customer's adoption of new technologies are remaining scarce especially in backward area/undeveloped areas of nation.

According to Uppal R.K. and Kaur Rimpi (2007)[46] banking is one of the most affected sector among the service sector of the economy. There is less business around and stiffer competition as banks flight to keep market share. This is because of implementation of new technology, new systems and a fresh approach which resulted in transformation in Indian banking system in recent years. For last many decades banking sector has faced many difficulties and the first phase of reforms laid the basis for sound banking system to remove these difficulties and make the banks more strong. New Indian banking is operating in highly deregulated, liberalized and competitive environment.

Janardhanan V.K (2008)[47] focused on growth and development of banking sector. The sector has been growing at an annual growth rate of 28% during the last 5 years. According to conventional classification, an economy is divided into three sectors namely agricultural (Primary),

Industrial (Secondary) and service (territory). The share of service sector in the total GDP has increased considerably from 49.8% in 2000-2001 to 55% in 2007-08.

Kumbhar V.M (2008)[48] studied that banks have done tremendous changes in the working system by adopting modern technology. Banks have shifted themselves from traditional banking to modern banking. Due to lack of funds, all types of banks have not yet adopted new technology and are not providing these services to the customers. Due to automation, numbers of customers have increased but their direct contact with bank employees have restricted. Direct contact between customers and bank employees resulted into keeping permanent customers but e-banking technology affect this relationship. Today banks need to create direct contact with customers for increasing their numbers and for keeping them permanently as a satisfied customer.

RBI report (2008)[49] published that today Indian banking sector are facing many problems but are also accepting new challenges on national/international level. Growth rate of all banks are upward slopping from 2009 to 2014. Indian banks are developing by adopting new technology, increasing capital, reducing NPA, controlling administrative expenses, and restructuring organization. GoI try to merge small banks into big banks for facing global competition among banks through effective management, qualitative services and adoption of recent technology. But still Indian banks are facing various problems in providing e-banking services and attracting customers.

Editorial, JIBC (2009)[50] viewed that transactional errors or transactional hacking plays a significant role in diverting the customers at traditional banking system than electronic banking system. The Bill Clinton defined that the information technology is affecting the whole world. Thus the customers are grouped into electronic banking adopters and traditional banking defenders and so they have significant influence on the customers' adoption of e-banking services. The presidential incentives and awareness of customers for e-banking benefits, numerous respondents are still using the conventional banking.

Arti Sharma, Navgeet Kaur (2009)[51] opined that there should be qualitative changes in staff composition skills required latest training and retain staff to face competition. Today's success mantra for achieving excellence is managed with customer expectations of excellent customer service. According to report titled, 'banking in 2050: how big will the emerging markets get?' Banking sector growth in the major emerging economies of the world would outstrip in the developed nation before 2050. It has also emphasized that India can rise from relatively low levels today to emerge as the third largest domestic banking market in the world by 2040.

Bimal Anjum, Sofat Rajni, Sridhar Rajan (2011)[52] observed that Banking business in India is facing various challenges and opportunities especially beyond 2009 when banking would be fully exposed to foreign competitions. Banks in India are ready through adoption of new technologies; strengthening their capital base, reducing NPA, bringing down operating cost, enhancing corporate governance and alignment of regulatory and accounting requirements undertaking organizational restructuring and sharpening their customer centric initiatives. Impact of globalization in Indian banking can be visualized from the challenges faced by the Indian Banking Sector.

Ashwani Kumar Bhalla (2011)[53] defined strong growth in deposits and advances and in consumer finance. This growth is coupled with growth in number of new financial products offered to meet different consumer requirements, which are according to their specialized needs. Now banks are emphasizing on mass-marketing. Due to globalization, new generations of private sector banks and many foreign banks have entered the market and they have brought with them several useful and innovative products. Due to forced competition, PSB are also becoming more technology savvy and customer oriented.

Dutta and Sundaram (2013)[54] opined that in 1991, Narsimhan committee introduced NEP for development in banking sector. This committee has recommended that GoI should have to accept the policy of LPG; small banks should have to merge in other banks, minimize the financing pattern of PSL, terminate the bank recruitment board, provide administrative and financial rights to PSBs and minimize excess control of RBI. GoI and RBI have adopted some recommendations and focused on the development in banking sector.

According to Garewal, Prakash and Nandini Garewal (2013)[55] a recent national survey shows that 60% of young Indians are opting for careers in web-related activities and India is also now a potent hub for web-development. IT plays the prime role in providing improved services to the customers; i.e. e-Financials, e-business, e-marketing, e-infotainment etc. E-Financial includes financial services including capital markets and banking. Banking are highly document intensive thus image processing technology can have a far reaching impact for such applications for its less paper handling characteristics.

Mishra & Puri (2013)[56] examined the rapid advancement in various information delivery systems, IT refers to the entire media and devices used to transmit and process information for use of various target groups in the society. IT is known as 4th factor of production. In the knowledge economy IT is recent origin but it is spreading fast in India.

According to Takle Dinkar (2014)[57] an impact of globalization PSBs, private sector and foreign banks have adopted new technology, but cooperative banks are less active in adopting this technology and so customers are neglecting to cooperative sector. LPG is worship for banking sector for making improvement in their banking business by reducing time and cost, quick services and branch expansion especially in rural areas. Banks have to provide various e-banking services to customers and have to attract new customers by keeping old.

Thakur Vishwas (2015)[58] defined an impact of globalization on banking sector. He noted that all types of banks are providing e-banking services to their customers. Cooperative banks are also facing the challenges in the competition of banking sector. Today 90 per cent cooperative banks have adopted e-banking technology for attracting the customers and for increasing their business. Now banks have to use CMR process to attract customers. RBI has newly introduced Internet Mobile Phone Service and cooperative banks will also introduce this service shortly.

E. Opportunities and Challenges

Tripathi S.N. (2000)[59] has examined democratic functioning of cooperative banks and e noticed that the directors are generally not well educated and have less knowledge and managerial skill. As a result cooperative banks are not able to achieve desired result. Thus there is need of regular managerial audit which will help in deciding the functions of respective persons and about delegation of authority.

Ruchi Trehan, Niti Soni, Arti Verma (2009)[60] focused on fast development of electronic technology in banking sector which convert brick banking into electronic banking. The working of Indian banks till 1990s was under very comfortable and protected environment. But the LPG has created opportunities for financial sector and tremendous pressure was put on various banks to remain competitive. Usage of technology is due to the challenge of competition, rising consumer expectations, and shrinking margins of banks which leads to reduction in cost and enhancement of productivity, efficiency and consumer convenience.

Chakrabarti Rajesh (2009)[61] reported that banks are providing innovative services which save time and improve customer satisfaction level. Online banks system is very popular among the customers and banks so it has higher approval of new technologies and progressively more understanding of transactions. Now banks are also providing mini-statement having information of last few transactions, online bill payment facility, money transfer facility, etc which attract the customers at banking services.

Karunaniathal (2009)[62] examined that many positive developments made in Indian banking sectors are mainly in the last decade of 20th century. Establishment of new private sector banks have large quantities which could reach the next level of their growth in the Indian Banking Sector by continuing to innovate and develop business models to profitably serve segments and reaching the next level of performance in their service platforms.

An article published in Lokmat (2011)[63] noted that RBI has ordered to all the banks to change the system of withdrawal of money from ATM Card. For controlling the transactions of misuse of ATM Card, every customer should have to use the permanent number while withdrawing the money from ATM Centre and also should have to use the same number at any ATM Centre at all withdrawal transactions and also while depositing the cash into the Bank with the help of ATM Machine. This number will work as the password of the customer. So no one can make misuse of ATM Cards. This password number system is ordered by RBI and which will be implemented soon.

An article in Sakal (2011)[64] focused on new system of ATM machines that the tax-payer can pay the amount of tax with this machine by using any ATM Centre of the Axis Bank, Bank of Maharashtra, Corporation Bank, Union Bank of India, etc. This facility is available for 24*7 days of a week, so the tax payer can pay the particular amount of tax at any time, in any ATM Centre, and at any place of any bank.

According to R.K. Uppal (2012)[65] Indian financial market is presently undergoing dynamic transformation with many new financial products and delivery systems. The Indian banking industry has to re-orient its strategy towards marketing to accommodate the changes and challenges that are taking place in the present globalised scenario. The growing competition, growing expectations led to increased awareness amongst banks. The arrival of foreign and private banks with their superior state of art technology based services pushed Indian banks to follow suit by using technologies so as to meet the competition and retain their customer base.

F. Competitive strategy

Rangarajan C. (1997)[66] evaluated the banking sector reforms that have led to an increase in the competition among banks and this has spurred the heightening of customer-orientation in most of the banks. Banks have instituted redressal machinery for customers' grievances. The banks now take serious cognizance of customers' complaints and try to rectify the deficiencies, because maximum satisfaction of the customer is the motto of all progressive banks, both in the private as well as in the public sector.

Uppal R.K. and Rimpi Kaur (2007)[67] opined that Indian banking system is facing a pressure of competition from inside and outside financial and non-financial companies. After the successful implementation of banking sector reforms in two phases i.e. IT act and other regulations. Banks witnessed excellent improvement in performance but still not become competitive internationally. So there is need to do SWOT analysis to make appropriate strategies to make them competitive at global level.

Jayalakshmi. S. and Asok. A. (2008)[68] defined that banking sector plays an important role in the economic development of nation. A sound efficient, effective, vibrant and innovative banking system stimulates economic growth by mobilizing savings. Indian banking sector has many positive and significant transformation and developments in the last half decade. India needs to perform successful financial services through reforms, because only private sector banks and PSB in India are changing perceptions of customers.

Patel, Ranjana (2009)[69] highlighted the situation of fast developing and over populated economy like India. The ever increasing work-force can find gainful employment more in the service sector as compared to other sectors.

With the introduction of new technologies; primary sector is shrinking and secondary sector grows slowly. In service sector, there are always immense possibilities for absorbing workforce, provided proper cautions are taken. Proper caution is needed while inviting FDI in the service sector. It should aim at providing creating tangible assets so that service sector growth becomes sustainable.

Maheswari and K. Govindrajan (2009)[70] examined that LPG have resulted in sea changes in time and cost effective consumers' banking services. These competitive innovations have male customers more concerned about money and its value leads to high customer expectations rise with the use of latest technology as online services. Service quality is related to customers' perception and satisfaction. For customer satisfaction banks have to provide qualitative services to its customers for survival and competitive advantage.

Nigamananda Biswas (2009)[71] studied poor performance of public sector banks during the 18th century. It provided necessary platform to the banking sector to operate on the basis of operational flexibility and functional anatomy which resulted into efficiency, productivity and profitability in banks. Advancement of IT has become an important pillar for banking revolution which created a lot of opportunities for banking business in India and also invited many challenges for the bankers.

Selvaraju R. and Vasanthi G. (2009)[72] noticed four components of marketing strategy i.e. product, place, price, promotion in classical marketing but bank need seven components such as product, price, place, promotion, people, procedure and physical evidence. The production of qualitative service is important because customers raising expectations and its fulfillment attract the attention of customers. Due to the tangible nature of service products, making the intangible products in to tangible becomes important.

Pravin Kumar Tayal and Sugan Jain (2009)[73] defined various challenges before banking industries i.e. de-regulations, new rules introduced by RBI for smooth conduct of e-transactions, working efficiency, diffused customer loyalty, mis-aligned competency gap etc. Thus banks have to control the problems faced by customers and have to provide qualitative services to the customers. The provision of quality service products is crucial because of the strong presence of human factor.

According to Dwivedi Shyam Mohan and Mishra ridyanarayan (2011)[74] different strategies are developed for different segments. Retail banks are increasing their cross selling and up scaling activities for increasing their customers relation. Product innovation is another strategy applied by retail banks. The different client segments are offered other services like Insurance/leasing services. The latest strategy is in the use of debit/ATM cards, means a single debit/credit/ATM card which can be used in any of the ATM machine without any processing/transaction fee.

Gurpreet Kaur, Niti Soni, Arti Verma (2011)[75] focused on the advent of e-business, technological innovations and globalization that are increasingly driving businesses to change their traditional modes of operation. The internet banking offers many opportunities to financial services providers in terms of modified value chain and disintermediation, which are redefining the financial services market place. Numerous factors including competitive cost, customer service, and demographic considerations are motivating banks to evaluate their technology and assess their e-commerce and e-banking strategies.

Padhye Kishor C. and Rakesh Roshan Mishra (2013)[76] defined that banking ombudsman scheme was setup w.e.f. 14/06/1995 to provide public forum for grievances against a bank which are not resolved within a period of two months provided their complainant pertain to any of the matter specified in the scheme. The scheme covers all scheduled commercial banks (excluding RRB) and all scheduled primary co-operative banks having a place of business in India whether incorporated in India or outside India.

Economic Survey (2013-14)[77] published that the banks in India using IT not only to improve their internal processes but also to increase facilities and services to its customers. Efficient use of technology has facilitated accurate and timely managed of the increased volume of transactions of banks consistent with larger customer base. Today 97.8% PSB are fully computerized. ATMs growth is 37.8% in 2009-10 and 44.6% in 2010-11.

G. Benefits and Problems

R.P. Gupta (2003)[78] has highlighted as per his study that there are some weaknesses in cooperative banks i.e. duality of control, frequent changes in top management and board of directors, limited product base, inadequate infrastructures, adverse publicity etc.

Kaptan S.S. (2005)[79] defined that e-banking services provide various benefits to its customers and to the banks also. Customers can enjoy the benefits of time saving transactions, quick and 24*7 accessibility, one step or one click on mouse transactions, cashless transaction, quick balance information, etc. and the banks can enjoy the benefits of lower transaction cost, time saving transactions etc. Bank employees may increase the number of customers by giving reliable services and by advertising services with the help of internet facilities.

Sharma Naina (2007)[80] committed to protect interests to stakeholders, shareholders, customers, employers and society, ensure transparency in communication and also ensure accountability of performance to achieve excellence.

Goyal B.B. and Kumar Nitesh (2007)[81] opined that E-banking helps the banker in reducing the cost of transactions and cost of administrations and to provide better and efficient services. The banks are interested to retain their customers to offer different alternatives and they must adopt new technologies. The sources of innovations are customers, employers, consultants, business partners and competitors.

Soni Niti and Kaur Gurpreet (2007)[82] viewed that bank customers use internet banking to access accounts and general information on bank products and services through personal computers and other intelligent device. The advent of e-business, technology, innovations and globalization are increasingly changing their traditional modes of operation. Internet offers many opportunities to financial service providers in redefining the financial services market place. Numerous factors include competitive cost, customer services and demographic considerations are motivating banks to evaluate their technology.

Ashwini gupta (2009)[83] opined that maximum number of branches providing CBS in recent years is increasing rapidly. Under CBS the services are provided as anywhere banking and everywhere access and quick transfer of funds in an efficient manner and at reasonable cost. New private sector banks, foreign banks and a few old private sector banks are already put in place of CBS. PSBs are also increasingly adopting a similar system and providing these services through their branches.

Sofat Rainy, Singh Amarpreet and Kaur Inderpreet (2009)[84] observed that technology has emerged as a key driver of growth for banking sector in India. During the last decade, technology has been dramatically transforming banking in India driven by the challenges of competition, rising customer expectations and shrinking margins. Technology intensive delivery channels have created a situation by expanding great convenience and multiple options for customers while providing tremendous cost advantages to banks.

Sathiya and Jay Kumar (2009)[85] highlighted that banking is service oriented industry. It works mainly for accepting deposits and to make loans and advances. Customers need changing value-added services with technological aspects which is providing anytime-anywhere banking to the demanding customers. So e-banking has introduced to face the imminent challenge competition in modern Indian Economy. Many banks are providing techno-based customer services to provide flexibility in banking operations for the benefits of customers.

According to Sundaram V. (2009)[86] IT has recorded compounded annual growth rate of 8.4% that any person can operate his transactions from his own place. Transactions are paperless and time saving and cost saving also. Banks are also highly documents intensives, image processing technology can have a far reaching impact for such applications. In banks, image technology could be used for automatic identification or character recognition to read text and diagram and to scan cheques and documents.

Vashistha, V.K. (2009)[87] opined that banks are providing various e-banking services but customers are facing many problems in using the services. It means qualitative services are most important for development of banks through the qualitative and quantitative dimensions. In modern era demand of customers are increasing from financial institutions thus relevant technological services and proper implementation of customers' requirements are essential. In developed countries there are different mechanisms but India does not have any mechanism. Thus it's become difficult to such financial institutions to struggle and to stable in competitive markets. Due to absence of proper management and sufficient financial assistance, financial institutions can't do high-tech arrangements.

Pathania Kulwant Singh and Sharma Mamta (2010)[88] Customers are facing various problems while operating the New Technologies. The awareness and satisfaction of customers while using the services are found low. Due to managerial and technological problems and absence of knowledge, many customers are not using the services.

According to Amit Barak (2010)[89], usage of IT for financial system is fundamental to the survival and growth of the institutions. IT helps banks to hold and reduce cost of operations, several developments in the ICT enables the institutions for highly profitable products and services to their constitutions. It also provides competitive advantage and edge to its users.

Kaustubh Kelkar (2010)[90] gave hints of awareness while using the credit cards and how such cards are to be misused at the time of purchasing and why banks collect excess amount as penalty.

S. Valli Devasena and M. Gurupandi (2010)[91] studied that banking services are essential in the society for making availability of cash and cash payment services to the customers. An interesting feature of basic banking account scheme is the element of transparency i.e. the banking institution should prior to opening the account, minimum availability of balance, charges for providing various services, maximum number of withdrawal transactions without any additional charge and other charges imposed on transactions for availing electronic facility not operated by the account holder's banking institutions, etc.

From the information of Maharashtra Times (2010)[92] any bank customer may transfer cash from mobile from any banks. These transactions will be completed with the help of National Payment Corporation of India. And these transactions will be known as Interbank Mobile Payment Service (IMPS). Customers may transfer cash up to Rs. 50,000/- in a day but the sender and the receiver both must have Mobile Money Transfer Identifier Number (MMID).

An article of Bhagwat Ashwini in Daily Loksatta (2011)[93] noted that there is facility of insurance for Debit and Credit cards which has been provided by the Insurance Company in case of loss of cards. The card holder should have to get this facility from own bank by making special registration for insurance facility and also should have to pay the particular amount of the services as annual installment. With the help of this service any card holder who has lost his card can get the particular amount used after missing the card from the bank within 24 hours.

As per an article of Daily Sakal (2011)[94] noted that modernization has taken place in banking sector so it becomes easy to withdraw the cash from ATM Centers.

With the help of CBS any cheque of same bank has been cleared within a minute and without charging any amount as the service commission. Now with the help of 'Milestone of Modern Banking Services', it will become possible to clear the cheque by any bank without charging any amount as service commission. It also provides depositary and withdrawal facility from National and Merchant Banks on international level also.

Dasgupta (2012)[95] defined that E-banking is providing more efficient, faster and much easier way of completing transactions without face to face communication. For technological development banking sector is known as ideal platform for successful implementation of electronic media. At virtual level of banking sector, online services are completed with the help of internet facilities and use of high technology system.

Revathy Shriram (2013)[96] defined features of Core Banking Solution that these services are of 24*7 processing capacity, Central customer information system, independent platform and data base, availability of multi-currency, support for multiple delivery channel and have Global exposures.

Poonia M. S. (2013)[97] noted that ICT is playing very important role in the development of banks by providing online transaction facility and by reducing transactional cost. E-banking is most important for achieving long-term goals and for survival of banks. The banks which are not providing these services would lose their customers thus the banks are providing essential e-banking services to their customers.

H. Working Groups/Committees

Jalan (2002)[98] has defined that ICT has brought fundamental revolution in banking sector. The banks using e-banking technology have more profitability. He also noted that internet as being a supplementary distribution channel for their products and service. In addition to other forms of distribution channels such as ATMs, Phones, mobiles and bank branches. Basic transactions and securities trading are the most popular types of operations that customers carry out in internet banking.

Ministry of Information Technology (GoI-2003)[99] defined that since last 5 years, majority of transactional services will be provided by way of internet. Net-based banking comes at only 10 per cent of the operating cost of conventional banking practices and services. Banks are going to play a key role in IT enabled public services involving electronic money transactions. MIT feel that cooperative banks should consider Net banking in a big way.

RBI committee chaired by Gandhi[100] (Chairman of working group of RBI-2007) focused on IT initiative in UCBs. This committee reviewed Annual Report of 2007-2008 of RBI and examined the various areas where IT support is provided by RBI and it is realized that till March 2007, 16 out of 1853 banks had implemented core banking solutions and 50 banks had no computers. Most of the banks have based on Total Branch Automation. Several banks have implemented locally developed and customized application solutions. Committee found that the major cause behind this was that the computerization does not include networking among branches, since the sector is largely dominated by unit banks with only a few branches.

C. Rangarajan (2013)[101] committee report stressed the need for mechanization of operations and suggested adoption of modern banking technology in Indian Banks.

An article published in Sandhyanand (2014)[102] defined that RBI permit new banking licenses for economic reforms in banking sector. Banks are motivating customers to open new accounts in their banks and to increase number of account holders (customers). New Bank Licensing Committee chaired by Nachiket More defined that RBI is working for controlling drawbacks and removing technical problems on national level. RBI also trying to permit incenses to new branches which are opening in rural and village areas as well as in tribal areas. RBI is also trying to adopt new policies for improving customer services and for increasing the financial transactions smoothly and safely with the help of banks.

In the budget of 2015-16, Finance Minister Arun Jetli103 focused on the use of plastic money instead of paper currencies such as cheques, cash, etc. To motivate the customers at e-banking transactions and for maximum use of debit/credit cards for retail transactions, many banks have adopted the 'cash back policy' and 'Reward Point Policy'. These policies are free of cost and customers have to register for this policy. In the competitive era, banks are giving the reward from 2.5% to 10% per transaction. If the plastic cards are used for household purpose, customers can save Rs. 400 to Rs. 500 for per transaction of Rs. 10000/ - Use of plastic money is boon to those customers which are doing online shopping/e-trading.

Conclusion

From the reviews given above, it is clear that e-banking is working as change agent. It has changed the fact of traditional/manual banking into modern/techno-based banking. The key factors of using e-banking services are; to improve customer access towards e-banking, to facilitate the offering of more services, to increase customers' loyalty at techno-based services, to attract new customers, to provide services offered by competitors, to reduce customers' attrition, etc. Further it cleared that people have knowledge of the concept and they are availing it. The results are drawn on the basis of techniques of sampling. This was due to reason that people are not aware of the concept and they are unable to give the desired information. Thus technology in banking sector is yet to overlap traditional system.

References

1. Bhatt Sanjeev (1988), 'Bank Marketing', An article in The Economic Times, dated 1st Sept., 1988
2. Kohok M. A. (1993), Financial Services in India, 'Credit Cards', First Edition, Digvijay Publication, Nashik, Pp-257-261
3. Jhingan M.L., Cooperative Banks in India, 'Money, Banking, International Trade and Public Finance', 7th Edition, 2008, Vrinda Publications, pp-605-606
4. Ahluwalia Rupali (2008), Service Sector in India, 'Banking Services-Vision and Prospects', Adhyayan publication, New Delhi, editorial, , pp-70-72
5. Ganesan, S., (2009), E-banking: Opportunities and Challenges, Editorial-R.K. Uppal, 'Mahamaya Publications, New Delhi, Pp-37
6. Uppal R.K., Jatana Rimpi, (2009), Editorial, 'E-banking: Opportunities and Challenges', Mahamaya Publications, New Delhi, Pp-6
7. Maheshwari V. & Govindrajan K. (2009), 'Modern Banking Technologies', Southern Economist, Vol-48, No-16, Dec., 2009
8. Bhaskaran R. (Chief Executive Officer-RBI-2011), Know Your Banking, 'Electronic Banking', Pp-111
9. Padhye, Kishor C. and Mishra Rakesh Roshan (2013), A to Z banking and finance, Himalaya Publishing House, First Edition, 2013, Pp. 15
10. Editorial, Vikalpvedh, Vol-17, No-3, 2011, Pp-19
11. Govilkar Vinayak, 'Rural Development', An article in Daily Lokmat, dated 13th Sept., 2011, Pp-8
12. Mishra Rabindrakumar, Economic Development in India, AVON Publication, New Delhi, 1st Edition, 2013, Pp-110
13. S.S. Sisodia (1995), Cooperative Banks in India, New century Publication, New Delhi, First Edition, Pp-42-43.
14. Aggarwal, 2002, E-Banking for Comprehensive Democracy; An Indian Discernment, www.JIBC.Com/e-banking 2002
15. Acharya & Shankar, 'Macro Economic Management in the 90s', Economic & Political Weekly, 2002, Vol-37, No-16, Pp-15-38
16. Avadhani V.A. (2008), Marketing of Financial Services, Himalaya Publications House, Mumbai, Pp-642-649
17. S. Sanmuga Pria, (2009), E-banking: opportunities and challenges, Editorial R.K.Uppal and Rimpi Jatana, Mahamaya Publishing House, New Delhi, First Edition, Pp-49-53
18. Joshi Shrinivas, Banking Sector Towards Global Competition, Yojana, March-2009, Pp-26 -29
19. Puja Arora, (2009), E-banking: Opportunities and Challenges, Editorial R.K.Uppal and Rimpi Jatana, Mahamaya Publishing House, New Delhi
20. Keyur Nayak (2009), Retail Banking In India, 'Indian Banking Sector: Its Efficiency', New Delhi, Editorial R.K. Uppal, Pp-270-283

21. Biswas Nigamananda, 'Biometric ATM: Boon to Indian Rural Bank Customers', Southern Economist, ISSN-0038-4046, Vol-48, No-19, Feb-2010, Pp-29
22. Kaur Gian, (2011), New Trends in Finance, 'Risk, Efficiency & Return of PSBs and Private Banks in India', Editorial, Pravin Kumar Toyal, Sugan Jain, RBSA Publishers, Pp-256-272
23. Dongre Yashwantha (2011), Banking for rural development in India 'Rural reconstruction through co-operative resurgence', Editorial: G.V.Joshi, P.A.Rego, Sinam M., Bangalore University, Published by Macdonald & Evans, Pp-147-156
24. H. Rajeshwari, (2011) Banking sector reform in India: A critical evaluation, R.K.Uppal, editorial, Adhyayan publication, pp- 87-99
25. Gupta, O.P. and Poonam Nagpal (2011), Banking Sector Reform, 'Banking Sector Reform in India in the Phase of Globalisation', Uppal, R.K. editorial, Mahamaya Publishing House, New Delhi, Pp- 76-86
26. Dutta-sundaram (2012), 63rd edition, Indian Economy (2013), 'IT Industry', S.Chand Publication, New Delhi, Pp- 675-686
27. V.S. Deshpande (2013), Developmental Strategies in India, Status of Human Development', Editorial-Vidya Prakashan, Nagpur, Pp-123
28. C. Padhy Kishor and Rakesh Roshan Mishra, (2013) A to Z Banking and Finance, 'Eligibility for Autonomy', Himalaya Publishing House, First Edition, 2013, Pp-16
29. Govilkar, Vinayak, 'Rural Development', An article in Daily Lokmat, dated 13th Oct., 2013 Pp-6
30. Iyer, V.R. (2013) BOI, Chairperson's speech, 17thAnnual General Meeting of Shareholders at Mumbai, 29thJune2013, published in Economic times on 1stJuly, 2013
31. Jack Ewing, New York Times News Service, 'Bank Resists Pressure to Scale Back Global Ambition', The Economics Times, Page 7, Dated 31st May., 1992
32. The Economic Times, dated 23rd Jan., 2007
33. Pravinkumar Tayal & Sugan C. Jain (2007), New trends in Finance, 'Financial Reporting of Banking Companies in India- an Evolutionary Stage', Editorial- Dangwal R.C.& Kashmira Singh, RBSA Publishers, Pp-305-320
34. Chetia Dilip Kumar, Indian Journal of Commerce, 'Banking Infrastructure in North-East India', Vol-61, No-03, July-Sept-2008, Pp-49
35. Goyal Ritu & Kaur Rajinder, Indian Journal of Commerce, 'Performance of New Private Sector Banks in India', Vol-61, No-03, July-Sept-2008, Pp-1-5
36. Ram Mohan T.T., Indian Journal of Commerce, 'Performance and Development of Indian Banking', Vol-63, No-01, Jan-March-2010, Pp-21-25

37. Syal Ginni & Gulati Sonu (2011), Indian Banking Industry in 2020, Editor-R.K.Uppal, an article on 'Indian Banking: Role of Financial Growth', Mahamaya Publishing House, New Delhi.

38. Gandatra Navdeepkumar & Rama (2011), 'Banking Sector Reforms: A fresh Outlook', Editor-R.K.Uppal, an article on 'Competition in Indian Banking Sector-Issues and Strategies in Global Scenario', Mahamaya Publishing House, New Delhi, Pp-125-128

39. Kumar Navdeep (2011), Indian Banking Industry in 2020, Editor-R.K.Uppal, an article on 'FDI in Indian Banking Sector', Mahamaya Publishing House, New Delhi, Pp-158-167

40. Mishra RabindraKumar, (2013), Economic Development in India, 'New Avenues in Banking sector', AVON publication, New Delhi, 1st Edition

41. Economic Survey, 2013-14, Technological Banks in India, 'Financial Intermediation and Markets', Pp-110-111

42. John H. Dunning, Elsevier, 'Trade And Foreign Direct Investment', Reserve Bank of India, Occasional Papers, Globalization, Vol-20, No-2, Monsoon-1999, Pp-339-340

43. Herbst 'Trade And Foreign Direct Investment', RBI, Occasional Papers, Globalization, Vol-20, No-2, Monsoon-2001, Pp-207-208

44. Bhasin T.M., 2001, 'E-Commerce in Indian Banking', IBA Bulletin, Vol-XXIII, No. 4-5

45. Reddy Y.V., 'Asian Perspective on Growth: Outlook for India', RBI Bulletin-2006, Pp-11

46. Uppal R.K. and Kaur Rimpi (2007), Indian banking in globalised Era, Editorial-Mahamaya Publishing House, pp-2

47. Janardhanan V.K., 'Relevance of Service Sector Growth in India', Southern Economist, Vol-47, No-14, Nov., 2008

48. Kumbhar V.M., Arthasanvad, Dec., 2008, Vol-32, No-3, Pp-214-222

49. Report on Trend and Progress of Banking in India, 2008-2009, Pp-124

50. JIBC, Editorial, December 2009, Vol. 14, No. 3, Pp-2

51. Sharma Arti & Kaur Navneet (2009), Indian Banking sector: Its Efficiency 'Indian Banking Challenges in Liberalized Era', , New Century Publication, New Delhi, Pp-195-206

52. Bimal Anjum, Sofat Rajni, Sridhar Rajan(2011), 'ndian banking industry in 2020, 'Impact of Globalization on Indian Banking', Editorial: R.K.Uppal, Mahamaya Publishing House, Pp-247

53. Bhalla Ashwani Kumar (2011), Indian Banking Industry in 2020, 'Indian Financial Services', R.K.Uppal, Editorial, ,Mahamaya Publishing House, Page No. 266-276

54. Dutta-sundaram(2013), 'Indian Financial System', Indian Economy, 64th edition, S.Chand Publication, New Delhi, Pp- 854

55. Prakash Garewal & Nandini Garewal(2013), Banking sector Reform: A fresh Outlook, Editor-R.K. Uppal, Adhyayan publication, Pp- 76-86

56. Mishra & Puri (2013), Indian Economy, Himalaya Publishing House, Pp-745

57. Takle Dinkar, 'Challenges in Banking Sector After Globalization', Arthasanvad, July-Sept., 2014, Vol-38, No-2, Pp-204-209

58. Thakur Vishwas, (Chairman-Vishwas Cooperative Bank limited, Nashik), an article, 'Dynamic Changes in Banking Sector', in Daily Deshdoot, supplement of Banking Special, dated 20th Feb., 2015, pp-1

59. Tripathy S.N. (2000), 'Cooperative: Growth and New Dimensions', Discovery Publishing House, New Delhi

60. Ruchi Trehan, Niti Soni, Arti Verma, Indian Banking Moving Towards Better Tomorrow, 'Innovations in Banking', R.K. Uppal, Editorial, Mahamaya publishing house, New Delhi, 2009, pp-43-47

61. Chakrabarti Rajesh (2009), 'The Financial Sector in India-Emerging Issues', Oxford Publications, Pp-154-177

62. Karunaniathal (2009), Banking, Micro Finance and SGs in India, 'Performance of Private Sector Banks in Erode District', New Century publication, New Delhi, First Edition

63. An article in Daily Lokmat dated 6th Jan., 2011, Pp-06

64. An article in Daily Sakal dated 9th March, 2011

65. R.K.Uppal (2012), editorial, Indian Banking Industry in 2020, 'Globalization', Mahamaya Publishing house, Pp-19

66. Rangrajan C., (1997), Governor's Speech, RBI Bulleting, Pp-51

67. Uppal R.K & Rimpi Kaur (2007), 'Indian Banking in Globalised Era: Moving Towards Better Tomorrow', Editoriral, Mahamaya Publishing House, New Delhi, Pp-01

68. Jayalakshmi. S. and Asok. A., 'WTO and Indian banking sector: An Overview', Southern Economist, vol-47, No-15, Dec., 2008

69. Patel Ranjana (2009), Service Sector in India, 'Service Sector in India: Growth & Potential', Editor-Shyam Mohan Dwivedi & Hridyanarayan Mishra, Adhyayan Publications, Jaipur, Pp-46-51

70. Maheswari V. & Govingrajan K. (2009), 'Modern Banking Technologies', Southern Economist, Vol-48, No-16, Dec., 2009

71. Biswas Nigamananda (2009), 'Banking Sector in India: Challenges Ahead', Southern Economist, Vol-48, No-14, Nov., 2009,

72. Selvaraju R. & Vasanthi G., Marketing Mix Strategy of Banking Services, Southern Economist, Vol-47, No-20, Feb-2009

73. Pravinkumar Tayal & Sugan C. Jain (2009), New trends in Finance, 'Financial Reporting of Banking Companies in India- an Evolutionary stage', Editorial- Dangwal R.C.& Kashmira Singh, RBSA Publisers, New Delhi, Page no. 255

74. Shyam Mohan Dwivedi & Hridyanarayan Mishra (2011), Service Sector in India, 'Role of IT & Internet in Service Sector', Editor-Shyam Mohan Dwivedi & Hridyanarayan Mishra, Adhyayan Publications, Jaipur, Pp-127-133

75. Gurpreet Kaur, Niti Soni, Arti Verma (2011), Indian Banking Moving Towards Better Tomorrow, 'Banking With Technology', Editorial, R.K.Uppal, Mahamaya Publishing House, New Delhi, 2009, Pp-54

76. PadhyeKishor C. & Mishra Rakesh Roshan, A to Z Banking & Finance, 'Banking Ombudsman', Himalaya publishing house, First Edition, 2013, pp-41

77. Economic Survey- 2013-14, 'Technological Developments in Banks', Financial Intermediation and Markets, Pp-110-111

78. R.P.Gupta (2003), 'Dynamics Of Banking Technology', Journal of Internet Banking and Commerce, Vol-3, No-2, June 2003,

79. Kaptan S.S., (2005), New Concepts in Banking, Sarup & Sons Publications, New Delhi

80. Sarma Naina (2007), Banking and Social Change in India: The early Decades, Aalekh Publishers, Jaipur

81. Goyal B.B. & Kumar Nitesh (2007), Indian Banking Industry in 2020, 'Globalisation: a Paradigm Shift in Indian Banking System', Mahamaya Publishing House, New Delhi, Editor-R.K.Uppal, Pp-138

82. Niti Soni and Gurpreet Kaur (2007), Indian Banking Moving Towards Better Tomorrow, 'Banking With Technology', Editorial R.K. Uppal, Mahamaya Publishing House, New Deli, Pp-17-24

83. Ashwini Gupta (2009), Editorial R.K.Uppal and Rimpi Jatana, E-Banking: Opportunities and Challenges, New Century Publication, New Delhi, Pp-

84. Rainy Sofat, Amarpreet Singh and Inderpreet Kaur(2009), Indian Banking Moving Towards Better Tomorrow, 'Indian Banking Challenges in Liberalized Era', Editorial, R.K. Uppal, Pp-175-194

85. Sathiya & Jay kumar (2009), 'E-banking services', Southern Economist, Vol-48, No-8, August-2009

86. Sundaram V. (2009), 'Banking Development', Alfa Publication, New Delhi, Pp- 27-33

87. Vashistha, V.K. (2009), Indian Economy and Regional development, Pratiksha publications, Jaipur, Pp-202-211

88. Singh Kulwant, Pathania & Sharma Mamta (2010), 'Adoption of Banking Technology', Indian Journal of Commerce, Vol-63, No-01, Jan-March-2010,

89. Amit Barak (2010), Cooperative banks in India, New century Publication, New Delhi, First Edition, Pp-42-43

90. Kelkar Kaustubh, An article in Daily Lokmat dated 16th Sept., 2010

91. S. Valli Devasena and M. Gurupandi (2010), 'Service Quality Analysis of Banks', Indian Journal of Commerce, Vol-63, No-01, Jan-March-2010, Pp-21-25

92. Maharashtra Times, 4th June, 2010, An article on 'E-transactions', Pp-7

93. Bhagwat Ashwini, An article on 'Security of Cards', in Daily Loksatta, dated 19th Nov., 2011, Pp-6

94. An article in 'Modern Banking', in daily Sakal, dated 4th March, 2011

95. www.projectshub.com Dasgupta, P. (2012), 'Future of E-Banking In India', An Article

96. Sriram Revathy 2013, Core Banking Solution: Evaluation of Security and Controls, PHI Learning Private Limited, New Delhi,

97. Poonia,M.S. (2013), 'Development Banking in India', Pratiksha Publication, Jaipur, Pp-143-149

98. Bimil Jalan, 'Strengthening Indian Banking and Finance; Progress And Prospects', Bank Economist Conference, Mumbai, RBI Bulletin, 2002

99. Http://Www.Mit.Gov.In/Eg/Home.Asp MIT 2003, Official Website of MIT, GoI,

100. RBI Committee Report chaired by Gandhi, published in 'The Economic Times', on 19th Dec., 2007

101. C. Rangrajan, 'RBI-Reports on Trends and Progress of Banking in India, 2013

102. Sandyanand dated 16th April, 2014Ashish Thakur, 'Development-Qualitative or Quatitative', Loksatta-Arthbramha, No-2, 2015-16, Pp-74

Socio-Economic Profile of Study Area

3.1 Introduction

Maharashtra is one of the leading state; playing an important role in the development of nation through social, political, economic and cultural aspects. According to CM Devendra Phadanvis, Nashik is the third leading and dynamic city of Maharashtra[1]. Nashik is located on the bank of river Godavari (Second largest river in the Indian plateau) and in the mountain ranges of Sahyadri; making it one of the holiest places for Hindus. From ancient period, Nashik is referred in various religious, historical and as a tourism center. Mountain Bramhagiri (origin of river Godavari), Panchavati, Anjaneri (birth place of Hanuman), Temple of Renuka Devi and Saptashrungi Devi, Workplace of Samarth Ramdas, Lord Shiva's temple at Tryambak, West Kashi Dharmapeeth are famous places from the age of god and goddess. Thus Nashik is known as one of the most famous religious place where Kumbhamela is organized once in every 12 years[2].

Prominent authors of Marathi drama poets and world class literature writers, Vasant Kanetkar and V.V. Shirvadkar have done their creative work in Nashik. Museum, memorial place of Dadasaheb Phalke is famous in the Art of film making and originator of films in India. Earthen Dam of Gangapur, Nashik Dhol, Music, Bird Sanctuaries of Nandur Madhyameshwar, are some of the key-points of attraction for tourists. Nashik is also famous for agricultural products as onion, grapes, sugarcane etc. and also for industries as winery, sugar factories, Paithani etc.

3.2 Historical features of Nashik District

No one knows when the city of Nashik came into existence. According to the mythology, Laxmana cut the nose ('Nashika' in Sanskrit) of 'Shurpnakha' and hence the city got the name 'Nashik'. Long ago, Brahmadeva had meditated in 'Padmasana' here, so the city was also called 'Padma-Aasana' for some time. Nashik was 'Trikantak' in Kritayuga, 'Janasthana' in Dwaparyuga and later it became 'Navashikh' or 'Nashik' in Kuliyuga. Renowned poets like Valmiki, Kalidas and Bhavabhooti have great contribution for Nashik. Nashik in 150 BC was believed to be the country's largest market place. It was also known as the 'Land of the brave' during the regime of Chhatrapati Shivaji Maharaj[3].

A. Ramayana Period

Nashik has a personality of its own, due to its mythological, historical, social and cultural importance. Nashik has a rich historical past, as the mythology; that Lord Rama (the King of Ayodhya) stay at Nashik during his years in exile. At the same place Lord Laxmana (brother of lord Rama) cut the nose of 'Shurpnakha' (sister of Ravana) by the wish of Lord Rama, and thus this city was named as Nashika, a Sanskrit word thus the name was originated as 'Nashik'. Nashik has been a famous holy pilgrimage Centre known for both Rama (Nashik) and Shiva (Tryambak).

B. Maratha Rule

During that period of Maratha rule the rich families like braves, Vaishampayans and Gadres of the locality started their financial activities and provided advances to military campaigns of feudal Sardars and in their later times their Pedhi's gradually began to finance the flourishing trade in metal ware and fabrics as well as grapes and onions.

During those days a person named Dev Mamledar (God like Tehsildar) lived in Nashik whose real name was Yashawant Mahadev Bhosekar. He began his career as a humble clerk in the revenue department and gradually rose to the position of Mamaledar. A severe famine affected the area and Bhosekar generously helped the people to alleviate their sufferings. In less time he became so famous that princes and people began to respect him as a saint and called him Yashwantrao Maharaj. Upon his death in 1887 people raised a small beautiful temple for his Samadhi on the ban of the river where his last funeral rites were performed.

C. Peshwa Period

In the recent past, the Moguls were fascinated by the beauty of the city and renamed it as 'Gulshanabad' (city of gardens). Beautiful fresh flowers were sent to Aurangzeb from Gulshanabad i.e. Nashik. But it was during the rule of the Peshwa, when the place was finally renamed as Nashik. During this period, Raghobadada and his wife Anandibai settled down at 'Anandwalli' in Nashik. There are some forts of Anandibai. There is also a temple called 'Navasha Ganapati' built by Anandibai.

D. British Rule

By the middle of 19th century the British Rule was firmly established and the public life of Nashik began to pulsating with activities suited to the times. During the British rule (pre-independent period), many freedom fighters were also fought for freedom from Nashik District. Swa. Sawarkar (Bhagur), Tatya Tope (Yeola), Ahilyabai Holkar (Chandwad). In April 1818, a British officer named Mr. Jackson was killed in Vijayanand Film Theater and so Anant Laxman Kanhere and other nationalists were hanged by the British, then Nashik once again regained its importance. The British fell in love with the beauty of the city and developed it in various fields. The Golf course, developed by the British, was one of the largest in Asia.

National Movement In 1869 made Nashik as a full-fledged district with its present Talukas. With the return of peace Nashik flourished into prosperity due to political, religious and commercial activities led to its rapid development. With the construction of the railway, going from Bombay to north-east, from very near the city, religious minded devotees came to be attracted to the town in ever increasing numbers where they made their purchases of various artistic and useful articles. This made Nashik a great trade Centre where artisans skilled in manufacturing utensils and smiths excelling in workmanship in silver and gold crowded to ply their trade.

At that time, the present territory of Nashik District was partly distributed in Khandesh and Ahmednagar. During the British rule Nashik region witnessed some revolutionary insurgencies against the British rule. Bhagoji Naik's rebellion 1857, (We Indians call it a revolution for independence against British Rule) were a few of those revolutionary actions. The roots of Nationalist movement in India were also shown in and around Nashik. Early in 1899 a secret society known as Rashtra-Bhakta-Samuha (a body of devoted patriots) was started by Savarkar, Mhaskar and Page (Nashik District Gazetteer). Nashik was also a center of Abhinav Bharat. Many patriots sacrificed their lives for the Nationalist appeal.

During the British rule Nashik was also known for the movements of socio-cultural transformation. For example; Kalaram Mandir Satyagraha led by Dr. Babasaheb Ambedkar, Bhoomi Mukti Andolan by Dadasaheb Gaikwad, the making of Dabhadi Prabandha –a Manifesto of Shetkari Kamgar Paksha (Party of Peasants and workers). In Post Independence period Nashik developed as one of the leading districts of Maharashtra. Development in agriculture and industry boosted its socio-economic development.

3.3 Milestones in the History of Nashik

Nashik Road Railway Station, Indian Security Press, Nashik Artillery Centre, HAL (Hindustan Aeronautical Limited), Air Force are leading factors of Nashik.

Table 3.1

Major events in the history of Nashik

Development/Changes	Year
Establishment of SarvajanikVachanalaya (Native Library Nashik)	1840
Formation of Sharanpur Colony	1854
Formation of Deolali Cantonment (Anglo-vernacular school)	1861
Construction of Nashik Road Railway Station	1862
Formation Nashik Municipality	1864
Formation and Declaration of Nashik District	1869
Construction of Saint Andrew Church	1894
Construction started for Victoria Bridge	1894
Establishment of Police Training School	1910
Distillery started at Nashik Road	1922
Construction and formation of Security Press at Nashik Road	1927
Shifting of Artillery Center from Quetta (Pakistan) to Nashik	1941
Establishment of Revenue Department	1981

Source: http://www.nashik.nic.in

Nashik is also educationally rich that two universities are established in Nashik as Yashwantrao Chavan Maharashtra Open University, Health Science University. Mahindra and Mahindra, Mico, Glaxo, Crompton Greaves, VIP, Asian Paints are leading companies located in Nashik. Import and Export is also comparatively more from Nashik.

3.4 Geographical features of Nashik district

3.4.1 Location

Nashik District is located at North area of Maharashtra between 19° 35' and 20° 52' North Latitude and 73° 16' and 74° 56' east longitude, with an area of 15,582'0 km.2 (6,015 sq. miles). East-West average length is 200 km and of South-North is 120 km and at 565 meters above mean sea level. Its area is 5.04% of the area of Maharashtra.

It is located in three different rivers; Godavari, Tapi and Daman ganga at west side in the Tehsil of Surgana and Peth. All the rivers have their sources in the rock ranges of Sahyadri and flow from East to West. Nashik has boundary of five districts of Maharashtra and two districts of Gujarat. Boundaries are Dhule (north), Jalgaon (North-east), Aurangabad (South-east), Ahmednagar (south) and Thane (south-west). As this Surat and Dang is at north-west. Nashik is surrounded by nine hills, namely: Durga, Ganesh, Chitraghanta, Pandav, Dinger Ali, Mhasarul, Jogwada, Pathanpura and Konkani.

3.4.2 Temperature

The climate of the district is generally dry except during monsoon season. As per the Nashik District Gazetteer, "the maximum temperature in summer is 42.5 degree centigrade and minimum temperature in winter is less than 5.0 degree centigrade. Relative humidity ranges from 43% to 62%. Climate of the Nashik is generally compares with that of Bangalore and Pune because of its pleasant nature. However in recent years it is noticed that the temperature is increasing and the rainfall is decreasing due to industrialization and fast deforestation.

3.4.3 Forest

Total forest area of Nashik district is 2622.23 hectares (20.74%) to total land of which 2373.4 is reserves and 242.18 sq. km is secured and remaining 6.65 sq. km is unclassed. The ratio of forest in Nashik district is highest in Maharashtra state. The forest areas in the district lie in the western part of the district. Surgana, Kalwan, Peth, Dindori, Nashik, Igatpuri, Tryambak Talukas have a number of forests. Teak, Sissov trees are found in large number of these forests. The forest area is mainly located in the western, northern and south-western regions of the district. Teak is the main species; other species are Sadala, hed, Haldu, Sisum, Khair, Tiwas, Bibla, and Dhavada Bamboos. There is a bird sanctuaries center at Nandur-Madhyameshwar (Niphad Tehsil) and many birds come and stay there in winter. The total area of bird sanctuary is 100.12 sq. kms.

3.4.4 Water Resources

Nashik district is drained by two chief rivers, i.e. the Girna and Godavari. Godavari, which rises near Tryambak and drains Nashik and Niphad Tehsil, is the most celebrated river and is known as "Southern Ganga". Other rivers of the district are Darna, Mosam, Aram, Vaitarna, Manyad and Kadwa. The main feature of rivers of Nashik District is that all the rivers of the district have their sources in Nashik and no any river comes in Nashik from any other districts.

Nashik has also reputed hill stations which are at the east side of rock ranges of Sahyadri. As a result of new technology in many industries the demand for water has increased greatly. Consequently, the problem of securing usable water at reasonable rate is now a major one. An adequate water supply is necessity in choosing a site for industries including poultry farming.

3.4.5 Rainfall

Website from Irrigation department holds that, 'the average rainfall of the District is between 2600 and 3000 mm, but there is wide variation in the rainfall received at various blocks. Most of the rainfall is received from June to September'. Nashik has been the best District as compared with the other districts in the Nashik Division for scores in rainfall. Average rainfall in Nashik District is 1125.4 mm and an average height of land is 5 to 55 ft. from sea level.

3.4.6 Irrigation Projects

Gangapur, Ozarkhed, Karanjwan, Darana, Girna are some of the major water projects. In 2013-14 these entire projects brought total 3,37,522 hectors (44.08 %) land in the district under irrigation. Out of this 32.82% land is under natural irrigation and remaining 67.18 % base on wells.

13 major irrigation projects, 8 medium size projects, 811 small storage projects, 692 dipping ponds, 23 dams, 153871 water wells are available. Major water projects are mostly concentrated in the Talukas of Dindori, Kalwan, Baglan, and Nashik. The data reveals the fact that Peth, Surgana, Igatpuri, Yeola, Tryambak, most of the part of Nandgaon are agriculturally (irrigation wise) most backward sections of the district as against irrigated and agriculturally rich sections like Niphad, Kalwan, Sinner, Chandwad, Nashik, Baglan and some part of Dindori. About 92% of irrigation was available from underground water resources like wells and from canals or dams.

3.5 Economical Features

3.5.1 Land-use and Land Holding Pattern

A) Land Use Pattern

According to 2013-14 Land Survey Report, the total land of the district is 1426000 hectors out of which 16.87% was forest-land, 10.04% was non-cultivable land (hilly, rocky) 6.63% was cultivable but unused land and 8.25% was non-cultivable land due to its poor quality and remaining 61.75% is use for cultivation.

Table 3.2

Taluka-wise Distribution of Irrigated and Cultivable Land

Nashik District Total	Actual Cultivable area	% of Cultivable area to total area	Irrigated area	% of Irrigated area to total area
	880258	87.51	206741	24.21

Source: Nashik District Census Report-2011, page 54

Out of 1426000 hector, 880000 hectare is cultivated land of the district out of which 9.92 per cent land has used for cultivation of more than one time. Irrigation facilities to agriculture have been unequally distributed in the district and thus created developed and undeveloped agricultural zones.

B) Land Holding Pattern:

The Nashik district Agricultural survey data base of 2013-14 showed that total agricultural land holders are 642662 and total agricultural land holding in the district is 982889 hector and average land holding is 1.53 hector.

Table 3.3

Land Holding Pattern (Hectare)

Sr. No	**Size of holding**	**Total holdings**		**Average Land holdings**
		Number of families	**Area in Hectare**	
1.	0.0 to 0.5	139489	37886	0.27
2.	0.5 to 1.0	149007	110459	0.74
3.	1.0 to 2.0	203932	288742	1.41
4.	2.0 to 5.0	126860	366755	2.89

5.	5.0 to 10.0	20164	132641	6.58
6.	10.0 to 20.0	2895	36527	12.61
7.	20.0 +	315	9879	31.36
	Total	642662	982889	1.53

Source: District Socio-Economic Survey- Nashik District, 2013-14

3.5.2 Occupational Pattern

The proportion of the marginal workers to total workers is 12.54%. The number of marginal workers is still high despite the development of cities at faster rate. As per census 2011, 27.63 lakh are workers which is 42.25 per cent from total population in which 32.60 per cent are farmers, 23.31 are labours, 1.66 per cent are small businessmen, and 33.74 per cent are engaged in other work. However, the proportion of both cultivators and land laborers, it differs from Taluka to Taluka. The primary sector is large in Nashik. But the secondary and tertiary sectors together went on enlarging in last few decades which resulted in decline in primary sector in both Maharashtra and Nashik district also.

Table 3.4

Sector-wise distribution of workers

Area	Maharashtra	Nashik
Primary	61.51	68.73
Secondary	15.80	13.99
Tertiary	22.69	17.28
Total	100	100

Source- HRD-Maharashtra 2006-07

3.5.3 Crop and Cropping Pattern

A) Crop Pattern

The crops like wheat, Bajra, Maize, paddy and other cereals are grown in various parts of the District. Paddy has mainly grown in Tribal area i.e. Igatpuri, Peth, and Surgana. Vegetables and Onion were main cash crops since last 30 years. Various types of vegetables are supplied to Mumbai so the district is known as Backyard of Mumbai. After establishment of sugar factories, Sugarcane has acquired important position in the agriculture economy of the district. One sugar factory under private sector at Ravalgaon and other sugar factories under co-operative sector at Niphad, Ranwad, Palse, Materewadi and Vithewadi are functioning. Economic development in the rural area with speed started only after establishment of sugar factories.

The Government has granted permission for starting four sugar factories under private sector as a result of the liberalization. One sugar factory in private sector has started functioning in Satana Since last 20 years. Another agriculture product of grapes has acquired dominance on the agricultural economy of district. Due to water shortage in Kalwan, Deola, Baglan and Malegaon blocks the farmers have shifted to Pomegranate from sugar cane and grape crops and also cultivating flowers in green houses. These developments also indicate that the farmers in the district adopt new technology and methods of cultivation very fast. The district has been identified for the purpose of establishment of Wine Park and Food Park.

Onions is a major crop in Nashik especially in the Niphad taluka. The total Onion plantation in Nashik is more than 100,000 acres. Onion is one of the important crops for exports in the Middle East. The major trading for the domestic sale is done in the markets of Lasalgaon and Pimpalgaon. Lasalgaon market is the biggest trading house in Asia for Onions.

3.5.4 Industrial Workers

Table 3.5 indicates number of workers working in various industries in Nashik district. It is noted that the number of workers are 54303 per cent which are decreasing in decadal years and it is noted that the growth rate of workers is decreased with 9.19 in the year 2011-12. From the year 2012-13 the numbers of these workers are increasing and the average growth rate is 26.41 per cent.

Table 3.5

Number of Industrial Workers

Particulars	1990-91	2000-01	2011-12	2012-13	2013-14	Average
No. of workers	54303	82832	75222	76957	100601	389915
Growth rate in %	55.65	52.54	-9.19	2.31	30.72	26.41

Source: Socio-economic survey of Nashik District, 2011

3.5.5 Self-employment

It is noted that total 9900 educated unemployed candidates have taken self-employment opportunity with the financial support of employment center, district rural development schemes, lead bank and local corporation bodies. The highest numbers of self-employed persons are from lead bank (50 %) available in the nearest area, followed by district employment center (21.8 %) and educationally unemployed candidates get financial support from bank and have got self-employment opportunity.

Table 3.6 shows the number of beneficiaries under various self-employment schemes of state and central government.

Table 3.6

No. of Beneficiaries under self employment

Tehsil-places	District Employment Center	District Rural Development Scheme	Lead Bank	Local Corporation Bodies	Total
Malegaon	363	590	1003	50	2006
Satana	93	290	396	13	792
Kalwan	40	0	51	11	102
Nandgaon	127	3	140	10	280
Surgana	30	200	230	0	460
Nashik	928	10	1078	140	2156
Dindori	66	24	93	03	186
Igatpuri	87	110	197	0	394
Niphad	137	260	417	20	834
Peth	5	14	19	0	38
Sinnar	97	330	462	35	924
Yeola	116	30	152	06	304
Chandwad	36	260	306	10	612
Tryambak	3	330	333	0	666
Deola	26	24	73	23	146
Total	2154 (21.8)	2475 (25)	4950 (50)	321 (3.2)	9900 (100)

Source: Socio-Economic Survey of Nashik District, 2013-14

3.6 Industrial Features

3.6.1 Agro based Industries

On the basis of agriculture, many cash crops like Sugarcane, Grapes, Onions, Pomegranates, Roses, and Carnations are being planted on large scale. Sugarcane growing provided major thrust for the growth of agriculture in Nashik district. The Sugar factories today form a strong footing for the politics of Maharashtra. There are six sugar factories working in Nashik district, in which one sugar factory is working in private sector and other are working on cooperative basis. The sugar factories located in Nashik District are;

1 Ranwad Cooperative Sugar Factory Limited

2 Niphad Co-Operative Sugar Factory Limited

3 Nashik Co-Operative Sugar Factory Limited

4 Kadwa Cooperative Sugar Factory Limited

5 Vasantdada Cooperative Sugar Factory Limited

6 Rawalgaon Sugar Private Limited

Grapes prove to be one of the largest fruit exported from India and the majority of it comes from Nashik. The grape plantation is around 45,000 acres in Nashik. The grapes are also exported from Nashik to Middle East, South East Asia, United Kingdom and Europe. There are around 100 grape export units in Nashik and most of them are based on the farms. They have learnt new techniques in growing, thinning, canopy management, girdling, etc. Many farmers have started planting on rootstocks, which gives a good vigor to the development of wines. The grape industry is set to develop and is progressing in the right direction to achieve international standards. Pomegranates are another good crop from Nashik. This has a very good domestic market.

Floriculture is a very recent development in Nashik. Many poly houses have coming up in Nashik for flower exports. Roses and Carnations are the most popular flowers for exports. Carnations have recently lost their charm as the risks involved are very high and they no longer prove viable. Different varieties of roses are still in demand. The major markets for Indian roses are Holland (the-biggest flower market in the world), Singapore, United Kingdom and Japan.

3.6.2 Other Industries

Since last 6-8 years, industrial development has picked up the speed, particularly after declaration of a five-star mega industrial estate on 2700 hectare land in Sinnar block. Till March 2014, total 2105 industries are registered out of which 1933 are working smoothly. There are nearby 100601 workers working in industries. Many reputed and large companies like Mahindra and Mahindra, MICO, Siemens, Crompton Greaves, Kirloskar, and Raymond steel, Jindal, Brook Bond, L and T, Ceat, VIP, Carbon Everflow, Garware, Jyoti Structures, Samsonite, Datar Switch Gears, and Glaxo India etc. have established their units in the District. Prestigious project IDEM of Mahindra and Mahindra is established in Nashik very recently. These industries have brought the District on the National and International map. Musalgaon, Malegaon, Gonde, Satpur, Ambad are famous for large industrial development corporations.

In addition to these industries the District also has national level institutes like;

(i) Dr. Babasaheb Ambedkar Institute of Rural Technology and Training run by KVIC

(ii) Indian Institute of Numismatic Studies and Research at Tryambak.

Table 3.7

Working Industries and Number of Workers

Particulars	1990-1991	2000-2001	2011-2012	2012-2013	2013-2014	Average
Working Industries	1086	1416	1997	2105	1933	8537

Growth rate	73.48	30.39	41.03	5.41	-8.17	28.428
No. of workers	54303	82832	75222	76957	100601	389915
Growth rate in %	55.65	52.54	-9.19	2.31	30.72	26.41

Source: Statistical Data of Nashik District 2012-13

3.7 Demographic features

Various demographic features of population as observed in census 2011 are presented in this section.

3.7.1 Population in Nashik District

As per census 2011, population of Nashik district is 5.44 per cent with population of 61.07 lakhs in which 3157186 are male and 2950001 are female. Amongst Maharashtra State Nashik is the fourth largest district in terms of population having with growth rate of 22.29 per cent density of 393 sq. km. The population of the district has almost doubled between 1981 and 2001.

Out of 15 tehsils, largest number of population 28.74 per cent population is living in Nashik and the least 1.96 per cent population is living in Peth. 15.65 per cent population is living in Malegaon, Niphad have 8.08 per cent population whereas Satana have 6.13 per cent population. 58.60 per cent population is living in Nashik, Malegaon, Niphad and Satana and remaining population is living in other 11 tehsils.

Table 3.8

Population in Nashik District

Census Year	Total Population	Growth Rate %	% of Rural Population	Growth Rate %	% of Urban Population	Growth Rate %
1961	1855246	25.87	74.39%	32.83	25.61%	-12.88

1971	2368691	27.71	71.38%	22.54	28.62%	42.74
1981	2,991,739	26.26	68.98%	22.00	31.02%	36.87
1991	3,851,352	28.75	64.45%	20.31	35.55%	47.52
2001	4,993,796	29.68	61.19%	23.13	38.81%	41.56
2011	6107187	22.29	57.47%	14.86	42.53%	34.00

Source: WWW.nashik.nic.in, Nashik District Census 2011

Table 3.9

Decadal Variations of Population Density

Year	Density Per Sq. kms.	Female Per 1000 males	Decadal rate		Total
			Rural	Urban	
1951	92	715	0.00	0.00	0.00
1961	119	945	30.22	28.39	29.75
1971	152	920	22.49	42.84	27.20
1981	193	937	22.05	36.80	26.28
1991	248	940	20.25	47.52	28.73
2001	321	927	22.93	41.49	29.52
2011	393	931	22.30	29.66	NA

Source: Nashik District Census 1991 to 2011

As per census 2011, density of population in Nashik district was 393 per sq. km which is greater than Maharashtra state which is 365 sq. km. Nashik district is at 7th rank in the state for highest density. Density of Nashik tehsil is greatest with 2166 sq. km and lowest is of Tryambak tehsil with 190 sq. km.

3.7.2 Urban and Rural Population

In Nashik District, out of the total population, 42.52 percent (25.93 lakh) are living in urban area. 57.48 percent population is living in rural area. Population density in urban area is 4447 per sq. km. The urban population has increased by 441 lakhs during the decade (2001-2011).Population density in rural area is 202 per sq.km. Means in India around 72 percent population is living in rural area and 28 percent in urban area. Economic developed is generally associated with the growth of urbanization. Some writers say that acid test of development lies in the shift of population from the rural to the urban areas.

Table 3.10

Decadal Urban Population (lakh)

Census Year	Urban Population			Rural Population		
	Male	Female	Total	Male	Female	Total
1951	194	176	370	517	523	1040
1961	253	222	475	700	680	1380
1971	356	322	678	865	826	1691
1981	491	437	928	1053	941	1994
1991	715	654	1369	1270	1212	2482
2001	1023	914	1937	1569	1482	3051
2011	1352	1245	2597	1805	1705	3510

Source: District Socio-Economic Survey – Nashik District 2013-14

Out of the total Nashik population for 2011 census, 42.53 percent lives in urban regions of district. In total 2,597,373 people lives in urban areas of which males are 1,352,474 and females are 1,244,899. Sex Ratio in urban region of Nashik district is 920 as per 2011 census data.

3.7.3 Tehsil-wise population

As per census 2011, rural population of Nashik district is 3509814 which is 57.47% of the total. Out of this, 24% are tribal and 8.5% are dalits. In terms of occupation, there are

51% cultivators and 33 % as engaged as agriculture labourers. There are 6 blocks with more than 50% tribal population. Kokana, Mahadev Koli, Bhill, Warli, Thakur, Katkari are some of the leading tribes of Nashik district. 9.08 per cent population is of scheduled caste and 25.62 per cent are of scheduled tribe.

Table 3.11 shows the age-wise population of Nashik district. Child sex ratio in Nashik district was 890 in 2011 census. Child population (0-6) in urban region was 331,875 of which males and females were 175,568 and 156,307. This child population figure of Nashik district is 12.98 % which was 34.86% in 2001. The younger population is more in 2001 and in 2011 recorded as 14.43% and 17.38% respectively.

Table 3.11

Age-wise Population

Particulars	0-14	15-19	20-29	30-39	40-59	>60	Total
Male	9044	2844	4535	3605	4112	1709	25849
Female	8326	2327	4123	3470	3676	2052	23974
Total	17370	5171	8658	7075	7788	3761	49823
Percentage	34.86	10.38	17.38	14.20	15.63	7.55	100

Source: Socio-Economic Survey of Nashik District, 2013-14

As per census 2011, population in the district is; Hindu i.e. 86.53 percent; whereas lowest population was of Sikh religion i.e. 0.14 percent. Population of other religions to the percentage of total population of district was Buddha 1.90 percent, Christian 0.38 percent, Jain 0.71 percent, Muslim 10.17 percent and others were hardly 0.14 percent.

3.7.4 Rural and Urban Literacy ratio

The district literacy ratio has improved as 82.31 percent (2011) from 77.3 percent (2001 census). Table 3.12 indicate literacy ratio of the district. From total number of literate male population.

Table 3.12
Rural/Urban Literacy Ratio

Nashik District	Rural Literates	Urban Literates	Total Literates
Male	1306464 (56.16)	1091074 (54.04)	2397538 (55.17)
Female	1019968 (43.84)	927860 (45.96)	1947828 (44.83)
Total	2326432 (100)	2018934 (100)	4345366 (100)

Source: Socio-economic survey of Nashik district, 2011

The district has 77.19 percent literacy in rural area and 89.12 per cent in urban area, in that 88.17 percent males and 76.08 percent females. The district is 20thrank in the state in respect of literacy. Literacy and population growth are two factors, which bring about a change in nation. Female literacy rate, however around 12 counts lower than the male literacy rate.

Table 3.13

Gender-wise Literacy Ratio

Year	Particulars	Male	Female	Total	Growth Rate
2001	Literates	1,823,366	1,302,822	3,126,188	7.95%
	Literacy Rate	83.65%	64.35%	74.36%	
2011	Literates	2397538	1947828	4345366	
	Literacy Rate	88.17%	76.08%	82.31%	

Source: Nashik District Census 2001 and2011.

3.8 Educational Development

The first school in the Nashik was opened in 1861 as 'Superior Anglo vernacular school', which was transformed into Nashik High school in 1871 and was the first Secondary School in the district. Qualitative education facility is also available in the district. Private educational institutions are playing enormous role in education field.

3.8.1 Schools and Colleges

Till 2013-14, there are 4164 Primary schools, 1070 secondary schools, and 46 colleges are giving education to 13.08 lakh students. Out of the total students in primary, secondary and higher secondary schools 9.83 percent and 20.67 percent students were from scheduled caste and scheduled tribe respectively in the district.

Table 3.14

Educational Institutes in Nashik District

Sr. No	Year	Primary Schools	Secondary & Higher Secondary Schools	Colleges	Total
1	2000-2001	3269(83.65)	607(15.53)	32(0.82)	3908(100)
2	2005-2006	3461(78.75)	908(20.66)	26(0.59)	4395(100)
3	2010-2011	4359(78.30)	1164(20.91)	44(0.79)	5567(100)
4	2013-2014	4164 (78.86)	1070(20.27)	46(0.87)	5280(100)

Source: Education Department, Nashik District, 2013-14

3.8.2 Renowned Institutions

Following renowned institutions are also established in Nashik District

Table 3.15

Renowned Institutions in Nashik District

	Name of Institutions
ISP	India Security Press
CNP	Currency Note Press
HAL	Hindustan Aeronautics Limited
AC	Artillery Center

TPS	Thermal Power Station
MERI	Maharashtra Engineering Research Institute
MUHS	Maharashtra University of Health Sciences
YCMOU	Yashwantrao Chavan Maharashtra Open University
MPA	Maharashtra Police Academy

Source: field survey

3.8.3 Government Institutions

Instead the below mentioned educational institutions Engineering colleges, Polytechnic institutions, Industrial technical institutions, Medical College and Research Center, Ayurvedic College, Dental College and Research Center, B. Ed., D.Ed. and Law colleges are also in Nashik. Apart from this the district has education institutes in the areas like Management, Computer Science, Hotel Management and Catering Technology etc. Two universities named Yashwantrao Chavan Maharashtra Open University and Arogya Vidnyan Vidyapeeth are also in Nashik.

3.9 Financial institutions

3.9.1 Bank Offices

Table 3.16

General Information (Taluka-wise) of Banks in Nashik District

Sr. No	Tehsils	No. of villages covered by banks	Scheduled banks		* Other bank offices/ branches
			No. of banks	No. of branches	
1.	Surgana	07	3	3	05
2.	Kalwan	22	3	10	11

3.	Deola	16	3	4	19
4.	Satana	38	6	17	21
5.	Malegaon	59	11	30	23
6.	Nandgaon	24	8	14	14
7.	Chandwad	22	2	8	18
8.	Dindori	35	11	19	09
9.	Peth	07	3	4	04
10.	Tryambak	10	5	6	13
11.	Nashik	193	38	146	43
12.	Igatpuri	23	9	13	14
13.	Sinnar	43	13	23	27
14.	Niphad	85	14	37	35
15.	Yeola	25	8	13	11
	Total	609	40	347	267

Source: Socio-economic survey of Nashik district, 2011

*indicate data from field visit

There are 609 offices of Scheduled banks in allover district including city, towns and villages. There are 40 scheduled banks, 347 branches of scheduled banks and 267 branches of other banking sectors including bank offices. Scheduled banks have deposits of Rs. 2113243.62 lakh and agricultural advances are of Rs. 584795 lakh and non-agricultural advances are of Rs. 602634 lakh.

3.9.2 Self-Help Groups (SHGs) and Post Offices

Till March 2013, there are 2163 Self Help Groups working in the district in which 2106 are established till Marc 2012 and 57 SHGs are newly added.

Table 3.17

Number of Self Help Groups and Post-Offices

Sr. No	Tehsils	Self Help Groups			Post-Offices
		2011-12	2012-13	Total	
1	Surgana	343	3	346	28
2	Kalwan	437	7	444	30
3	Deola	50	3	53	27
4	Satana	0	0	0	53
5	Malegaon	155	18	173	69
6	Nandgaon	0	0	0	32
7	Chandwad	198	3	201	43
8	Dindori	60	0	60	66
9	Peth	39	0	39	21
10	Tryambak	46	0	46	42
11	Nashik	256	7	263	75
12	Igatpuri	0	0	0	30
13	Sinnar	155	0	155	45
14	Niphad	240	16	254	41
14	Yeola	127	0	127	37
	Total	2106	57	2163	639

Source: Socio-economic survey of Nashik district, 2014

From this 1943 are women's SHGs and are working actively. All the SHGs are engaged in various types of entrepreneurs i.e. 1050 in primary sector, 719 in secondary sector and 394 in territory sector. There are 639 Post-offices in the district.

3.9.3 Life Insurance Corporation (LIC)

There are 8 branches of LIC in Nashik district. Total numbers of Policies are 1278232 and amount is Rs. 319308 lakh. There are 6848 LIC agents in which 2423 are female.

3.10 Cooperatives in Nashik District

Up to March 2012, there are 11,876 Co-operative institutions having 23.65 thousands of members. The total advances provided through PCSs to the farmers are Rs.1053.30 Crore.

Table 3.18

Table showing number of Cooperative Banks

Categories	Number of Banks	No. of Branches
District Central Co-operative Bank	1	213
Urban Co-operative Banks	42	42
Urban Credit Cooperative Societies	596	596
Land Development Bank	49	NA
Agricultural Credit Co-operative Societies	870	870
Non-Agri. Credit Co-operative Societies	596	596
State Agricultural & Rural Development Bank	01	01
Lamps Cooperative Societies	172	172

Source: Socio-economic survey of Nashik district, 2011

3.10.1 Nashik District Central Co-operative Bank

This bank is established in 1955, NDCC Bank plays an important role as a central financing agency. This bank is working as an agency for providing short term and medium term loans to PACs within the district and this is the principal function of this bank.

The maximum limit of the loan to be granted to each individual is based on the statements provided by them to the bank and financial position of the individual for proper recovery of loan. This bank accepts deposits from cooperative societies, financial institutions and individual persons and gives advances to PACS which are not accepting funds required by their members. Bank also provides loans for establishment of processing industries as well as small manufacturing plants. It has also plays a vital role in establishing co-operative sugar factories in the district.

3.10.2 Urban Co-operative Bank

Urban Co-operative Bank is another bank which is providing banking services in the district. This bank accepts deposits from public and provides advances to public also. This bank performs all functions of a co-operative bank as well as a commercial bank. This bank had 18 branches at various places in the district in the year 1960-61, it has increased by 29 branches and it has recorded 47 in the year 2010-11. The growth of UCB is nearby triple in the last half century.

3.11 Conclusion

Nashik is known as perfect city among all the cities. Most of the populations are living in tribal areas i.e. in the east and central area of district. The quantity of agricultural products is more (vegetables, fruits, grapes, onions, sugarcane, pomegranate, etc) and all these things are exported daily. Animal husbandry and milk dairy is the secondary occupation of these people. Rich agriculture, relatively developed industry, better water resources, rapid urbanization and growing tertiary sector are its strengths in economic sector. The economic inequalities are revealed by the land holdings, irrigation facilities, development of industries and agro-industries and occupation pattern. On the basis of Socio economic conditions, Nashik District can be conveniently divided into three broad sections –

1) Developed areas
2) Semi developed areas and
3) Backward-Tribal areas.

Nashik city, most part of the Nashik Taluka, most part of the Niphad Taluka, some part of Sinnar, Chandwad and Dindori can be seen to constitute the developed areas because it is industrially and agriculturally advanced. Nashik city has been a famous religious, cultural center of Maharashtra. There are following reasons for Maratha domination in the district.

1) The caste Maratha has substantial number to influence electoral politics. The Maratha-Kunbi caste group is the highest numbered caste in the district comprising about 30 to 40% of the total population of the district. They are dominant in almost all non-tribal areas of the district.
2) Marathas are the land owning caste, after 1970s become dominant in cultivation of cash crops in cooperatives and sugar-industries.
3) The anti-Brahmin drive with the Satyashodhak, Non-Brahmin Movement in 1920s created both Maratha leadership and Non- Brahmin conscience in the district.

Some Talukas in Nashik district could be categorized as semi developed areas. They are neither developed nor very backward. They can be included into semi developed areas. These areas include semi tribal zones of Satana, Deola, Chandwad, Dindori and Kalwan. The drought prone areas like Yeola, Sinnar are developing their industries and thus some parts of those Talukas exceeded from the backwardness generated due to drought.

Nashik district has higher percentage of tribal population compared with percentage of tribal population in Maharashtra state. These tribal areas are known as undeveloped areas or backward areas. Tryambak, Peth,

Surgana, Igatpuri, and some area of Dindori is known as tribal because the agricultural productivity is comparatively less and migration ratio is comparatively high which affect the literacy ratio, employment ratio as well as standard of living of the people. Their awareness towards technological development is also very low. It indicated that the overall progress of the district is developed in developed areas and is slowly developing in backward areas.

Appendix 3.1

Tehsil wise population of Nashik District

Sr.No	Tehsil-places	Total population			Rural population			Urban population		
		Total	Male	Female	Total	Male	Female	Total	Male	Female
1	Malegaon	955594	490303	465291	368137	191267	176870	587457	299036	288421
2	Satana	374435	193072	181363	336734	173623	163111	37701	19449	18252
3	Kalwan	208362	106130	102232	208362	106130	102232	0	0	0
4	Nandgaon	288848	149507	139341	185186	96561	88625	103662	52946	50716
5	Surgana	175816	87862	87954	169553	84667	84886	6263	3195	3068
6	Nashik	1755491	922060	833431	175948	90889	85059	1579543	831171	748372
7	Dindori	315709	161500	154209	315709	161500	154209	0	0	0
8	Igatpuri	253513	128999	124514	197686	100466	97220	55827	28533	27294
9	Niphad	493251	254768	238483	418853	216293	202560	74398	38475	35923
10	Peth	119838	60292	59546	119838	60292	59546	0	0	0
11	Sinnar	346390	180001	166389	281091	145368	135723	65299	34633	30666
12	Yeola	271146	139990	131156	221320	114408	106912	49826	25582	24244

13	Chandwad	235849	122098	113751	210508	108814	101694	25341	13284	12057
14	Tryambak	168423	85298	83125	156367	78128	77239	12056	6170	5886
15	Deola	144522	75306	69216	144522	75306	69216	0	0	0
	Total	6107187	3157186	2950001	3509814	1804712	1705102	2597373	1352474	1244899

Source: Socio-economic survey of Nashik district, 2013-2014

Appendix 3.2

Tehsil-wise Literacy Ratio

Sr. No	Tehsil-places	Total population			Rural population			Urban population		
		Total	Male	Female	Total	Male	Female	Total	Male	Female
1	Malegaon	674065	364037	310028	244116	138446	105670	429949	225591	204358
2	Satana	249465	137866	111599	219457	121843	97614	30008	16023	13985
3	Kalwan	121538	67852	53686	121538	67852	53686	0	0	0
4	Nandgaon	200844	112698	88146	119105	68901	50204	81739	43797	37942
5	Surgana	100634	55379	45255	95947	52871	43076	4687	2508	2179

6	Nashik	1374928	752594	622334	122939	68802	54137	1251989	683792	568197
7	Dindori	210976	117947	93029	210976	117947	93029	0	0	0
8	Igatpuri	169629	96116	73513	126320	72707	53613	43309	23409	19900
9	Niphad	359841	198373	161468	301187	166817	134370	53654	31556	27098
10	Peth	72139	40379	31760	72139	40379	31760	0	0	0
11	Sinnar	248838	139980	108858	199255	112487	86768	49583	27493	22090
12	Yeola	194171	108066	86105	154370	87005	67365	39801	21061	18740
13	Chandwad	168068	93616	74452	148457	82929	65528	19611	10687	8924
14	Tryambak	97662	55422	42240	88058	50265	37793	9604	5157	4447
15	Deola	102568	57213	45355	102568	57213	45355	0	0	0
	Total	4345366	2397538	1947828	2326432	1306464	1019968	2018934	1091074	927860

Source: Socio-economic survey of Nashik district, 2013-2014

References

1. Daily Sakal dated 21st August, 2015
2. Morvanchikar R.S. (1993), 'History of Maharashtra', First Edition, Pratima Publications, Pune, Pp-172
3. http://www.nashik.nic.in
4. Nashik District Census Report-2011, page 54
5. Nasik District Gazetter, 2014
6. HRD-Maharashtra 2006-07
7. Ibid, Pp-267
8. Ibid, Pp-284
9. Statistical Data of Nashik District 2012-13
10. WWW.nashik.nic.in,
11. Nashik District Census 1991 to 2011
12. Ibid, Pp-254
13. ABP News, 27th August, 2015, Time 7.35Pm
14. Daily Lokmat, dated 28th August, 2015
15. Ibid, Pp-256
16. Education Department, Nasik District, 2013-14
17. www.cooperatives-nashik.ac.in

E-Banking Services: A Theoretical Framework

4.1 Introduction

In this chapter researcher has defined the emergence and innovations in banking sector on national as well as international level with special reference to e-banking services provided by banks to its customers and development of these services on the platform of globalization. This chapter starts with e-banking concept, its objectives and ends with its future. The researcher also discussed the origin of these services in India and some statistical data is also presented for showing the present status of e-banking services in India and in other developed nations. The Banking Ombudsman Scheme and Basel introduced by RBI are also discussed in this chapter.

4.2 Origin of E-Banking

Finland is the first country in the world to have taken a lead in e-banking technology and ICICI is the leading bank of India which has taken initiative for the progress of e-banking technology under the branch name of 'Infinity'. After Globalization Indian Economy have witnessed with highest growth rate with the performance in service sector and today finance, insurance and real estate are the star performers. Integration of Indian Economy with the global economy, free movement of capital and financial services are promoted with globalization process as well as provided the means to the Indian Banking Sector to spread its wings beyond geographical borders[1].

4.2.1 E-Banking

"E-banking means providing banking products and services through e-channels".

E-banking is more efficient, faster and much easier way of completing transactions without face to face communication. For technological development banking sector is an ideal platform for successful implementation of electronic media. At virtual level of banking sector, online services are completed with the help of internet facilities and use of high technology system.

"E-banking is offering, supplying and delivering banking products and services through various electronic delivery channels via electronic devices".

In short E-banking is an umbrella term where bank do process with technology and a customer may perform banking transactions without visiting a brick and mortar institutions. In the views of customers e-banking services are convenient and valuable that they access their account by 24*7 at anywhere and anytime. Banks can also perform technology for achieving the goals and for taking the technological advantages[2]. These services are increasing the profit level of banks by providing technological services at best level having characteristics of awareness, safety, privacy, protection, time-saving, reliability, efficiency, substantially lower costs, technological readiness etc.

Electronic transactions need less transaction cost. According to Booz Allen and Hamilton, cost needed for various services are; CBS Rs. 1.07, phone banking- Rs.0.54, ATM- Rs. 0.27, Debit card- Rs. 0.20, Internet Banking Rs.-0.01 and Online banking- Rs. 0.015 per transactions.

Example. A typical customer transaction cost is about Rs. 1 in a traditional brick and for ATMs it is maximum Rs. 0.60 but in case of phone banking it is only 0.20 paisa. E-banking makes it easier for customers to compare banking services and products and can increase competition among banks and allow banks to penetrate new markets and thus expand their geographical reach. Some customers in such countries can access services more easily from banks abroad and through wireless communication systems, which are developing more rapidly than traditional wired communication network.

Though e-banking services have rapid growth in India, but the customers who are illiterate or the problems of lack of trust, non-availability of services/infrastructure facilities, security and having more changes on delivering services are not using these services. Like SEBI (controlling share market, money market, capital market), there is no any mechanism for supervising and controlling and regulating bank transactions and for solving the problems of customers raised while using the services[3]. If any problem occurred with customer, he has to file his problem and has to visit or to contact with particular bank till getting the solution on his problems.

4.2.2 Brick Banking Vs Click Banking

E-banking is a generic term which includes internet banking, phone banking, mobile banking, etc. It is a process of delivery of banking services and products through electronic channels such as telephone, internet, mobile etc. The concept and scope of e-banking is still developing i.e. quick banking, home banking, etc. E-banking facilitates an effective payment and accounting system enhancing the speed of delivery of banking services. E-banking has improved efficiency and convenience, but still it has to face several challenges to the regulation and supervisors[4]. Click banking need less time and less cost for performing transactions. It allows customers the facilities such as anytime any where banking, cashless transactions, 24*7*365 services, and other transactions with the help of internet (e-banking) technology.

Table 4.1

Alternative Banking Channels and Available Services/ Facilities

Brick Banking	Click Banking	Means	Available services/Facilities
Traditional calculations	Automated calculations	PC & LAN	Instant calculations of balances, interest, dividends, loans, etc.
Branch Banking	CBS & Internet Banking	PC & Internet	Quick deposits &withdrawals, easy cheque clearing system, quick lock system and clearance of a/c, balance enquiry, mini statement.
Manual Note counting	Money counting machine	Electronic device	Instant currency note counting and verification of currency.
Formal cheques	MICR Cheques	MICR technology	Quick and cost-free clearing of cheque
Demand	EFT	CBS	Instant fund transfer system from one Drafts branch to another with CBS
Manual cash withdrawal / deposits	ATM, Debit cards	ATM	Cash withdrawal, cash deposits, balance enquiry, mini statement, online payment of bills, cash transfers, cashless shopping
Letter of credit	Plastic money	Credit cards	Shopping and payment of bills
Counter Receipts	SMS	Mobile	SMS of cash withdrawal, cash deposits, quick banking facility, account information about any transactions.

Source: www.rbi.org

4.2.3 New avenues (emerging trends) in banking sector, Electronic banking is one of the latest emerging trends on the Indian banking scenario. Prior to liberalization of banking system in 1991, the usage of e-banking in India is restricted to foreign banks and specialized foreign exchange branches of some leading banks in public sector. Private sector banks began to operate it from 1994 onwards with fully computerized operations that spurred the entire banking system towards full computerization and electronic banking[5]. Today, most of the PSB branches in metros and cities have computerized and their operations are also managed with computer system. Now all three major types of commercial banks in India viz, PSB, private sector Indian banks and foreign banks are now providing e-banking services to customers in metros, cities and also a number of small towns. As this most of the Urban Cooperative banks also continue to use the manual system of banking.

Table 4.2

Committees for Use of IT and Development of Indian Banking Sector

Name of Committee and Chairman		Year
Consumer services in Banks	Talwar R.K.	1979
Feasibility for introducing MICR technology useful for cheque clearing process	Damle Y.B.	1982
Mechanization in Banking industry	C. Rangarajan	1984
Implementation of Communication technology and SWIFT	Iyer T.N.A.	1987
Bank automation/computerization	C. Rangarajan	1988
Customer related e-banking services in banks	Goiporia M.N.	1990
Banking Sector Reform I	R. Narsimhan	1991
Frauds and malpractices in banks	Ghosh A.	1993
Payment system, cheque clearing and securities settlement	Saraf W.S.	1994
Legislation on EFT and other e-payments	Shere K.S.	1995
Technology upgradation	Vasudevan A.	1996
Banking Sector Reform II	R. Narsimhan	1997
Working group on e-banking technology	Khan S.H.	1998

Suggesting benefits of e-technology	Barman R.B.	2000
Working group on Internet Banking	S.R.Mittal	2001
Suggested on payment and settlement system	Bhide M.G.	
Legal aspects of bank frauds	Mitra N.L.	
Working group on electronic/plastic money	Cama Zarir	2002
Online payment system	Patil R.H.	
Cheques truncation and e-cheques	Barman R.B.	2003
Internet Deployment of Central Database Mgt. system	Vaidyanathan	2004
Regulatory mechanism for cards	Gandhi R.	2005
Preparing guidelines for access to payment systems	Gandhi E.	2007
Technology upgradation of RRBs	Srinivasan G.	2008
IT support for UCBs	Gandhi R.	
To review business correspondent model	Vijaya Bhaskar	2009

Source: www.rbi.org,in

4.2.4 Innovation and Imitation in E-banking

Innovation is the base of services according to the need of customers, but for service satisfaction. Imitation has also become one of the most important changing parts of Banking Services, because services are provided for all customers who are living in rural and urban areas or in backward area. In India, various technological Banking Services are primarily provided by public sector banks for urban customers according to their socio-economic conditions. But after 1990s, adoption of New Economic Policy necessitated commercial banks to adopt various policies and programs for the development of backward regions[6]. But though the policies and programs were launched for backward area, they have failed in exciting customers because of the changing psychology of customers, increasing level of earnings, inclusion of more items in the family budget and growing culture, inter-communication between east and west, but for becoming successful in providing Banking Services, it is essential to follow the following guidelines[7]

1) To provide facilities according to the need of customers with technical perfection.
2) Proper implementation process of the services rendered to its customers for better feedback and success of policies.

Only to provide services are not goal of the Banks, but also to create new products according to the need of customers. Thus it is necessary to create attractive schemes for the satisfaction of customers.

Rural prospects are in intensive care due to liberal attitude of government towards rural development programs. So banks have to be careful that customers buy solution to their problem.

The next important dimension in the formulation of the product mix is making of decisions and framing of policies regarding the implementation of development and welfare programs. Following key points need intensive care while formulating Banking Services policies.[8]

Objectives of E-Banking

i. Anywhere anytime banking (Branchless Banking)
ii. To provide speed, accuracy and confidentiality of customers' transactions
iii. Enhancing customers' convenience
iv. Minimize cost of transaction

4.2.5 Computerization in Banking sector

In Indian banking sector 100 per cent computerization is made in the banks of SBI and its associated groups and old private sector banks and new private sector banks are also fully automated with their branches. Foreign banks are fully computerized from their establishment. In cooperative banking sector Regional Rural Banks (RRBs), Urban Cooperative Banks (UCBs) and State cooperative banks (SCBs) and other cooperative banks are developing with the percentage of 94.6 %, 97.3%, 99.9 % and 89.6% respectively. In short the development of cooperative bank is in process and today their adoption ratio is more than 90 per cent. Till 2020 all banks will be fully computerized with their branches including cooperative banking sector[9].

Number of bank offices and percentage of computerization of banks with bank name and category are given in table 4.3.

Table 4.3

Number of Bank Offices: (31st March, 2012)

Name of Banks/ category	No. of Bank offices	Number of Branches	No. of Rural Branches	% of Rural Branches	% of Computerized Banks
Public Sector Banks	27	83207	28665	34.85	100
Nationalized PSB	19	61164	20802	34	100
SBI & its Associate Banks	08	22043	7863	35.7	100
Private Sector Banks	25	18859	4042	21.4	100
Old PVT Banks	17	18859	4042	21.4	100
New PVT Banks	08				100
Foreign Banks	39	321	4042	21.4	100
RRBs	357	19082	14242	74.6	*94.6
Sch. Co-op. Banks	53	121469	46956	38.7	*97.3
Non-Sch. Co-op. Banks	31	66	20	30.3	*99.9
*Local Co-op. Banks	NA	66	20	30.3	*89.6
All Commercial Banks	NA	121535	46976	38.7	NA

Source: Economic survey of India, Report-2013, Pp-A-60

* Thakur Vishwas, (Chairman-VCB, Nashik), an article, 'Dynamic Changes in Banking Sector', in Daily Deshdoot, supplement of Banking Special, dated 20th Feb., 2015, pp-1

4.3 Elements of E-banking services

Banks are delivering e-banking services with the help of internet which is by-product of IT sector. All e-banking services are accessible on internet. Thus the internet becomes one of the most important factors working between banks and bank customers. Banks are also charging some amount for providing these services. With the help of Internet, banks are offering branch-based services such as free of cost services (Phone Banking, Internet Banking, Mobile Banking, online bill payments, EFT/NEFT) as well as new value added services i.e. ATMs, Debit/Credit Cards, electronic commerce, RTGS (Real Time Gross Services), real-time brokerage, financial information menus, e-mail alerts and third party services (tax payments, bill payments, money transfer etc.)[10]

E-banking services are broadly categorized into different classes as shown in table 4.4

Table 4.4

Classification of E-banking Services/Products

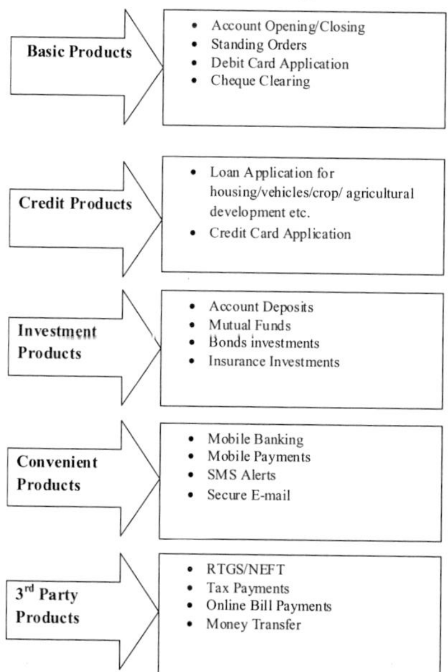

4.3.1 ATM (Automated Teller Machines)

ATM is cash rendering teller machine. This helps a bank customer to withdraw many from his account without having to go to bank. ATM is a user friendly, computer driven system, which operates 24 hours a day, 7 days a week. A totally menu-driven system, it displays easy-to-follow, step by step instructions for the customer. ATM can be accessed by a customer by using an ATM card that gives entry into the ATM room. The Personal Identification Number (PIN), exclusive to each customer, has to be keyed-in for carrying out desired transactions.

ATMs can be installed on the bank's premises (on-site ATMs) for which no license is required from the RBI[11]. However, for ATMs to be erected at public places (off-site ATMs), banks have to obtain a license post-facto. Many banks have opened off-site ATMs at airports, railway stations, petrol pumps, market centers, universities etc. A full-fledged ATM is well equipped to perform the following functions; however, only a few of these are being provided by ATMs of most of the banks in India.

1 Cash dispensing
2 Generating statement of account
3 Account balance enquiry
4 Request for cheque book
5 Deposit of cash/cheques etc.
6 Issue of gift cheques/traveler's cheques
7 Utility payments like telephone bills, electricity bills.

Features of ATMs[12]

1 Round the clock banking for 365 days a year, banking can be done by the customer at any time on any day of the week.
2 Quick and efficient service.
3 Response is uniform and fixed for all customers as

per the programme set, thus leaving no scope for discourteous or subjective behavior as may happen with human interaction at bank's counters.

4 Cash withdrawals are restricted to certain amounts as fixed by bank and as notified to ATM card holders.

5 Cash dispensation is restricted to certain denomination of currency notes-usually Rs. 50/100/500.

6 ATM can perform only particular functions. For other functions, the customer has to visit the branch or direct one's enquiries to the concerned call centre.

Table 4.5

ATM Centers of Banks

Type of Banks	On-site ATMs		Off-site ATMs		Total ATMs in 2013
	2005	2013	2005	2013	
All Scheduled Banks	12134	55760	11019	58254	114014
PSBs	20727	40241	6021	29411	69652
Nationalized Banks	4812	20658	2353	14701	35359
SBI and Associates	1775	18708	3668	13883	32791
Private Sector Banks	4309	15236	4350	27865	43101
Old Private Banks	1054	4054	493	3512	7566
New Private Banks	2255	11182	3857	24353	35535
Forcign	232	283	648	978	114014
Total	47298	166122	32409	172957	452032

Source: RBI Annual reports of 2006, 2011, 2014

Big banks can afford to install their own ATMs on-site and off-site. The banks which do not have their own ATMs or which have only a few ATMs and want to expand their ATM network enter into arrangements with other banks to facilitate such usage, on a mutually sharing arrangement and fee basis. The arrangement, referred to as the Shared Payment Network System (SPNS) is used by the participating banks, which are connected to the network through a host computer. SPNS was especially in vogue in 1990s amongst the commercial banks of Mumbai, when the number of ATMs was limited due to high capital cost of installation[13]. SPNS enables one bank/branch's customer to access another bank/branch's ATM, for putting through the permitted transactions. It also helps better utilization of resources for a larger section of customers.

4.3.2 Debit Cards/Credit Cards

Credit cards are known as plastic money. Credit card frauds are increased according to the frequency of its utility. Thus it becomes necessary to study the terms and conditions for proper use of credit cards and to control frauds. Credit cards includes the information of customer i.e. Name of card holder, card number, validity, bank logo, CVV number, Magnetic strip, signature and some instructions[14].

Table 4.6
Debit/Credit Cards

Types of Cards	Year-wise Frequency (in millions)			Year-wise Amount (in Billions)		
	2011-12	2012-13	2013-14	2011-12	2012-13	2013-14
Debit Cards	327.5 (50.58)	469.1 (54.19)	619.1 (54.88)	534.3 (35.61)	743.4 (37.68)	954.1 (38.26)
Credit Cards	320 (49.42)	396.6 (45.81)	509.1 (45.12)	966.1 (64.39)	1229.5 (62.32)	1539.9 (61.74)
Total	647.5 (100)	865.7 (100)	1128.2 (100)	1500.4 (100)	1972.9 (100)	2494 (100)

Source: RBI Annual Report, 2014, Pp-110

Numbers of customers are increasing day by day so it needed to take information from particular bank for taking the card as well as for using the card, because after that there is no any opportunity for solving the complaints of the customers[15].

1 Though the cards are looking same but they have different features, so be aware about the terms and conditions and charges of banks.

2 After taking cards banks have no interest in solving the problems of customers regarding the charges, so take care and complete information regarding the bank charges.

3 The service charges are depending on the policies of banks and the service charges are not fixed, so each and every customer has to take details of bank charges of that particular bank.

4 While using these cards or for scratching the cards card-number and CVV number (password) is called so the card holders have to take proper care while providing such information.

5 Some customers take cards from banks but not using it due to any cause. Though the customers are not using the cards but banks recover charges on these cards also according to their rules.

6 If any customer fails to pay cash in particular period fine is also charged so be aware about the fine charges also.

7 Don't permit to others for using your card.

8 Put signature on the card for security purpose as per the rules and regulations of RBI.

Banks are also providing discount on using credit cards for online payment of LIC premium, Electricity charges, phone charges etc. So study the terms and conditions of banks and take proper information of such discount offers. On 1st July, 2009 RBI as introduced new guidelines to control credit cards fraud and consumer protection[16].

4.3.3 Phone Banking

Tele-banking requires authorized computers to use a special telephone number of the bank. Tele-banking can be done from anywhere, at any time. In fact, the absences of geographical or time restrictions for the customer are the main advantages of tele-banking.

Types of Tele Banking: There are major two types of tele-banking[17];

a) Public Enquiry: General information about banking services/facilities can be obtained by customers and non-customers alike, by dialing a special enquiry number of the bank (call centre) and the desired information can be obtained after reaching the concerned extension number/desk.

b) Private Enquiry: This relates to account-specific information and can be accessed only by the account holder by disclosing his/her secret Personal Identification Number (PIN) and customer ID.

c) Facilities available via tele-banking: Following facilities are available through tele-banking;

   i. Balance enquiry.

   ii. Request for cheque book/statement of account which can be couriered to the customer.

   iii. Stop payment services.

   iv. Talk to phone banker.

   v. Check status enquiries.

   vi. Request for draft or cash withdrawal: These facilities are made by a few banks and to selected clients by using a special telephone number.

The customer gives his PIN and customers ID and specifies the amount of the withdrawal draft and other particulars. The cash or draft is sent by the bank to the customer at the recorded address and delivered to him/her in exchange of a cheque for the amount as also in addition to services charges.

4.3.4 Mobile Banking

The traditional 'brick and mortar' banking is done from a fixed branch premises, wherein customers have to go personally for carrying out transactions. Mobile banking tries to reach the customer to enable them to transact banking. Mobile banking is carried out in two different ways, as follows[18]:

a) Banking through a mobile van (mobile bank), with or without computerized banking system: The mobile van moves from place to place on designated routes at designated hours and the customers can transact their banking business, such as cash deposit, withdrawals, draft issuance, cheque book issue, pass book update etc.

b) ATM on ship or airliner: This can be even lighter than an on-road ATM and should be able to meet specific travel needs, e.g. main currency exchanges relating to the destination, acceptance of certain kings of credit cards (global cards), debit cards for payments/purchases. This requires communication with a central data base that is compatible with the navigational system of the aircraft/ship.

Features of Mobile Banking [19]:

i. Lower capital investment as compared to 'brick and mortar' bank.
ii. Larger area coverage.
iii. Novel concept with the banker visiting the customers for banking, rather than the other way round.
iv. It serves as a tool for marketing on special events, like exhibitions, metals, festivals.
v. Disadvantages of Mobile banking: Following major issues are connected with mobile banking;
vi. Safety and security of cash, equipments and records,
vii. On-line communication with base office,
viii. Wireless technology for data communication and on-line back-up for transactions.

4.3.5 Internet Banking

Internet banking means, on-line banking from home or anywhere. It provides 'anywhere and anytime' banking access to one's account as well as to the public information updated by the bank on its website.It has been introduced in India by most commercial banks which have fully computerized their operations. Just as the bank staff accesses the account of a customer on-line, the customer can also access his/her account on-line via internet[20]. For accruing Internet a customer requires:

i. A Personal Computer,

ii. A Telephone link

iii. A Modem

iv. An arrangement with one of the Internet Service Providers, e.g. VSNL, BSNL, Satyam etc.

Table 4.7

Internet Banking users in India

Year	2005-06	2010-11	2013-14
Population (in millions)	1,11,22,25,812	1,15,68,97,766	12,63,43,76,113
Internet Service users	50,60,0000	8,10,00,000	1,25,16,95,584
Users in %	4.5 %	7.0 %	19.4%

Source: www.internetworldstats.com

Utility of Internet Banking [21]:

1) In internet banking, the customer himself accesses his account through the internet connected to the bank's data base. The account details are displayed on the PC screen and can be browsed by him.

2) The customer cannot order cash withdrawal through internet banking, but he can transfer money from one of his accounts to another and even to a third party's account.

3) Security issues in Internet Banking:

4) Confidentiality of transactions has to be ensured as the account can fall prey to Internet hackers. Hence, stringent log-in procedures are prescribed by banks in this regard.

5) Integrity of transaction is done by encryption standards.

6) Non-repudiation of the transaction by the customers which is done by building a suitable certificate authority.

7) Privacy when the account is accessed by a customer from some public place, like cyber café. Once a customer logs out of his account, there are some traces of the transaction in the form of history files. These need to be removed by certain programmes, e.g. cookies or other devices, in order to ensure privacy of the customer's transaction. However, this can be done only by the customer, and not by the bank; thus making the account vulnerable to fraudulent practices.

4.3.6 Electronic Funds Transfer (EFT)

Traditionally, funds are transferred by banks from one place to another by mail transfer and telegraphic transfer, the latter being faster. In both kinds of transfer, banks use the post and telegraph departments' services and use certain codes to ensure confidentiality and safety in transmission of the messages[22].

Under this facility, the customer has to provide the details of beneficiary account at other centers. In turn, the customer will then send the particulars to local clearing centre, which subsequently processes the transactions and will pass on the instructions of local bank in the bank's network to credit the account of the respective beneficiaries.

Table 4.8

Number of banks providing NEFT Service (as on June 2010)

Sr. No	Name of Bank	Number of Branches	% of Branches
1	SBI	13051	57.30
2	IDBI	772	3.39
3	Bank of Baroda	3098	13.60

4	Corporation Bank	1139	5.00
5	Axis Bank	1003	4.40
6	ICICI Bank	1973	8.66
7	HDFC Bank	1741	7.64
	Total	22777	100

Source: RBI Annual Report, 2010

This electronic fund transfers millions of dollars per day with the help of electronic system of communication; transmission is much faster and safer. Several banks have started the EFT/NEFT systems for funds transfer. RBI has introduced EFT service in 1997 and up to Rs. 5 lakh is transferred from one account to another account on same day in any bank and in any city. NEFT is introduced in 2003 and 77 bank offices with 3000 branches have adopted this technology by covering 500 cities[23].

Table 4.9

Annual frequency and amount in EFT/NEFT Transaction

E- Banking Service	Year-wise Frequency (in millions)			Year-wise Amount (in Billions)		
	2011-12	2012-13	2011-12	2012-13	2011-12	2012-13
EFT/ NEFT	226.1 (8.93)	394.1 (13.41)	661.0 (18.24)	17,903.5 (14.78)	29,022.4 (21.64)	43,785.5 (30.52)
Net Retail Payments	2,532.4 (100)	2,939.5 (100)	3,624.4 (100)	121,149.9 (100)	134,114.4 (100)	143,447.4 (100)

Source: RBI Annual Report, 2014, Pp-110

4.3.7 Real Time Gross Settlement (RTGS)

RTGS transfers funds from one bank to another on a 'real time gross settlement basis.' It mainly used for large amount transactions system from the 26th March, 2004 but it is introduced in 2002. This system is used for transferring large amount and operations are cleared by RBI. This system includes inter-bank as well as customers' payments. Only the banks under CBS are providing this facility[24]. In 2010, 11,172 banks were linked for RTGS facility but today 90 per cent banks are linked with it. RTGS includes four types of Inter-bank transactions;

1. Call money Transactions
2. Rupee payment of Foreign Currency Transactions
3. Bank to bank transfers for funding upcountry requirements
4. Bank to bank transfers for Inward Remittances

Table 4.10

Annual frequency and amount in RTGS Transaction

E- Banking Service	Year-wise Frequency (in millions)			Year-wise Amount (in Billions)		
	2011-12	2012-13	2011-12	2012-13	2011-12	2012-13
RTGS	55.0	68.5	81.1	539,307.5	676,841.0	734,252.4
	(96.66)	(96.75)	(96.89)	(57.05)	(57.44)	(54.16)
Total SIFMIs	56.9 (100)	70.8 (100)	83.7 (100)	945,378.7 (100)	1,178,439.5 (100)	1,355,822.0 (100)

Source: RBI Annual Report, 2014, Pp-110

Other than RTGS, the RBI has implemented 'Cheque Truncation System' for cheque clearing in less time. In this process the physical cheques are converted into electronic image (scanning) and scanning image of cheque is sent to the drawee branch with the relevant information such as the name of bank, MICR number, date of presentation of cheque, presenting banks to its clearance. This process works through the INFINET with proper authentication given by RBI. The time required for clearing the cheque via cheque truncation system is T+0 (same day) for Local area Clearings and T + 1 (one day) for inter-city clearing[25].

4.3.8 Online Bill Payment[26]

4.3.9 Indian Banking Financial Network

A. BANKNET

RBI has introduced electronic payment system called STEPS whereby funds can effectively be remitted electronically from one customer's account at one centre to another customer's account at another centre on the same day. Under this system seven cities named Mumbai, Deli, Calcutta, Madras, Nagpur, Bangalore and Hyderabad are connected for financial transactions. This project has been worked out in two stages i.e. BANKNET I and BANKNET II. Today all the cities are connected with this system[27]. Under core banking solutions, where the technology platform connects several branches of a bank located at distant places, transfer of funds from one account to another account at different places can be easily done between the inter-connected branches.

B. SWIFT

The society of World-wide Inter-bank Financial Telecommunication is an International Society for enabling inter-national electronic fund transfer between member banks world-wide. SBI and several other banks in India are members of this Society. Member banks are connected through a high-speed closed used group communication system. Structured and codified messages are sent by the remitting bank to the receiving bank for crediting the beneficiary's account situated with it[28]. The inter-bank settlement of account is done via the correspondent banks. The funds' transfer system is fast, secure and efficient.

4.3.10 Electronic Clearing System (ECS)

Electronic Clearing System (ECS) has following three features:

i. Clearing House System

ii. Debit Clearing System
iii. Credit Clearing System

1) Clearing House System

Inter-bank cheques drawn on branches of a city/town are cleared/paid through a system of 'clearing house'. Out-station cheques are sent for collection through a different system. Clearing house is a common service provided by RBI in metros and by scheduled banks in other cities. Clearing house functions in all cities/towns where there are 5 or more banks. In big cities and metros, service branch of each bank carries out the clearing house operations require huge expenditure by way of premises, equipment and staff. The number of cheques in clearing house transactions is very large and the volume of transactions is huge[29].

Table 4.11

Number of Clearing Houses with its management

Managed by	Year			
	2000-01	2005-06	2010-11	2013-14
RBI	14	16 (15)	16 (16)	16 (16)
SBI	649	684 (9)	728 (19)	728 (19)
SBI & associates	316	327 (2)	312 (4)	312 (4)
Nationalized Banks	07	18 (13)	46 (25)	46 (25)
Other Banks	-	-	1 (0)	1 (0)
Total	986	1045 (40)	1103 (64)	1103 (64)

Source: Department of Payment and Settlement system of RBI

Figures into bracket indicate number of MICR cheque processing centers.

For speedier processing, manual systems have been replaced by Automated Clearing System (ACS). The main elements of ACS are as follows;

A. MICR Cheques:

Magnetic Ink Character Recognition (MICR) cheques are used for clearing system in India. As these are processed on high speed machines, the cheques are printed on a specific type of paper and meet other specifications, including two white bands on top and bottom, which should be free from any marking or impressions. In these bands details are encoded with special magnetic ink.

The details encoded on the lower band are as follows;

i. First 6 digits- Cheque no. in a 6 digit code is pre-printed.

ii. Centre code in 9 digits: first 3 digits represent city code, next 3 digits represent the bank code and the last 3 digits are for the branch code.

iii. A 2 digit transaction code indicating the type of the account (e.g. savings/current)

Table 4.12

Year-wise MICR and non-MICR centers

(in millions)

Particulars	**2010-11**	**2011-12**	**2012-13**	**2013-14**	
MICR Centers	Number of cheques	114.971	934.9	823.3	439.0
	Amount	85315.159	65,093.2	57,504.0	31,129.8
Non-MICR Centers	Number of cheques	23.057	227.0	215.3	225.7
	Amount	18784.247	18,815.1	20,898.3	17,681.8
Total	Number of cheques	138.03	1161.90	1038.60	664.70
	Amount	104099.415	83,908.30	78,402.30	48,811.60

Source: RBI Annual Reports, Statistical tables related with Banks in India.

B. Encoder:

This machine is used to write details of the cheque in the lower band with magnetic ink. In power encoder, the data on the cheque is keyed at the branches and sent to the service branch along with a floppy/CD containing the information. When the cheques are passed through the power encoder, the data from the floppy gets encoded on the cheque.

C. Cheque Reader-cum-sorter:

Cheques in the clearing house are run through this machine, which records the drawee bank-wise/branch-wise presentation of cheques from the magnetic ink impression on the lower white band. The sorter portion of the machine automatically sorts the cheques, drawee bank-wise/branch-wise and also lists out the cheques in the same order. Cheques segregated into packets that are sent to the service branch of each bank for further processing. Payee branch process the payments on the next day and all returns are submitted to the clearing house in the next day clearing. The customer therefore gets the credit on the third day.

2. Debit Clearing System

Under this system, the utility service provider (like telephone, electrically, gas and insurance company) obtains an authorization from the customer to debit his specified bank account with the amount of the bills at regular intervals. The letter of authority is submitted by the service provider to his banker which raises a debit for the amount listed on the other bank maintaining the client's account.

Table 4.13

Debit clearing in India (ECS)

(In millions)

Particulars	**Years**				
	2005-06	**2010-11**	**2011-12**	**2012-13**	**2013-14**
Frequency	35.95	149.28	164.7	176.5	192.9
Amount	129.865	695.238	833.6	1,083.1	1,268.0

Source: RBI Annual Reports

Customer is not required to keep a track of his bills for ensuring that he pays before the due date. Customer also need not take effort of writing the payment cheques. The service provider need not print out the bills and send it to the customers for payment. The system helps the banker in cutting down on expenses as cheques are not used for payment of the bills.

3. Credit Clearing System

This is a total contrast to the Debit Clearing System. It is used by a company for paying the dividends/interest of its shareholders/depositors at periodic intervals. Instead of sending out cheque to the investors, the company directly credits the amount through the clearing system of its bank, to the customers' accounts, in keeping with a letter of authority (or mandate) obtained from the customers. The letter of authority contains all the relevant particulars, e.g. bank, branch, account number, etc.

The company need not print the dividend/interest warrants and reconcile the paid and outstanding amounts. The investors need not deposit the cheques to their bankers every time and wait for the credit clearance. Under the credit clearing system, credits to the customers' account are made on a fixed date. The bank saves a lot of time spent in processing the large number of cheques/warrants deposited by the customers' as is done in the manual system.

Table 4.14

Credit clearing in India (ECS)

(In millions)

Particulars	**Years**				
2005-06	2010-11	2011-12	2012-13	2013-14	
Frequency	44.21	98.13	121.5	122.2	152.5
Amount	323.24	1176.12	1,837.8	1,771.3	2,492.2

Source: RBI Annual Reports

4.4 E-Banking: Risk and Management

Recent developments in information and communication technologies, maximum banking operations have been computerized by most of the commercial banks, both in Private sector as well as in Public sector especially in the last ten years and the process is still on for extension and up gradation of computerization by banks in India. The computerization is done for front office operations involving internal interface with customers as well as back office operations involving internal housekeeping i.e. accounting and books balancing, external accounting and settlement with other branches and banks/institutions. E-banking provides a bouquet of new channels like internet banking, telephone banking, ATM banking-which are different from the traditional 'brick and mortar' branch banking and which have made possible 'anywhere and anytime banking' and contributed to speed, accuracy and confidentiality of customers' transactions while enhancing customers' convenience. Funds transfer, cheques clearing and collection of bills of exchange are also done electronically with accuracy, speed and safety31. Internal housekeeping is done accurately and much faster through programmed packages/ software at the branch and also at centralized platforms involving several branches of a region or zone.

4.5 Banking Ombudsman Scheme

RBI has introduced banking ombudsman scheme in 1995. Though the customers are using techno-based services provided by banks, but still they are facing many problems in using these services. The general causes of arising the problems are; machine errors, light fluctuation problems, lack of proper knowledge, illiteracy, unskilled employees, etc. Banks have appointed customer relation officers for providing solutions of problems but customers are still reluctant to do online banking transactions. RBI has introduced this system for conducting and solving the problems of customers according to the provisions given in banking regulation act, 1949 and consumer protection act, 198632.

4.5.1 Functions of Banking Ombudsman Scheme

It deals with complaints regarding [33]:

1. Non-payment or inordinate delay in the payment or collection of cheques.
2. Non- acceptance without sufficient cause of small domination notes tendered for any purpose.
3. Non-issue of drafts to customers and others
4. Non-adherence to prescribed working hours by branches
5. Failure to honor guarantee or letter or credit commitments by banks.
6. Complaints pertaining to operations in SB/CA/NRT accounts.
7. Non-observances of RBI guidelines in respect of interest rates
8. Non-observance or instruction of RBI regarding prescribed time scheduled for disposal of loan application.

Table 4.15

Classification of complainants

Types of Complainant	2011-12		2012-13		2013-14	
	No of complainant	%	No of complainant	%	No of complainant	%
Individuals	66779	91	65808	93	70913	92.6
Proprietors	2635	4	2245	3	2163	2.87
Partnership firm	253	0.3	227	0.3	151	0.2
Ltd. Company	690	1	628	1	510	0.7
Trust	150	0.2	213	0.3	184	0.2
Associations	461	0.6	325	0.6	297	0.4
Govt. Dept.	521	0.7	390	0.5	287	0.4

PSU	80	0.1	222	0.6	266	0.3
Others	1820	2	483	0.7	1802	2.4
Total	72889	100	70541	100	76573	100

Source: Reports on Banking Ombudsman Scheme, 2011-12 to 2013-14

Table 4.16

Complaints registered under Banking Ombudsman Scheme

Types of Complainant	2011-12		2012-13		2013-14	
	Numbers	%	Numbers	%	Numbers	%
Deposit Accounts	8713	12	3913	6	4032	5.3
Remittances	3928	5	2664	4	2659	3.5
Related to Cards	14492	21	17867	25	18474	24.1
Loans and Advances	6016	8	5996	9	5655	7.4
Charges without notice	3806	5	3817	5	4547	5.9
Pension	5944	8	5740	8	6555	8.5
Failure to meet commitments	18365	25	18130	26	20368	26.6
DSA & DRAs	459	1	351	0.8	295	0.4
Notes and Coins	165	02	56	0.2	63	0.1
Others	7327	10	8635	12	9861	12.9
Out of subject	3674	5	3372	5	4064	5.3
Total	72889	100	70541	100	76573	100

Source: Reports on Banking Ombudsman Scheme, 2011-12 to 2013-14

4.5.2 Types of complaints under the Banking Ombudsman Scheme[34]

1. Complaints concerning deficiency in banking services: e.g. non-payment or inordinate delay in

payment/collection of cheques, failure to honor a guarantee or letter of credit commitment by a bank, fraudulent withdrawals from the account.

2. Complaints concerning loans in so far as these relate to non-observance of RBI directive on interest rates, or other matters concerning loans, delay in sanction of loans, etc.

Table 4.17

Complaints registered in India and Maharashtra

Year	Particulars	Maharashtra	India
2011-12	Number of Complaints	7650 ()	72889 ()
	Number of officers	14 ()	160 ()
	Number of complaint per officer	546 ()	454 ()
2012-13	Number of Complaints	8607 ()	70541 ()
	Number of officers	15 ()	157 ()
	Number of complaint per officer	574 ()	449 ()
2013-14	Number of Complaints	9965 ()	76573 ()
	Number of officers	19 ()	167 ()
	Number of complaint per officer	524 ()	459 ()

Source: Report on Banking Ombudsman Scheme 2013-2014

4.5.3 Settlement process of complaints under the BOS

The banking ombudsman will facilitate a settlement of customers' complaints by one of the following procedures provided under the scheme[35]:

1. By agreement between the complainant and the bank within one month from the receipt of complaint,
2. By making recommendation for settlement, which the complainant may accept within two weeks from the date of receipt of the recommendations.
3. By making an award after giving an opportunity to

both the parties submit further representations. The award shall not be binding on bank unless the complainant gives an acceptance to the award as full final settlement of his claim in the matter.

4.5.4 Bank group-wise complaints

RBI has received complaints regarding e-banking technology from various stakeholders and customers. The complaints are received through e-mail, manually, via bank units, etc.

Table 4.18

Bank Group-wise complaints registered under Banking Ombudsman Scheme

Bank Group	2011-12		2012-13		2013-14	
	No of complainant	%	No of complainant	%	No of complainant	%
SBI Group	25848	35	23134	33	24367	32
Nationalized Banks	22326	31	21609	31	24391	32
Private Sector Banks	15090	21	15653	22	17030	22
Foreign Banks	5068	7	4859	7	5016	6.5
RRBs & Sch. UCBs	1439	2	1489	2	1590	2
Others	3118	4	3797	5	4179	5.5
Total	72889	100	70541	100	76573	100

Source: Report on Banking Ombudsman Scheme

4.5.5 Area-wise complaints registered under BO Scheme

Till March, 2014, total 76573 complaints are registered under banking ombudsman scheme at its registered office. Table given below indicates that in the year 2012-13 and 2013-14, the complaints from the customers living in rural areas are increased with 1 percent whereas the complaints from urban areas are decreased with 1 percent[36].

Table 4.19

Area-wise complaints under BO scheme

Area	Rural	Semi-urban	Urban	Metro-Politian	Total
2011-12	8190	11982	24565	28152	72889
	(11)	(16)	(34)	(39)	(100)
2012-13	8598	10868	24246	26829	70541
	(12)	(16)	(34)	(38)	(100)
2013-14	9927	12314	25448	28884	76573
	(13)	(16)	(33)	(38)	(100)
% Increase / Decrease	+1	-	-1	-	-

Source: Report on Banking Ombudsman Scheme 2013-2014

4.6 Basel Policy

On 26 June 1974, a number of banks had given payments of Deutsche Marks (DEM - German Currency at that time) to Herstatt (Based out of Cologne, Germany) in exchange of US Dollars (USD) which was delivered in New York. Due to delay in payments, Herstatt ceased operations for the respective payments. German regulators forced the troubled Bank into liquidation. The counter banks had not received any USD payments. Responding to the cross-jurisdictional implications of the Herstatt tragedy, the G-10 countries formed a standing committee in 1974 under the Bank for International Settlements (BIS), which is called as the Basel Committee on Banking Supervision. Since BIS is known as a headquarter of Basel, The committee comprises representatives from central banks and regulatory authorities[37]

Objectives of Basel

Basel 1	Credit Risk
Basel 1.1	Credit risk and Market Risk
Basel 2	Credit Risk, Market Risk, Operational Risk,
Basel 3	Credit Risk, Market Risk, Operational Risk, Liquidity Risk

4.6.1 The Basel –I accord

This Basel I accord came into existence in 1988 in Switzerland, which gives its initiatives by the global banking industry to develop and standardized a risk management framework. It realized that its effect is limited due its large dealt with credit risk, ignored operational risk and paid lip services to market risk. A minimum capital requirement for banks is suggested by the Basel Committee on Banking Supervision (BCBS). It was implemented by Group of Ten (G-10) countries from 1992. It highlighted credit risk of counter party failure. It defined capital requirement of banks and structure of risk weightage for banks.

The assets of banks were classified and grouped in following five categories,

A. credit risk,

B. carrying risk,

C. risk-weighted assets (RWA) - (Equity Capital + retained earnings)

D. Capital risk

E. Target risk.

The major characteristic of Basel I norms is to standardize the banking practices on global stage, but there are major problems of Capital and Differential Risk Weights to Assets in different nations. Other problems included risk weights related to credit risk, viz., market risks, liquidity risk and operational risks. For withdrawing the errors in Basel I, a new set of rules and regulation introduced in 2003, which is known as Basel II and later on it is developed with the new intentions.

4.6.2 Basel II Accord[38]

Basel committee on banking supervision has released a consultative paper in April 2003 to improve capital adequacy framework. The new accord consists of three pillars According to Basel II, banks are facing new challenges and thus it requires banking supervision. Objectives of Basel II have control on the banking operations by quantifying each risk associated with its product, services and operations. The solution to the Basel II defined use of IT as an integral part of today's banking operations. This accord builds on an evolving framework from managing risk in banking and financial services transactions. In contrast to the first capital accord that addressed capital risk and market risk.

Basel II provided a common and stronger framework for risk management and includes operation risk. IT has become decisive factor in shaping modern banking operations as IT is no more a facilitator but now it's an integral part of banking operations which is evident from the fact that many banks have undergone a fundamental transformation in terms of IT infrastructures, applications and IT-related internal controls.

1. Minimum capital requirements- the ratio continues to be 8% by modifications have been made in the definitions of risk weighted assets.
2. Supervisory review- stress test of assets held by the bank may be held. Banks are to assess capital adequacy positions relative to their overall risks.
3. Market discipline- a set of disclosure requirements has been developed to allow the stakeholders, shareholders and market participants to assess key information about banks risk profile and level of capital resources to meet the unexpected losses.

4.6.3 Basel III

Basel III was developed due to the financial crisis created in banks; which focuses on different issues primarily related to the risk of a bank. The drawbacks in Basel II norms effects on the global financial crisis of 2008, because Basel II did not have any particular rules and regulation on the debt that banks could take on their accounts. To ensure that reliability of banks about debt on short term funds, Basel III norms are proposed in 2010 with following features[39];

i. To promote more flexible banking system by focusing on four vital banking parameters viz. capital, leverage, funding and liquidity.

ii. Capital Requirements of 4.5% for common equity and 6% for Tier 1.

iii. Banks require a buffer of high quality liquid assets as the liquidity coverage ratio (LCR) to deal with the cash outflows encountered in an acute short term stress scenario as specified by supervisors. The minimum LCR requirement will have to reach 100% on 1 January 2019.

iv. Leverage Ratio > 3%: (The leverage ratio = Tier 1 capital / the bank's average total consolidated assets).

RBI Deputy Governor, Mr. Anand Sinha noted that the implementation of Basel II have a negative impact on growth rate of India thus in FY 2012-13, Government of India has expected to provide Rs 15888 crores to recapitalize the banks as to maintain capital adequacy of 8% under old Basel II norms.

4.7 Some Major Developments under Basel III guidelines

On 30th October 2012, RBI in its Second Quarter Review of Monetary Policy 2012 13 has declared that[40];

(i) Requirements on Regulatory Capital Composition

The Basel Committee on Banking Supervision (BCBS) has finalized the proposals on disclosure requirements related to the composition of regulatory capital, aimed at improving transparency of regulatory capital and market discipline. On 30th June, 2013, National Authorities has been decided to issue guidelines on composition of capital disclosure requirements.

(ii) Banks' Exposures to Central Counterparties (CCP)

The Basel Committee on Banking Supervision has issued an interim framework of capital requirements of banks to CCPs. This framework is introduced as an amendment to the Basel II (capital adequacy framework) and is also intended to create incentives to increase the use of CCPs. These standards come into force from 1st January, 2013. Accordingly, it has decided to issue guidelines on capital requirements for bank exposures, which are based on the interim framework of the BCBS, by mid-November 2012.

(iii) Core Principles for Effective Banking Supervision

The Basel Committee has issued revised guidelines of the Core Principles in September 2012 to reflect the practices done during the recent global financial crisis. It is proposed to carry out a self-assessment of the existing regulatory and supervisory practices based on the revised Core Principles and to initiate steps to further strengthen the regulatory and supervisory mechanism. On 7th November, 2012, RBI has issued final guidelines regarding Liquidity Risk Management.

4.8 Strategy for progress in banking sector

All other banks witnessed better position in post e-banking period along with profitability and with increasing costs but it is also viewed that the progress of cooperative banks is also less compared to others, so there is need to adopt competitive strategies along with international standards to improve their performance and make them competitive in local as well as international markets. All or some of the following strategies should be attempting to draw some strategies for the better tomorrow of weak Indian cooperative banking sector[41]:

1. Adoption of New technology: Better position in terms of higher profitability, reduction in costs and non-performing assets, customer satisfaction in new private sector banks and foreign banks reflects the

favorable effect of the adoption of new technology. Now the Cooperative banks must adopt technology in full version with all advancements to improve their performance in the market and make them competitive locally as well as internationally. Adoption of technology will further help to reduce their increasing level of costs and will improve their share in fee based income.

2. Rural Branches: All bank groups have gained good share in rural branches but cooperative banks are losing their share continuously as facing competition from public sector banks, new private sector banks, etc. They should make appropriate strategies to improve their performance in rural areas and for this purpose they must follow consolidation of two or more branches especially week branches to make them strong enough to face competition from their counterparts and survive in the market.

3. Priority sector advances: There is growth in priority sector advances of all bank groups but share of public sector banks has declined from 82 percent in 2005-06 to 35 per cent during 2010-11 whereas new private sector banks and foreign banks have gained momentum share with excellent growth. Public sector banks are facing competition from new private sector banks and foreign banks to retain their share. They should advance loans in the priority sector with proper strategies for the evaluation of the financial position and security of loan seekers so that they can get recovery of their loans promptly and further continue to advance loans in priority sector.

4. Strong provisioning norms: Provision for taxes etc are mandatory for all the banks as these provide help to bear future uncertainties. There is a need to motivate the banks to maintain their provisions to the maximum extent. Therefore, the RBI should aging fix some amount for provisions that can help the banks to maintain their provisions at least to the required level.

5. Relief from Excessive Government Regulations: After the introduction of NEP, restrictions are still imposed by the RBI and Co-operative societies act, 1960 which become many times obstacles to take important decisions at the right time but they can't do that and loose that opportunity to perform better because it takes long time to take approval and to take important decisions. Therefore, cooperative banking sector should be awarded full autonomy to operate their business freely under the guidelines of RBI or there should be special Administrative Authority to operate their business freely in the market so that they can also avail the opportunities at the right time.
6. Customer Focus: The most important concern is customer satisfaction which is the strength of new private sector banks and foreign banks to gain a momentum share in the market. They serve their customers according to their needs with latest tech-savvy channels, innovative products/services but this lacks in public sector banks and old private sector banks. They should also focus on customers to retain them and so that they can't switch over to other banks for better services. And for this purpose, they must provide innovative products/services through new technologies as demanded by the customers which will definitely help them to retain their share in the market.

4.9 Future of Banking in India

With rapid advances in telecommunication systems and digital technology, it is difficult to predict how e-banking will improve and expand in the coming year. For example, internet banking via mobile phones using wireless application protocol (WAP) or banking services through the TV screen via the new interactive TV channels may become established it is likely that the number of customers wanting to bank online will increase which could lead to high street banks offering personalized services and better online customer care. To combat computer crime and increase security levels, banks may consider new security measures such as iris, voice and finger print recognition, smart cards and electronic signatures[42].

The banking sector, as a whole is undergoing a transformation, primarily because of the advent of the internet. Financial institutions are realizing that e-banking is not just another distribution channel for their services, but a revolution as the internet and its associate development challenges the traditional banking practices and core business units. Corporate banks are carefully considering the best way forward and many are viewing the e-banking phenomenon an opportunity and not a threat. Smaller banks need to look at how they can best compete in their market. Developing their own internet solutions is rarely possible and so they must look at other options to facilitate e-banking and e-commerce initiatives[43].

4.10 Perception of Indian banks in 2020

Change is the only certainty and it would govern the banking industry, graduating from financial intermediary into risk intermediary. The repetition and overlapping systems and procedures have given ways to simple key-press technology, ensuring accuracy and speed of data flow to improve overall efficiency through knowledge management. The emerging IT facilities in utilizing Knowledge management effectively and efficiently have to improve in product range and services quality in the banking sector.

Definitely by 2020, the vast and enormous differences are noticed between PSB and the new generation private sector banks and foreign banks. The dominance of PSB which accounts for nearly 80 % share in the banking sector wants to reduce considerably by 2020. Technology has played a vital role in the evolution of banking sector, through speed creation, accuracy and efficiency of operation and reduction in the transaction cost[44]. Banking services are now oriented to "anyhow, anywhere, anytime and any type banking with 24*7*365" days banking.

The regulatory requirements and compliance regime in post-Basel II scenario complicates the processing of data besides the process of their storage and retrieval in the desired speed. Banks have to move on behaviour analysis approach for fine-tuning products.

The key drivers in the banking industry are as follows[45]

1. Instead of merely providing what the bank concerned could offer from its fold, banking may encompass extension of all the services that are required and dictated by customers.
2. Clients should get services from the banks on a 24*7*365 basis on an online ATM connected to the network. Whosoever a customer should be able to access his or her bank account through a PC/laptop/mobile or an ATM around the corner.
3. The time spent by the bank with customers would be reduced, thereby improving profitability through low operational cost that would ensure time saving for the customers as a by-product.

4.11 Conclusion

The biggest impact of globalization is found mainly on banking sector which is resulted in adoption and effective use of technology. The main objective is to reduce operating costs by offering them new products and services with highly powerful data storage and analysis. RBI regulations are similar for public and private sector banks. Customers are also using these services in large quantity. But due to lack of proper technological installation, light fluctuations and other causes, all the customers are not using these services and many of them are using but also facing some problems.

For controlling and solving such problems, RBI has appointed a special Ombudsman Scheme which helps banks in reducing problems and plans for development of e-banking sector with providing better quality services. BOS has introduced various policies for development of banks through controlling technological problems. BOS also defined that Indian banking sector may be one of the developed unit in future. Indian banks should have to cover rural areas by establishing new branches, should have to increase profit by controlling transaction costs. Banks also have to make provision for technological development of banks and also have to reduce the ratio of NPA.

References

1. Uppal R.K., Jatana Rimpi, (2009), Editorial, 'E-banking: Opportunities and Challenges', Mahamaya Publications, New Delhi, Pp-6
2. Jhingan M.L., Cooperative Banks in India, 'Money, Banking, International Trade and Public Finance', 7th Edition, 2008, Vrinda Publications, pp-605-606
3. Iyer V.R., BOI, Chairperson's speech, '17th Annual General Meeting of shareholders at Mumbai', 29th June 2013, published in The Economic times on 1st July, 2013
4. Kundi and Shah, 2009, 'Indian Banking in Globalised Era', Indian banking moving towards better tomorrow, Editorial, R.K.Uppal ,Pp-5
5. Avadhani V.A. (2008), Marketing of Financial Services, Himalaya Publications House, Mumbai, Pp-642-649
6. Economic survey of India, Report-2013, Pp-60
7. Bhaskaran R. (Chief Executive Officer-RBI-2011), Know Your Banking, 'Electronic Banking', Pp-111
8. Bhatt Sanjeev (1988), 'Bank Marketing', An article in The Economic Times, dated 1st Sept., 1988
9. Thakur Vishwas, (Chairman-Vishwas Cooperative Bank limited, Nashik), an article, 'Dynamic Changes in Banking Sector', in Daily Deshdoot, supplement of Banking Special, dated 20th Feb., 2015, pp-1
10. R.K.Uppal (2012), editorial, Indian Banking Industry in 2020, 'Globalization', Mahamaya Publishing house, Pp-19
11. Ruchi Trehan, Niti Soni, Arti Verma, Indian Banking Moving Towards Better Tomorrow, 'Innovations in Banking', R.K. Uppal, Editorial, Mahamaya publishing house, New Delhi, 2009, pp-43-47
12. An article in Daily Sakal dated 9th March, 2011
13. Pravinkumar Tayal & Sugan C. Jain (2009), New trends in Finance, 'Financial Reporting of Banking Companies in India- an Evolutionary stage', Editorial- Dangwal R.C.& Kashmira Singh, RBSA Publisers, New Delhi, Page no. 255Indian Economy
14. Kohok M. A. (1993), Financial Services in India, 'Credit Cards', First Edition, Digvijay Publication, Nashik, Pp-257-261
15. Editorial, Vikalpvedh, Vol-17, No-3, 2011, Pp-19
16. Joshi Shrinivas, Banking Sector Towards Global Competition, Yojana, March-2009, Pp-26 -29
17. Gandatra Navdeepkumar & Rama (2011), 'Banking Sector Reforms: A fresh Outlook', Editor-R.K.Uppal, an article on 'Competition in Indian Banking Sector-Issues and Strategies in Global Scenario', Mahamaya Publishing House, New Delhi, Pp-125-128
18. Bank Reports

19. Ibid
20. Gupta, O.P. and Poonam Nagpal (2011), Banking Sector Reform, 'Banking Sector Reform in India in the Phase of Globalisation', Uppal, R.K. editorial, Mahamaya Publishing House, New Delhi, Pp- 76-86
21. The Economic Times, dated 23rd Jan., 2007
22. Ibid
23. Dutta-sundaram(2013), 'Indian Financial System', Indian Economy, 64th edition, S.Chand Publication, New Delhi, Pp- 854Newspaper
24. Ibid
25. JIBC, Editorial, December 2009, Vol. 14, No. 3, Pp-2
26. Ibid
27. www.internetworldstats.com
28. www.rbi.org.in
29. RBI Report on payment and settlement system, Sept., 2012
30. Ibid
31. Economic Survey of Maharashtra, 2013-14
32. Report on Banking Ombudsman Scheme of India, 2013-14
33. Ibid
34. www.banking_ombudsman.com
35. Ibid
36. NitiSoni, ArtiVerma, 'Innovations in banking', Indian Banking: Moving Towards Better Tomorrow, Editorial, , R.K.Uppal, RuchiTrehan, , Mahamaya Publication, New Delhi, pp-51
37. Reports of RBI on Basel Policy
38. Ibid
39. Ibid
40. www.rbi_baselpolicy.com
41. R.P.Gupta (2003), 'Dynamics Of Banking Technology', Journal of Internet Banking and Commerce, Vol-3, No-2, June 2003
42. Rangrajan C., (1997), Governor's Speech, RBI Bulleting, Pp-51
43. Singh Kulwant, Pathania & Sharma Mamta (2010), 'Adoption of Banking Technology', Indian Journal of Commerce, Vol-63, No-01, Jan-March-2010, Pp-91BOS Report 2013-14
44. Padhye, Kishor C. and Mishra Rakesh Roshan (2013), A to Z banking and finance, Himalaya Publishing House, First Edition, 2013, Pp. 15BOS Report
45. Dasgupta (2012), Future of E-banking in India, an article available at www.projectshub.com

Business Analysis of Banks

5.1 Introduction

Technological advancement in banking sector is a dynamic avenue which turned banks on the path of development on globalised era. It has the feature of real cost reduction in the production and transaction process. It has two major advantages of technological adoption i.e. reduction in banks' operational costs (the cost savings advantage) and assisting more efficient transactions among customers within the same network. While using and providing this services banks are facing problems and so in this research work, researcher focuses on the current and prompt technological revolution controlling the whole banking sector on state, national and on international levels.

These e-banking services have greater developmental impacts on the banking sector through reducing transaction cost, time saving, 24*7*365 days services, etc. Particularly, this study seeks some clues on which the researcher can rely in order to understand various problems faced by banks while adopting and providing these services as well as the customers' behavior regarding the adoption of electronic banking. This research study also focuses on those factors which are reflecting the progress of Co-operative banks after the adoption of e-banking technology.

Purposive sampling method has been used while selecting branches from the population of Banks. The banks which have adopted e-banking technology and providing e-banking services to their customers are selected for the study. Primary data was collected through structured questionnaires for each of the types of respondents. Simple statistical tools such as percentages, averages and ratios have been used to analyze data. The respondents to this inquiry are Managers of Co-operative banks from Nasik District, one branch each from 13 (20 per cent of 64) Banks. 13 branches of Co-operative banks which are providing e-banking services to its customers are selected.

The respondents are Branch Managers of branches with different age, gender, educational qualifications.

5.2 Profile of Branches of Banks

As per the report of Rural Bank Association of Nasik District, there are 49 registered Co-operative banks but very few banks have their branches elsewhere. For this reason, the researcher has based her selection on the seniority basis of adoption of e-banking technology. As per sample of 20 per cent from total number of banks which have adopted e-banking technology; 13 branches are selected.

Among these 13 Co-operative Banks, only 2 branches have their head-office in Nasik and 10 banks have their head office in Mumbai and another one branch has its head office in Akola. Except one cooperative bank, all the other sample branches are urban in nature.

5.2.1 E-Banking Services

After globalized era, the role of e-banking services is an important part of business of banking sector and for attracting the customers at bank unit. For being development of banking sector adoption of e-banking technology is one of the important system which provide technology based self-services to its customers and save time and money of customers as well as banks also. E-banking is one of the most important weapons of branch expansion. Thus it is necessary to study the year of adoption of e-banking services which shows the awareness and competitive ability of banks.

In the competitive era, it becomes necessary to provide e-banking services to the customers of banks. All these services are the by-products of IT department. All these e-banking services are known as technology-based self-services which are provided by banks to their customers. These services are time saving and cost reducing also. At first Public Sector Banks have adopted these services followed by Private sector banks because these banks are profit oriented. Cooperative banks have also adopted these technologies in their branches thus attracting to the bank customers by providing latest technologies.

Table 5.1

Table Showing Year of Adoption of E-banking Services

Sr. No	Name of Banks	Year of Establis hment of Bank	Year of adoption of E-banking services
1	SVC Bank Ltd	1905	2002
2	CC Bank Ltd	1906	2003
3	AC Bank Ltd	1965	2004
4	BMC Bank Ltd	1939	2007
5	SC Bank Ltd	1918	2007
6	MC Bank Ltd	1973	2008
7	PMC Bank Ltd	1984	2010
8	GPPJS Bank Ltd	1972	2010
9	JKS Bank Ltd	1974	2010
10	AUC Bank Ltd	1963	2011
11	NRDVS Bank Ltd	1961	2011
12	NMC Bank Ltd	1959	2011
13	MSC Bank Ltd	1904	2011

Source: Primary data

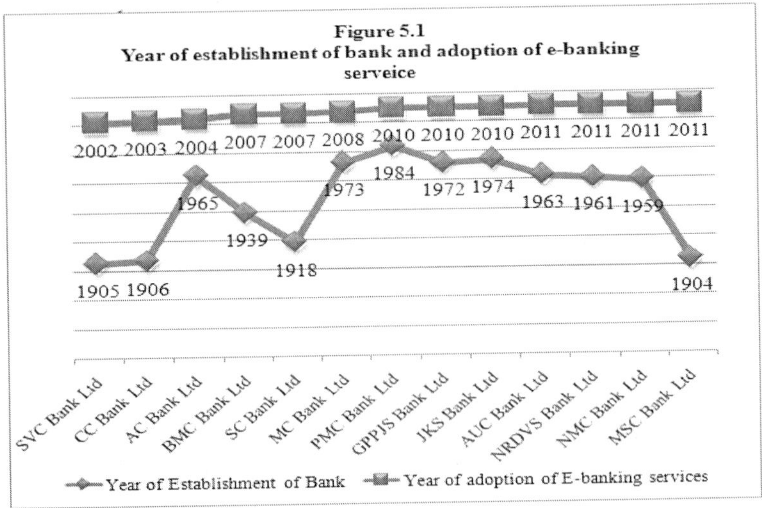

Without adoption of e-banking services, it is impossible to survive in banking sector and thus Co-operative banks have also adopted the e-banking technology and are providing these techno-based services to their customers.

5.2.2 Distribution of banks showing No of Branches

Co-operative banks are playing an important role in the development of rural areas and villages also. Most of the co-operative banks are only financing to farmers for agricultural development and the others are still comparing with PSB and Private sector banks by providing technological services to their customers. But technology needs more funds for development and more funds will be available only from the customers (from their deposits in current and saving accounts). It means when the number of customers using technological services are more, the establishment expenses of the technology and transactional costs are automatically decreases and vice-versa. Thus it becomes necessary to do study of banks as per number of branches.

Table 5.2

Table Showing Number of Branches and Number of States Covered by Banks

Sr. No	Name of Banks	No of States covered	No. of Branches			
			Nasik District	Maharashtra	Out of State	Total
1	SVC Bank Ltd	4	14	115	41	156
2	CC Bank Ltd	7	07	92	48	140
3	AC Bank Ltd	3	09	87	24	111
4	BMC Bank Ltd	1	81	81	-	81
5	SC Bank Ltd	6	19	149	118	267
6	MC Bank Ltd	2	03	47	-	47
7	PMC Bank Ltd	6	04	74	34	108
8	GPPJS Bank Ltd	1	07	62	-	62
9	JKS Bank Ltd	1	07	33	-	33
10	AUC Bank Ltd	1	02	21	-	21
11	NRDVS Bank Ltd	1	19	19	-	19
12	NMC Bank Ltd	10	01	32	20	52
13	MSC Bank Ltd	1	04	43	-	43
	Cooperative Banks	**Total**	177 (15.5)	855 (75)	285 (25)	1140 (100)

Source: Primary data

N.B: Figures in brackets indicate per cent to total

Figure 5.2
Number of Branches and states covered

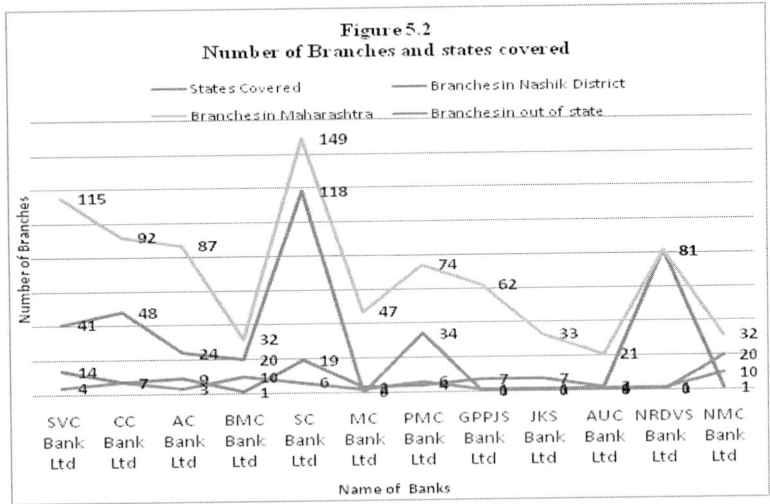

Table 5.3 indicates that the number of branch office of Saraswat cooperative Bank is far more than other Co-operative banks. All co-operative banks have their branches in Nasik District, of which, 46.15 per cent banks (6) have their branches in Maharashtra and 15.38 per cent banks (2) have their branches only in Nashik District and remaining 38.46 per cent (5) Co-operative banks have their branches in other states. Average 75 per cent (855) branches are working in Maharashtra state and 25 per cent (285) branches are located in other states.

5.3 Socio-economic characteristics of Bank Managers

Under this point, the personal and socio-economics of the bank managers' are presented. The distributions of respondents by Sex, age, annual income, education etc. are discussed in brief.

It is essential to study personal information, economic condition, educational status, because from these characteristics, we can observe their attitude towards the technological services provided by Co-operative banks.

5.3.1 Distribution of respondents by Sex, Qualifications and Age

Sex plays an important role in socio-economic activities of branch managers. When the researcher differentiate the sex group of respondents, the researcher find the major participation of male branch manager than the female branch managers.

Educational qualifications of branch managers show the developing attitude and the educational standard of managers, which is useful for accepting the challenges rising in banking sector. It also indicates the recruitment position of branch managers, whether they are directly recruited as branch manager or promoted by experience.

Table 5.3

Distribution of Branch Managers' by Sex, Qualifications and Age-wise

Sr. No	Name of Banks	Sex	Qualification	Distribution of Managers by Age Group			
				Upto 25	26-35	36-50	50 +
1	SVC Bank Ltd	M	DBM	0	0	1	0
2	CC Bank Ltd	F	Graduate	0	0	0	1
3	AC Bank Ltd	M	DCM	0	1	0	0
4	BMC Bank Ltd	M	MBA	0	0	1	0
5	SC Bank Ltd	M	PG	0	0	1	0
6	MC Bank Ltd	F	GDC&A	0	0	1	0
7	PMC Bank Ltd	M	Graduate	0	0	0	1
8	GPPJS Bank Ltd	M	Graduate	0	0	0	1
9	JKS Bank Ltd	F	PG	0	0	1	0
10	AUC Bank Ltd	M	GDC&A	0	0	0	1
11	NRDVS Bank Ltd	M	Graduate	0	0	1	0
12	NMC Bank Ltd	M	PG	0	0	0	1
13	MSC Bank Ltd	M	Graduate	0	0	0	1
	Cooperative Banks Total			0 (0)	1 (7.69)	6 (46.15)	6 (46.15)

Source: Primary data

N.B: Figures in brackets indicate per cent to total

Figure 5.3
Age-wise classification of branch managers

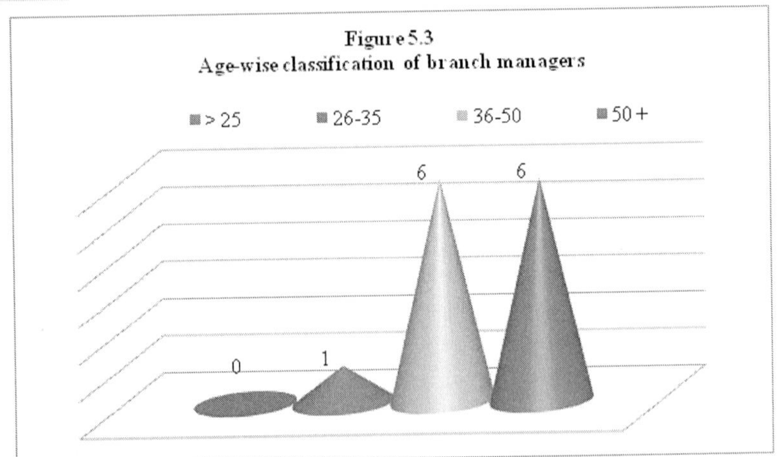

When we classify the respondents according to age group, it indicates the involvement of branch managers in business activity of branch.

Table 5.3 shows that the majority of Managers are males, out of 13branchmanagers, ratio of male managers are 76.92 per cent (10), and the female Managers are 23.1 per cent (3). It is clear that the branches are dominated by male Managers.

Distribution of Managers by age groups shows that maximum number of Managers (46.15 per cent each) are in the senior age groups of 36-50 and 51-60 age groups constituting 6 each, followed by one managers from Co-operative bank which is in the age group of 26-50 years.

If we look at the distribution of Managers by their level of education, maximum managers are post-graduates 23.1 per cent (3) and graduates 53.84 per cent (7), followed by diploma holders 15.38 per cent (2). Among the graduates, 15.38 per cent (2) are holding GDC&A diploma, which is an obligatory qualification for officers in Co-operative banks.

5.3.2 Distribution of banks by E-banking services provided

E-banking services are rendered by banks to their customers to attract them. Banks are providing maximum types of e-banking services. Increasing number of customers automatically decreases transactional costs. Thus banks give their preference for rendering maximum services. It is necessary to study the services which are provided by banks to their customers.

From the survey of researcher, it is noted that all the banks are providing all E-banking services through their branches to the customers. The banks are providing various types of e-banking services i.e. ATMs, Debit/Credit Cards, Phone Banking, Mobile Banking, Internet Banking, RTGS/EFT, Online payment of bills.

5.3.3 No. of Account holders using e-banking services

In globalized era, banks are providing various types of e-banking services to the customers. These services are techno-based and buy product from IT sector. All the services are time saving, cost reducing, cashless, anytime banking, etc. Customers use these services according to their need. The services provided by banks are depended on the number of service users. Thus it is necessary to study the number of customers using e-banking services provided by banks which shows the attitude of customers towards these services.

Table 5.4

No. of Account holders using e-banking services

Sr. No	Name of Banks	ATM	Debit/ Credit Cards	Phone Banking	Mobile Banking	Internet Banking	RTGS/ EFT	Online Payment of Bills
1	SVC Bank Ltd	926	536	926	926	926	94	73
2	CC Bank Ltd	686	588	686	686	686	83	16
3	AC Bank Ltd	718	354	718	718	718	42	78
4	BMC Bank Ltd	458	239	458	458	458	68	47
5	SC Bank Ltd	322	225	322	322	322	42	62
6	MC Bank Ltd	645	390	645	645	645	130	52
7	PMC Bank Ltd	478	276	478	478	478	68	42
8	GPPJS Bank Ltd	369	244	369	369	369	36	26
9	JKS Bank Ltd	286	184	286	286	286	42	42
10	AUC Bank Ltd	608	348	608	608	608	62	47
11	NRDVS Bank Ltd	421	358	421	421	421	62	42

12	NMC Bank Ltd	551	337	551	551	551	47	57
13	MSC Bank Ltd	416	356	416	416	416	31	62
Total Co-operative Banks		6885	4435	6885	6885	6885	806	646
		(100)	(64.42)	(100)	(100)	(100)	(11.72)	(9.38)

Source: Primary data

Figure 5.4
No. of Account holders using e-banking services

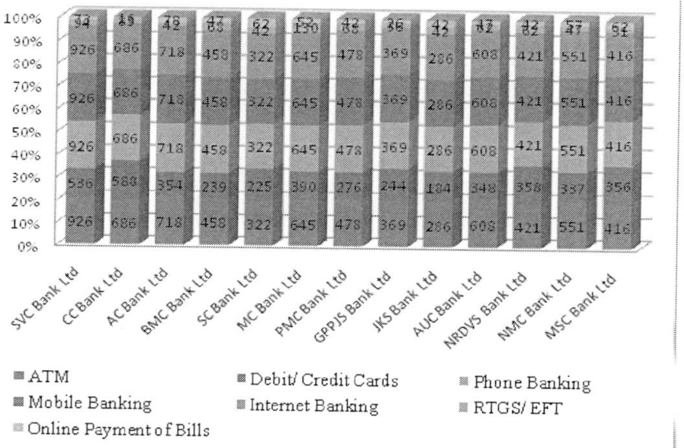

Table 5.4 shows that majority of customers are using ATM, Phone Banking and Mobile Banking and Internet banking services because except ATMs service other services are providing in free of cost and also provided to all the customers. Cent per cent customers from all the banks are using ATM, Phone Banking and Mobile Banking and Internet banking services. 64.42 per cent Customers are using Debit/ Credit Cards followed by 9.38 per cent customers who are using service of online bill payment.

It is observed that the customers show a tendency of underutilization for the services of RTGS/EFT, Debit/Credit Cards and for online payment of bills.

5.3.4 No. of Branches providing e-banking services

Though the e-banking services are useful for increasing the working capacity and profitability of banks, it needs huge funds for installation of technologies.

The banks having enough funds have adopted e-banking technology and providing these services successfully. All types of banks are not economically viable that they are not providing these services in all branches. PSB have more branches and more funds due to large number of customers and their positive attitude

Table 5.5

No. of Branches Providing E-Banking Services

Sr. No	Name of Banks	All Branches	More than 50%	Less than 50%
1	SVC Bank Ltd	v	-	-
2	CC Bank Ltd	v	-	-
3	AC Bank Ltd	v	-	-
4	BMC Bank Ltd	v	-	-
5	SC Bank Ltd	v	-	-
6	MC Bank Ltd	v	-	-

7	PMC Bank Ltd	v	-	-
8	GPPJS Bank Ltd	-	v	-
9	JKS Bank Ltd	-	-	v
10	AUC Bank Ltd	v	-	-
11	NRDVS Bank Ltd	v	-	-
12	NMC Bank Ltd	v	-	-
13	MSC Bank Ltd	v	-	-
Total of Cooperative Banks		11 (84.61)	1 (7.69)	1 (7.69)

Source: Primary data

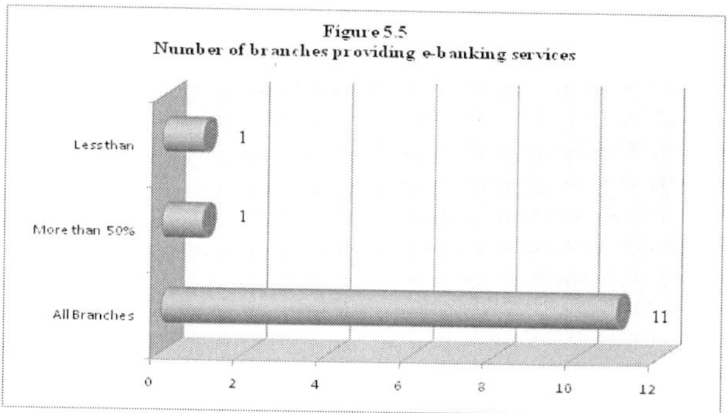

Table 5.5 indicates that84.61 per cent Branches of Co-operative banks (11) are providing all types of e-services through their branches, whereas another 7.69 per cent branch each (1 each) are providing these services trough more than 50 per cent services and in less than 50 per cent branches.

5.3.5 ATM Centers of Banks

For convenience of customers, banks have established indoor and outdoor ATM centers at nearest market places. It provides quick and near to door services to deposit and to withdraw cash. Thus the study of number of ATM centers is necessary that it shows the efficiency of banks. Table 5.6 shows distribution of Rural/Urban ATM Centers of branches of Co-operative and other banks.

Table 5.6

Number of ATM Centers in Banks

Name of Banks	No. of ATM Centers		
	In Rural Area	In Urban Area	Total
SVC Bank Ltd	0	173	193
CC Bank Ltd	0	23	53
AC Bank Ltd	0	27	127
BMC Bank Ltd	0	152	152
SC Bank Ltd	0	59	59
MC Bank Ltd	0	47	47
PMC Bank Ltd	0	137	137
GPPJS Bank Ltd	24	105	129
JKS Bank Ltd	0	64	64
AUC Bank Ltd	0	108	108
NRDVS Bank Ltd	2	47	49
NMC Bank Ltd	45	16	61
MSC Bank Ltd	0	139	139
Total of Cooperative Banks	71 (5.47)	1227 (94.53)	1298 (100)

Source: Primary data

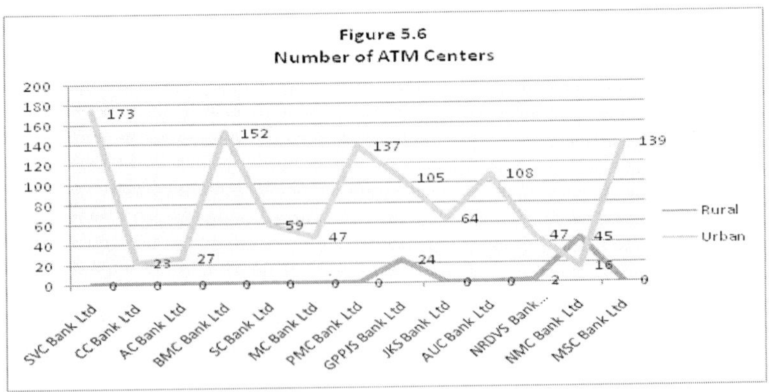

It is interesting to note that Co-operative banking network, though is expected to serve rural community, their branches providing ATM facility are more concentrated in urban area. Co-operative banks have 5.47 per cent ATMs in rural area and remaining 94.53 per cent in urban areas.

5.3.6 Time required for solving the problems of ATM Centers

Though these modern banking services are based on IT department these are being used extensively by the bank customers, still the researcher find some reservations on the part of customers using these services for one reason or the other. Thus the researcher analyzes the solutions of customers with regard to its problems.

Table 5.7

Average time required for solving the problems of ATM Centers

Sr. No	Name of Banks	Duration for solving problems of ATM Centers			
		Instantly	Within 3 days	Within a week	As per availability of technical staff
1	SVC Bank Ltd	1	-	-	-
2	CC Bank Ltd	-	1	-	-
3	AC Bank Ltd	-	-	1	-
4	BMC Bank Ltd	1	-	-	-
5	SC Bank Ltd	1	-	-	-
6	MC Bank Ltd	-	1	-	-
7	PMC Bank Ltd	-	-	-	1
8	GPPJS Bank Ltd	-	-	-	1
9	JKS Bank Ltd	-	-	1	-
10	AUC Bank Ltd	-	-	-	1
11	NRDVS Bank Ltd	1	-	-	-
12	NMC Bank Ltd	-	1	-	-
13	MSC Bank Ltd	-	-	1	-
Cooperative Banks Total		4 (30.8)	3 (23.1)	3 (23.1)	3 (23.1)

Source: Primary data

The banks which are solving the e-problems of customers in least duration are preferred by customers in large quantity. Table 5.7 indicates that, 4 branches (30.8 per cent) are capable of solving the ATM problems instantly. 3 Branches each (23.1 per cent) resolve the problems within 3 days, within a week and are unable to solve the problems due to absence of technical staff respectively.

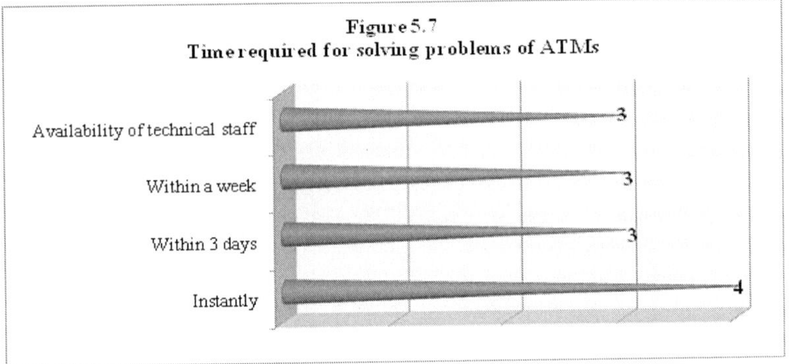

Figure 5.7
Time required for solving problems of ATMs

5.4 Services and security issue

5.4.1 Distribution of banks providing 24*7*365 helpline facility

Care of customers is playing an important role in the development of banks. Customers may need the help of banks at anytime and anyway for solving their query, thus banks are providing 24*7*365 helpline facilities but a very few banks have day time facility only (during office hours). Thus it is necessary to study that how many banks are providing 24*7*365 helpline facility.

Table 5.8

Distribution of Banks Providing 24*7*365 Helpline Facility

Sr. No.	Name of Banks	24*7 helpline facility	
		Yes	No
1	SVC Bank Ltd	v	-
2	CC Bank Ltd	v	-

3	AC Bank Ltd	-	v
4	BMC Bank Ltd	v	-
5	SC Bank Ltd	v	-
6	MC Bank Ltd	-	v
7	PMC Bank Ltd	-	v
8	GPPJS Bank Ltd	-	v
9	JKS Bank Ltd	v	-
10	AUC Bank Ltd	v	-
11	NRDVS Bank Ltd	v	-
12	NMC Bank Ltd	-	v
13	MSC Bank Ltd	-	v
	Total of Cooperative Banks	7 (53.8)	6 (46.2)

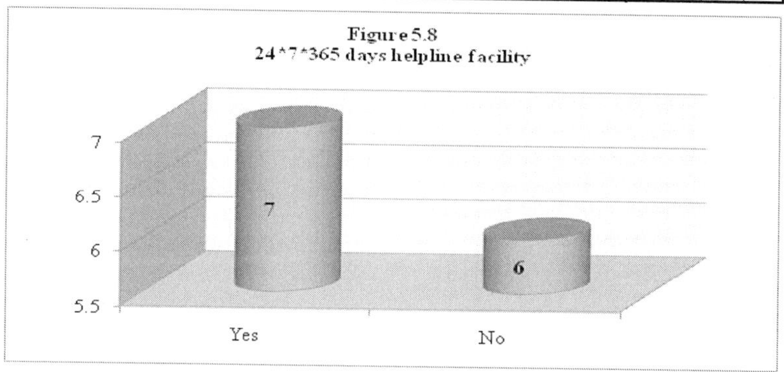

Figure 5.8
24*7*365 days helpline facility

Table 5.8 indicates that, 53.8 per cent (7) provide 24*7*365 helpline assistance but the remaining 46.2 per cent branches (6) provide helpline assistance only during office hours.

5.4.2 Number of Banks providing Guidelines of E-Banking Services

An attempt is made to find the status in this case and accordingly data collected on this issue is presented in Table 5.9

Table 5.9

Number of banks providing guidelines of e-banking services

Sr. No	Name of Banks	Guidelines/instructions of e-banking	
		Yes	No
1	SVC Bank Ltd	v	-
2	CC Bank Ltd	v	-
3	AC Bank Ltd	v	-
4	BMC Bank Ltd	v	-
5	SC Bank Ltd	v	-
6	MC Bank Ltd	v	-
7	PMC Bank Ltd	-	v
8	GPPJS Bank Ltd	-	v
9	JKS Bank Ltd	v	-
10	AUC Bank Ltd	v	-
11	NRDVS Bank Ltd	v	-
12	NMC Bank Ltd	-	v
13	MSC Bank Ltd	-	v
Total of Cooperative Banks		9	4
	(69.2)	(30.8)	

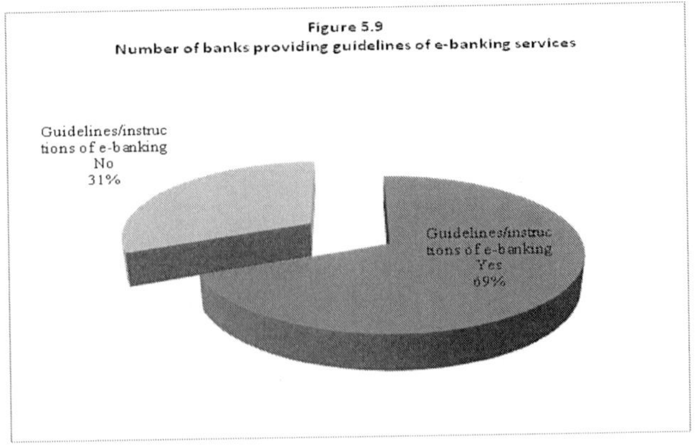

Figure 5.9
Number of banks providing guidelines of e-banking services

Table 5.9 shows that 69.2 per cent Co-operative bank branches (9) have their information or guidelines for using e-banking on website and 30.8 per cent branches (4) have not yet developed their website or have not given any information or guidelines for using e-banking services.

5.4.3 Perception of banks about awareness of customers

The e-banking services provided by banks are used by customers. The usage frequency of e-services is based on its utility and its convenience. The awareness of customers regarding security is playing very important role in the frequent use of services. Banks should have enough knowledge about the awareness of customers for using these services. According to the banks, awareness of customers' is classified into three categories; i.e. fully aware, aware to some extent and completely unaware about the awareness of customers'.

Table 5.10

Awareness of customers on Transaction Security: Bankers' Feedback

Name of Banks	Awareness of Customers' for transaction security		
	Fully Aware	Aware to Some Extent	Not at all
SVC Bank Ltd	v	-	-
CC Bank Ltd	v	-	-
AC Bank Ltd	-	v	-
BMC Bank Ltd	v	-	-
SC Bank Ltd	v	-	-
MC Bank Ltd	v	-	-
PMC Bank Ltd	-	v	-
GPPJS Bank Ltd	-	v	-
JKS Bank Ltd	v	-	-

AUC Bank Ltd	-	v	-
NRDVS Bank Ltd	v	-	-
NMC Bank Ltd	-	v	-
MSC Bank Ltd	-	v	-
Co-op. Banks Total	7 (53.8)	6 (46.2)	0 (0.0)

Source: Primary data

N.B: Figures in brackets indicate per cent to total

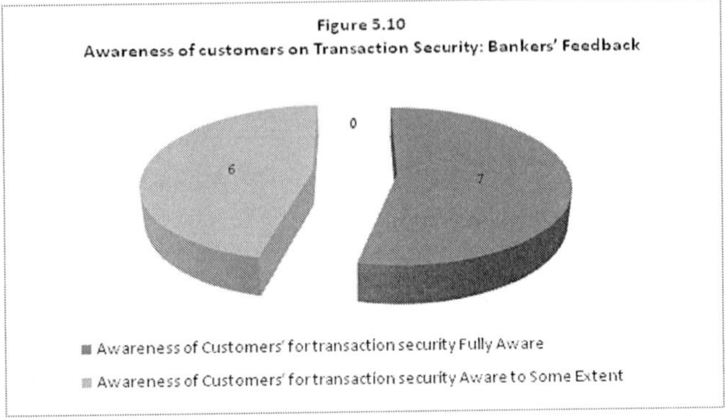

Table 5.10 indicates that though the customers are using e-banking services, only 53.8 per cent branches of Co-operative banks (7) customers are fully aware about their transaction security. Customers of remaining 46.2 per cent branches (6) are less aware about their transaction security or have less knowledge about their transactions. Thus their frequency for using these services is also comparatively less and they prefer for manual transactions.

5.4.4 E-Banking Awareness Programs to Customers for Making Online Transactions

Though the Banks are providing e-banking services to the customers, all types of customers are not using these services due to lack of sufficient knowledge and the fear that as a result of wrong operation, they may suffer from any trouble.

Banks have to motivate their customers for using these services. Banks are motivating to their customers by making face to face communication with customers, by organizing workshops and delivering lectures form experts, by showing videos or by giving demos relating to the use of services, by giving oral information or by using any mode according to the perception of customers. Thus it is essential to study means of motivation to the customers about using e-banking services which are provided by banks.

Table 5.11

E-banking awareness programs to customers for making online transactions

Sr. No	Name of Banks	Means of Motivation to Customers		
		Face to face talk with customers	Organizing Customers' Workshops	Demo Video
1	SVC Bank Ltd	v	-	v
2	CC Bank Ltd	v	-	-
3	AC Bank Ltd	v	-	-
4	BMC Bank Ltd	v	-	v
5	SC Bank Ltd	v	-	-
6	MC Bank Ltd	v	-	-
7	PMC Bank Ltd	v	-	v
8	GPPJS Bank Ltd	v	-	v
9	JKS Bank Ltd	v	-	
10	AUC Bank Ltd	v	-	-
11	NRDVS Bank Ltd	v	-	-
12	NMC Bank Ltd	v	-	v
13	MSC Bank Ltd	v	-	v
Co-operative Banks Total		13 (100)	0 (0.0)	6 (46.2)

Figure 5.11
Awareness programs for customers

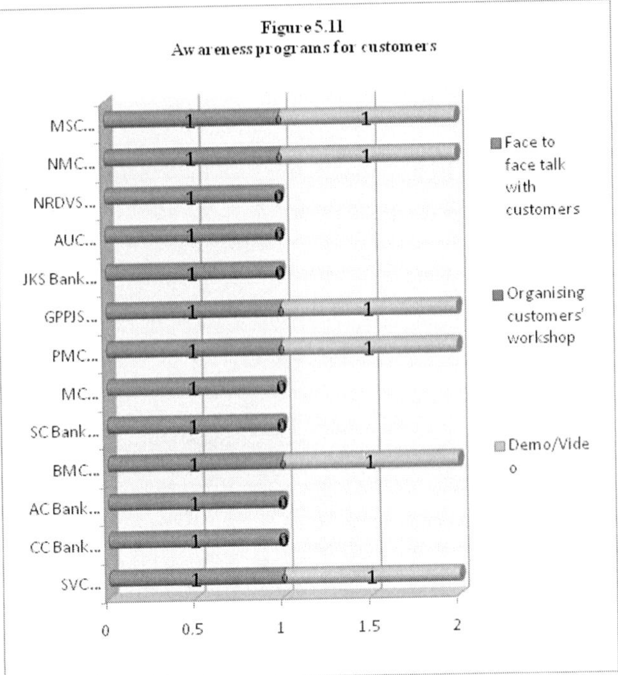

As per table 5.11 all the branches of Co-operative banks are making face to face communication with the customers to motivate them for using e-banking services by giving advertisement, by publishing advantages of these services in pamphlets', reports, newspapers, book-lets or in journals also.

Only 46.2 per cent branches of Co-operative banks (6) banks have prepared Demo Videos but remaining 53.84 per cent banks (7) branches did nothing to motivate the customers further such as organizing workshop for giving them proper knowledge of e-banking services and no attempt is evidently made for solving the queries, if any, of the customers.

A very few branches have taken every step that will result in customers' positive response at e-banking services. In fact, these services are relatively cheap and save time and money cost of the customers using these services.

5.4.5 Satisfaction of Bank Managers from technical support

Branch Managers often need technical support from internet services providers in order to maintain continuous supply chain of information needed to satisfy the requirements of e-banking transactions. In a way, efficiency of e-banking services provided by banks depends mostly on the prompt technical support received by the bank offices. A comparative study of availability of this support across Co-operative and non-Co-operative banks was undertaken by the researcher. Feedback received on this issue is presented in Table 5.12 below: Fortunately, majority of managers interviewed responded positively as their satisfaction is either very high or high.

Table 5.12

Satisfaction of Bank Managers from technical support of internet services providers

Sr. No.	Name of Banks	Bank's satisfaction from technical service providers			
		Very High	High	Moderate	Low
1	SVC Bank Ltd	v	-	-	-
2	CC Bank Ltd	-	-	-	v
3	AC Bank Ltd	-	v	-	-
4	BMC Bank Ltd	-	-	-	v
5	SC Bank Ltd	-	v	-	-
6	MC Bank Ltd	v	-	-	-
7	PMC Bank Ltd	-	-	v	-
8	GPPJS Bank Ltd		v	-	-
9	JKS Bank Ltd	-	-	v	-
10	AUC Bank Ltd	-	v	-	-
11	NRDVS Bank Ltd	-	v	-	-
12	NMC Bank Ltd	-	-	v	-
13	MSC Bank Ltd	-	-	-	v
Total Co-operative banks		2 (15.4)	5 (38.5)	3 (23.1)	3 (23.1)

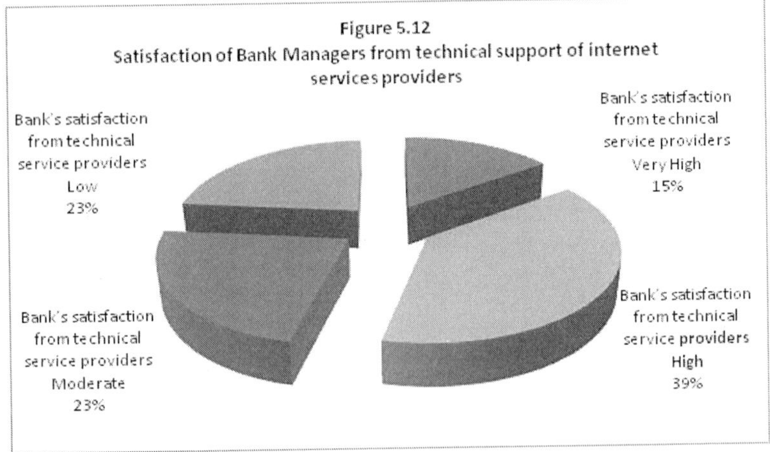

As per table 5.12, Managers of 15.4 per cent branches of Co-operative Banks (2) expressed very high satisfaction whereas another 38.5 per cent branch managers (5) expressed high satisfaction, followed by 23.1 per cent branch managers each (3) agreed to moderate satisfaction and low satisfaction respectively about technical service providers.

5.5 Special Facilities

5.5.1 Special facilities provided to disabled customers

One more aspect of researcher's interest in this study was to study the provision for special services, if any, made available by Co-operative banks to physically disabled persons as compared with Nationalized and Private sector banks. Her inquiry revealed that barring an exception of 30.76 per cent (4) branches of Co-operative banks, namely; SVC Bank and CC Cooperative Bank, Saraswat Cooperative bank and MSC bank limited, none of the remaining 69.23 per cent (9) branches of Co-operative banks provide any special assistance to physically disabled persons.

5.5.2 Special facility provided to illiterate customers

Literate and illiterate, both types of customers are using e-banking services. Literate have enough knowledge about using technologies, but illiterate have no knowledge but they have enormous curiosity in using these services. So the banks are providing special services to such type of customers, by using audio-visual narrator at the ATM. Researcher's inquiry revealed that this facility is available in all the branches of Co-operative and other branches in the from Nashik District. In case the illiterate customer is found incapable of grasping the message, any person on the nearby counter advises such customer with utmost care in any of the branch offices. Therefore, helping an illiterate customer is not at all a serious problem in the area under study.

5.5.3 Use of Cookies (software)

Cookie is one of the software which helps to the bankers and to the customers in identifying their customers. Which doing any e-banking transaction it identify its customer with his identification mark saved in the software. It actually identifies their customers according to the finger prints saved in the software. The transactions are completed only after clearing the identification of customers otherwise the transactions are retained by the machine. Thus it is necessary to study that how many banks are using the cookie software for security of e-banking transactions of customers.

However, researcher's inquiry during her survey revealed that identifying a customer at the bank is not so difficult a problem even in absence of e- banking practices. Though such cookies are available in the branches of banks, no one, either Banker or Customer was found insisting on use of these.

5.6 Business of Branches during recent times

Since the e-banking practices are of recent origin, it was a matter of curiosity for the researcher to trace the recent trends in normal banking activities of the branches after they entered into e-banking operations. This includes growth in deposits, loans and advances, capital and reserves, NPAs, composition of deposits, loans and advances etc. These recent developments in respect of branches of Co-operative and other banks cover a period of recent five years from 2008-2009 to 2012-2013.

(1) Deposits

It is difficult to trace growth rate of deposits with the help of absolute figures of deposit in Rupees. Therefore, a composite simple Index number with the base year 2008¹09 as 100 has been worked out.

Total deposit liabilities of branches are shown in Table 5.13

Table 5.13

Total Deposit liabilities of Branches of Banks

(Amt. in Rs. Lakhs)

Items /Years	**Deposits**				
Name of Bank	2008-09	2009-10	2010-11	2011-12	2012-13
SVC Bank Ltd	85,013 (100)	83,448 (124.1)	92,570 (150.1)	1,03,108 (180.2)	1,17,277 (220.7)
C Bank Ltd	24,598 (100)	26,892 (109.3)	30,834 (125.4)	33,703 (137.0)	38,301 (155.7)
AC Bank Ltd	83,470 (100)	87,973 (119.2)	89,715 (147.9)	93,449 (185.1)	98,081 (226.2)
BMC Bank Ltd	71,450 (100)	73,848 (103.4)	88,881 (124.4)	97,445 (136.4)	1,24,911 (174.9)
SC Bank Ltd	64,266 (100.0)	65,800 (102.4)	69,252 (105.2)	71,144 (102.7)	83,939 (118.0)
MC Bank Ltd	59,734 (100)	68,416 (114.5)	76,763 (123.5)	97,825 (163.8)	1,12,522 (188.4)
PMC Bank Ltd	78,694 (100)	78,775 (100.1)	90,804 (115.4)	93,328 (118.6)	93,915 (119.3)
GPPJS Bank Ltd	6,377 (100)	7,748 (124.5)	9,245 (145.0)	10,253 (160.8)	11,228 (176.1)
JKS Bank Ltd	62,731 (100)	71,354 (113.7)	77,791 (124.0)	87,753 (139.9)	92,327 (147.2)
AUC Bank Ltd	63,461 (100)	69,693 (109.8)	88,354 (139.2)	92,131 (145.2)	93,568 (147.4)
NRDVS Bank Ltd	51,701 (100)	57,018 (110.28)	71,351 (138.00)	80,574 (155.85)	1,01,428 (196.18)

NMC Bank Ltd	23,717 (100)	28,546 (120.4)	34,851 (147.0)	44,667 (188.4)	50,188 (211.7)
MSC Bank Ltd	57018 (100)	71351 (125.1)	80574 (141.3)	101428 (177.9)	140148 (245.8)
Index Number Co-operative Banks Base Year 2008-09	100.0	113.6	132.8	153.2	179.0

The growth trend clearly shows that the deposits of cooperative banks grown fastest during these 5 years from 100.0 to 179.0 during the same period. This is a clear indication that the progress in the growth of deposits is slowest among Co-operative banks. In other words, depositors feel less safe with their deposits in cooperative Banks.

(2) Advances

Advances are one of the parameters of measuring the growth of banks and financial institutions.

Table 5.14

Advances from Banks

(Amount in Rs. Thousands)

Items /Years	**Advances**				
Name of Banks	2008-09	2009-10	2010-11	2011-12	2012-13
SVC Bank Ltd	2,38,257 (100)	2,77,082 (116.3)	3,39,712 (142.6)	4,20,223 (176.4)	4,95,078 (207.8)
CC Bank Ltd	29,879 (100)	34,462 (115.3)	36,327 (121.6)	42,465 (142.1)	44,692 (149.6)
AC Bank Ltd	15,066 (100)	16,790 (111.4)	19,918 (132.2)	26,401 (175.2)	34,077 (226.2)
BMC Bank Ltd	36,209 (100)	41,239 (113.9)	48,137 (132.9)	56,504 (156.1)	73,679 (203.5)
SC Bank Ltd	92,503 (100)	115119 (124.4)	139527 (150.8)	150234 (162.4)	154700 (167.2)

MC Bank Ltd	31,497 (100)	36,015 (114.3)	48,201 (153.0)	56,992 (180.9)	62,423 (198.2)
PMC Bank Ltd	57261 (100)	61047 (106.6)	57895 (101.1)	66487 (116.1)	94598 (165.2)
GPPJS Bank Ltd	45,652 (100)	55,984 (122.6)	67,285 (147.4)	69,854 (153.0)	85,961 (188.3)
JKS Bank Ltd	54424 (100)	55151 (101.3)	54253 (99.7)	67974 (124.9)	62661 (115.1)
AUC Bank Ltd	28971 (100)	34441 (118.9)	46168 (159.4)	53045 (183.1)	59537 (205.5)
NRDVS Bank Ltd	2,39,623 (100)	3,22,643 (134.6)	3,69,771 (154.3)	4,85,210 (202.4)	6,80,585 (284.0)
NMC Bank Ltd	57,937 (100)	40,317 (69.6)	59,068 (102.0)	68,200 (117.7)	86,678 (149.6)
MSC Bank Ltd	36433 (100)	39774 (109.2)	48524 (133.2)	68859 (189.0)	91039 (249.9)
Index No. Co-op Banks	100.0	112.2	133.1	159.9	195.4

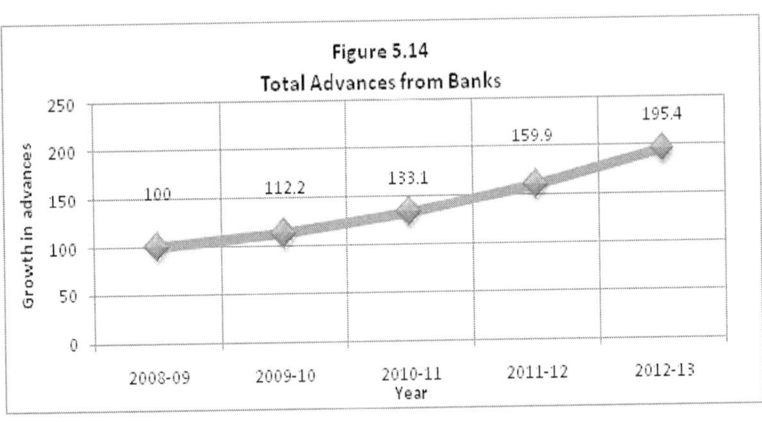

It is difficult to focus on the advances given by Co-operative banks to their customers with the help of absolute figures of advances in Rupees. Therefore, a composite simple Index number with the base year 2008¹09 as 100 has been worked out. The growth trend clearly shows that the advances of Co-operative banks grown fastest during these 5 years from

100 to 195.4. This is an indicator of credit deposit ratio being highest in case of Co-operative bank branches. To substantiate this statement further, Credit/deposit ratios for all the branches has been calculated below.

Credit/Deposit Ratio

Researcher has calculated credit deposit ratio of Co-operative and other banks on the basis of data on deposits and advances of all banks for the period 2008-09 to 2012-13 and presented in the form of Table below:

Table 5.15

Credit/Deposit Ratio Across Co-operative and Other Banks in Nashik District

Bank	Credit Deposit Ratio (Amount of Credit against re. 1 deposit)					
	2008-09	2009-10	2010-11	2011-12	2012-13	Average of 5 years
Total of 13 coop. banks	1.0	1.0	1.0	1.0	1.1	1.02

Source: Compiled from figures in Tables 5.13 and 5.14

Average C/D ratio for 5 years works out to 1:1.02 in case of Co-operative banks. Co-operative Banks may not be observing these norms strictly that might have enabled them to be more liberal. Researcher felt that this might be one of the reasons as to why Co-operative banks face the problem of high rate of NPAs.

One possible reason for this tendency is that co-operative banks are subject to duel control of; the Reserve Bank of India as well as the department of co-operation, Government of Maharashtra. RBI strictly enforces CRR in case of organized non-co-operative banks. Co-operative Banks might have been relaxed from this obligation assuming that the State Government might be taking care of appropriate CRR at the state level depending upon local conditions in the State.

(3) Reserves

As per the cooperative societies act every cooperative banks have to keep 25 percent amount of profit as reserves and the available amount from the reserves are utilized for development of banks.

Table 5.16

Reserves in Banks

(Amt. in Thousands)

Items /Years	**Reserves**				
Name of Banks	2008-09	2009-10	2010-11	2011-12	2012-13
SVC Bank Ltd	41,934 (100)	58,908 (140.5)	60,478 (144.2)	71,927 (171.5)	77,780 (185.5)
CC Bank Ltd	14,791 (100)	21,453 (145.0)	33,138 (224.0)	34,176 (231.1)	46,921 (317.2)
AC Bank Ltd	3,187 (100)	3,312 (103.9)	4,289 (134.6)	4,961 (155.7)	5,814 (182.4)
BMC Bank Ltd	8,670 (100)	10,423 (120.2)	11,718 (135.2)	13,667 (157.6)	15,994 (184.5)
SC Bank Ltd	12,703 (100)	14,765 (116.2)	17,156 (135.1)	19,613 (154.4)	21,418 (168.6)
MC Bank Ltd	6,678 (100)	7,806 (116.9)	8,821 (132.1)	9,424 (141.1)	9,826 (147.1)
PMC Bank Ltd	7703 (100)	8117 (105.4)	8387 (108.9)	8410 (109.2)	8706 (113.0)
GPPJS Bank Ltd	5,909 (100)	6,035 (102.1)	6,268 (106.1)	6,504 (110.1)	6,743 (114.1)
JKS Bank Ltd	16976 (100)	17305 (101.9)	19058 (112.3)	29064 (171.2)	39764 (234.2)
AUC Bank Ltd	17484 (100)	18616 (106.5)	21709 (124.2)	27851 (159.3)	29925 (171.2)
NRDVS Bank Ltd	14608 (100)	17347 (118.8)	19462 (133.2)	21772 (149.0)	26158 (179.1)
NMC Bank Ltd	9,842	11,066	12,018	15,564	20,003

	(100)	(112.4)	(122.1)	(158.1)	(203.2)
MSC Bank Ltd	19390 (100)	22375 (115.4)	25845 (133.3)	29972 (154.6)	36483 (188.2)
Index No. Co-operative Banks	100.0	115.8	134.3	155.6	183.7

Source: Primary data

N.B: Figures in brackets indicate per cent to total

Table 5.16 gives the position of reserves and the growth rate of reserves with banks. Provision for reserves made and accumulated by the Co-operative banks is growing fastest in case of Co-operative banks from 100 in 2008-09 to 183.7 in 2012-13.

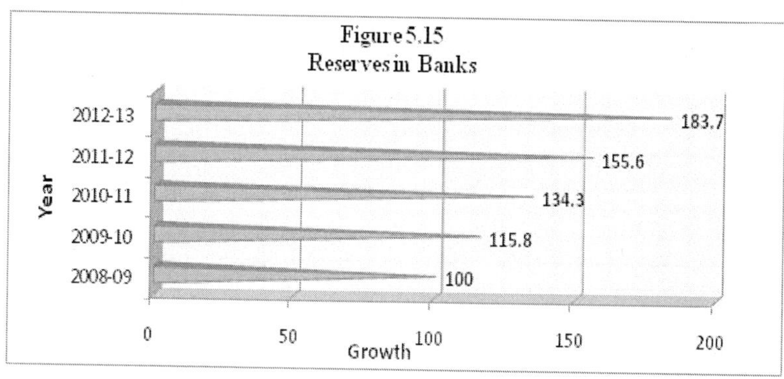

(4) Profit/Loss

Profit/Loss made by the branches of banks over recent past five years are shown in Table 5.17 below:

Table 5.17

Profit and Loss of Banks During Recent Past Five Years

(Amt. in Thousands)

Name of Banks	Profit/Loss				
	2008-09	2009-10	2010-11	2011-12	2012-13
SVC Bank Ltd	21,300 (100)	33,720 (158.3)	47,470 (222.9)	60,110 (282.2)	75,210 (353.1)
CC Bank Ltd	19,140 (100)	29,550 (154.4)	35,590 (185.9)	38,350 (200.4)	38,680 (202.1)

AC Bank Ltd	13,853 (100)	14,478 (104.5)	15,463 (111.6)	16,985 (122.6)	18,708 (135.0)
BMC Bank Ltd	10,960 (100)	14,304 (130.5)	16,568 (151.2)	20,410 (186.2)	25,871 (236.0)
SC Bank Ltd	11,967 (100)	21,227 (177.4)	23,557 (196.8)	11,209 (93.7)	14,709 (122.9)
MC Bank Ltd	5,215 (100)	6,473 (124.1)	6,884 (132.0)	8,721 (167.2)	11,422 (219.0)
PMC Bank Ltd	7231 (100)	6271 (86.7)	8279 (114.5)	9944 (137.5)	9044 (125.1)
GPPJS Bank Ltd	9,674 (100)	11,056 (114.3)	11,224 (116.0)	11,985 (123.9)	12,682 (131.1)
JKS Bank Ltd	42411 (100)	62176 (146.6)	63829 (150.5)	74918 (176.6)	81041 (191.1)
AUC Bank Ltd	35,125 (100)	38,365 (109.2)	38,683 (110.1)	44,341 (126.2)	58,655 (167.0)
NRDVS Bank Ltd	82,93 (100)	1,26,08 (152.0)	1,73,47 (209.8)	1,94,62 (234.7)	2,05,59 (247.9)
NMC Bank Ltd	1,502 (100)	2,183 (145.3)	2,526 (168.2)	3,623 (241.2)	3,923 (261.2)
MSC Bank Ltd	1268 (100)	1734 (136.8)	1946 (153.5)	2055 (162.1)	2519 (198.7)
Index No. Co-op. Banks	100.0	133.9	155.6	173.4	199.2

Table 5.17 clearly shows that all the banks are making profits during the period under review. If we compare the Index numbers of profitability, it is clear that the branches of Co-operative banks have made 99.2 per cent gain over the period of 5 years. It means no any bank is suffering from losses during last five years and the profit of 2012-13 is nearby double than the profit of 2008-09.

Table 5.18

Index Numbers of Profit and Loss of Banks During Recent Past Five Years

(Amt. in Thousands)

Name of Banks	2008-09	2009-10	2010-11	2011-12	2012-13	Average of 5 years
Index No. Co-operative Banks	(100)	(133.9)	(155.6)	(173.4)	(199.2)	(152.42)

Compiled from table 5.17

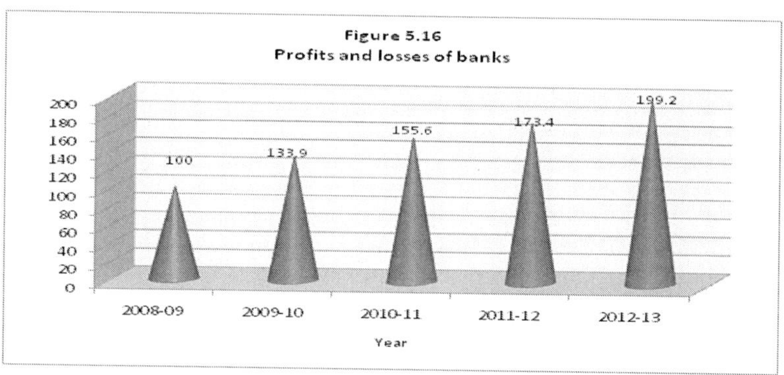

The Table 5.18 below gives average indices of recent five years also gives us same result that branches of Co-operative banks are at the top with 52.4 per cent gain over past 5 years.

(5) NPA (Non-performing Assets)

Table 5.19 shows proportion of NPAs reported by branches of Co operative and other banks.

Table 5.19

Non-Performing Assets of the Banks

(In Percentage)

Items /Years	**NPA Per cent**				
Name of Banks	2008-09	2009-10	2010-11	2011-12	2012-13
SVC Bank Ltd	8.4	7.2	5.7	3.6	3.2
CC Bank Ltd	4.2	3.9	0. 8	0.1	0.0
AC Bank Ltd	6.4	4.6	3.4	3.3	2.6
BMC Bank Ltd	8.1	4.6	1.6	1.2	0.2
SC Bank Ltd	2.1	1.3	0.8	0.0	0.0
MC Bank Ltd	4.8	2.7	1.6	1.0	0.9
PMC Bank Ltd	10.7	8.3	4.1	3.7	5.1
GPPJS Bank Ltd	6.4	4.9	2.6	1.6	0.5
JKS Bank Ltd	10.3	8.9	4.2	4.7	3.4
AUC Bank Ltd	4.4	3.9	2.3	1.3	0.8
NRDVS Bank Ltd	7.5	6.6	4.6	4.1	0.0
NMC Bank Ltd	6.4	5.6	5.5	3.1	2.9
MSC Bank Ltd	5.1	4.9	3.5	0.0	0.0
Co-operative Banks Average	6.5	5.2	3.3	2.1	1.5

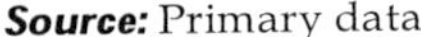
Source: Primary data

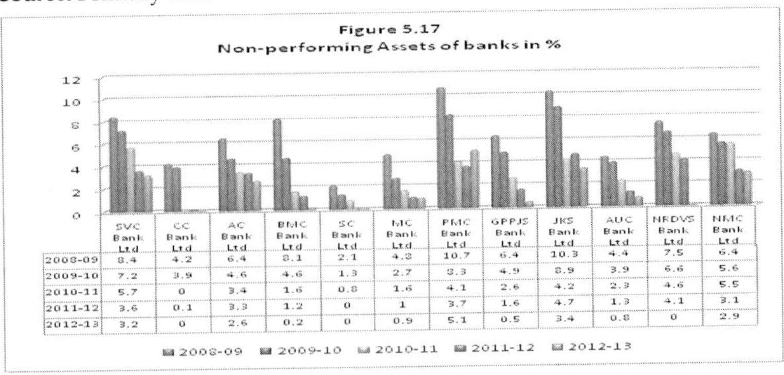

	SVC Bank Ltd	CC Bank Ltd	AC Bank Ltd	BMC Bank Ltd	SC Bank Ltd	MC Bank Ltd	PMC Bank Ltd	GPPJS Bank Ltd	JKS Bank Ltd	AUC Bank Ltd	NRDVS Bank Ltd	NMC Bank Ltd
2008-09	8.4	4.2	6.4	8.1	2.1	4.8	10.7	6.4	10.3	4.4	7.5	6.4
2009-10	7.2	3.9	4.6	4.6	1.3	2.7	8.3	4.9	8.9	3.9	6.6	5.6
2010-11	5.7	0	3.4	1.6	0.8	1.6	4.1	2.6	4.2	2.3	4.6	5.5
2011-12	3.6	0.1	3.3	1.2	0	1	3.7	1.6	4.7	1.3	4.1	3.1
2012-13	3.2	0	2.6	0.2	0	0.9	5.1	0.5	3.4	0.8	0	2.9

One of the important criteria in determining financial efficiency of a bank or financial institution is the low proportion of NPA to total earning assets of the bank. No doubt, NPAs of all banks are declining at a much faster rate during recent times. CC cooperative bank and Saraswat Cooperative bank is top most efficient in bringing down NPAs and reducing the same at zero till the end of 2012-13. Other Co-operative Banks are gradually bringing down their NPAs but could not reduce it to zero even in 2012-13.

5.7 Problems to Bank managers

5.7.1 Problems faced by banks in providing e-banking services

Though banks are providing e-banking services, the employees of banks are not well skilled in the technology. The qualities of service provided by banks are based on service providers. The researcher analyses these problems of banks with regard to each of the service discussed in this section. The classification of the problems is Technological problems, Managerial problems, Socio-cultural problems and Operational problems: From the feedback received from managers, it is observed that they had more than a single problem.

Table 5.20

Problems Faced by Managers while Providing e-Banking Services

Name of Banks	Problems faced by Banks in providing E-services			
	Technological Problems	Managerial Problems	Socio-cultural Problems	Transactional Problems
SVC Bank Ltd	v	v	-	-
CC Bank Ltd	v	-	-	v
AC Bank Ltd	v	-	v	v
BMC Bank Ltd	v	-	v	v

SC Bank Ltd	-	v	v	-
MC Bank Ltd	v	v	v	v
PMC Bank Ltd	v	v	-	v
GPPJS Bank Ltd	v	-	v	-
JKS Bank Ltd	v	v	-	-
AUC Bank Ltd	v	-	-	-
NRDVS Bank Ltd	v	-	v	-
NMC Bank Ltd	v	-	v	v
MSC Bank Ltd	v	-	v	v
Total Co-operative Bank	12 (92.3)	5 (38.5)	8 (61.5)	7 (53.8)

Source: Primary data

N.B: Figures in brackets indicate per cent to total

Most severe problem faced by 92.3 per cent (12) managers of Co-operative banks is technological, followed by socio-cultural problems faced by 61.5 per cent (8) managers, Transactional problems faced by 53.8 per cent (7) managers and the least 38.5 per cent managers had Managerial problems in providing e-services to their customers.

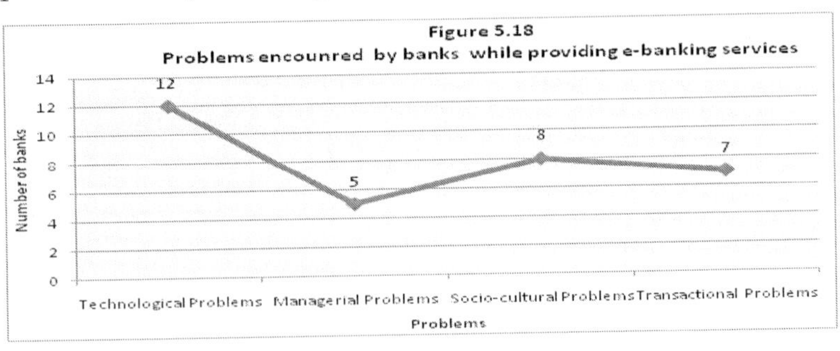

5.7.2 Feedback on utility of e-banking services

Banking services are techno-based and are also difficult to use in some extent, thus it needs to take feedback from customers. Banks are expected to get feedback from customers on the problems or drawbacks raised while using e-banking services or for being a non-user of e-banking services. Such feedback helps banks to adopt corrective measures for redressing customers' grievances.

The researcher found that no any bank has yet taken feedback from customers about utility of e-banking services which is an essential factor for the progress of e-banking technology and for transferring brick banking to click banking.

5.7 Summing Up:

Among these 13 Co-operative Banks, all the banks are urban in nature among which only 2 branches, one each of BMC and another NRDVS banks are from Nashik registered under Rural Bank Association of Nasik District. There are 3 branches of merchant banks. Today most of the cooperative banks are providing e-banking services. Without adoption of e-banking services, it is impossible to survive in banking sector and thus Co-operative banks have also adopted the e-banking technology and are providing these services to their customers. 9 branches of cooperative banks are providing e-banking services since 20th century and remaining have adopted this technology in 21st century. But Public and Private sector banks have adopted this technology in 20th century.

Results taken from analysis of primary data shown that age, education and profession and attitude of bank employees have affecting the satisfaction of customers in the sector of alternative banking. Income level of the respondents is not affecting the response of customers but the reliability of e-banking services, availability, attitude of bank employees and efficiency in transaction are the major features of satisfaction of customers. Mainly customers prefer and bank also providing efficient services, Security, Cost reduction, Problem solving attitude, service quality, and Accuracy are preferential factors and banks have to concentrate on all these features. ATM, Phone Banking and Mobile Banking and Internet banking services because except ATMs service other services are providing in free of cost and also provided to all the customers.

Management of Customer Services with E-Banking

6.1 Introduction

After discussing the result of Co-operative movement and current position of Co-operative Sector Banks from National level to Nasik District in chapter 3 and 4, this chapter shows the progress of Co-operative Sector Banks in Nasik District and also shows the response of customers regarding utility, benefits and drawbacks to the e- banking services rendered by sample branches of cooperative banks. This chapter also helps to show the position of Co-operative Banks in Nasik District with the help of collected samples. The relevant information pertaining to this study was collected from the sample units through structured questionnaires; fill up from the customers using the technical services from various cooperative banks. The collected data is classified, tabulated and analyzed according to the objectives of the study. The facts and findings derived after analyzing the information have been presented under the main heads of the objectives and discussed in succeeding pages.

The researcher has issued 100 per cent (9916) questionnaires (10 per cent from total number of account holders) to the bank customers who are using e-banking services but only 79.24 per cent (7858) customers have given response to questionnaires and return it back to the researcher. From the collected questionnaires only 87.61 per cent (6885) questionnaires were completely filled which are used for by the researcher for this study. This gave me sample size of 6.94 per cent of total sample population. Considering researcher as an individual, this sample size is quite reasonable and justifiable. Because of using direct contact method the response of customers is high which is used as sample size for analysis of this chapter and for taking findings.

6.2 Socio-economic characteristics of Customers

Under this head, the personal and socio-economic characteristics of the samples are presented. The distribution of respondents by sex, age, annual income, occupation, area, name of bank, type of account, education etc. are discussed in brief.

It is essential to study demographic features of respondents such as, gender, age, educational qualifications and socio-economic status, social attitude of the respondent because these characteristics are related with the use of Technological Services provided by Co-operative Sector Banks.

6.2.1 Distribution of respondents by types of accounts

Table 6.1 shows the population and sample units of customers holding current accounts and saving accounts.

Table 6.1

Table Showing Number of Respondents From Various Co-operative Banks

Sr. No		Name of Banks A/C Holders (Branch)			No. of Respondents		
		Current A/C	Saving A/C	Total	Current A/C	Saving A/C	Total
1	SVC Bank Ltd	6678	6468	13146	372	554	926
2	CC Bank Ltd	3885	6188	10073	268	418	686
3	AC Bank Ltd	4809	5502	10311	302	416	718
4	BMC Bank Ltd	2786	4186	6972	161	296	457

5 SC Bank Ltd	1918	2604	4522	135	187	322
6 MC Bank Ltd	3752	5264	9016	263	381	644
7 PMC Bank Ltd	3458	3325	6783	244	234	478
8 GPPJS Bank Ltd	2093	3409	5502	146	224	370
9 JKS Bank Ltd	2023	1946	3969	151	135	286
10 AUC Bank Ltd	4606	4053	8659	328	281	609
11 NRDVS Bank Ltd	2695	3346	6041	183	239	422
12 NMC Bank Ltd	3976	4109	8085	263	288	551
13 MSC Ltd	2583	3493	6076	169	247	416
Total Respondents	45262 (45.65)	53893 (54.35)	99155 (100)	2985 (43.35)	3900 (56.65)	6885 (100)

Source: Primary data

The distribution of population of customers between current A/C and saving A/C is in the ratio of 45.65: 54.35 per cent in aggregate. Since the population of saving account holders is quite large for an individual researcher, Ten per cent sample is quite significant for an individual researcher for being fairly representative of population. Furthermore, each sample unit was picked up by simple random method so as to keep the sample free of bias. Thus, inferences drawn from the behavior of sample units can be generalized for the entire population of respondents.

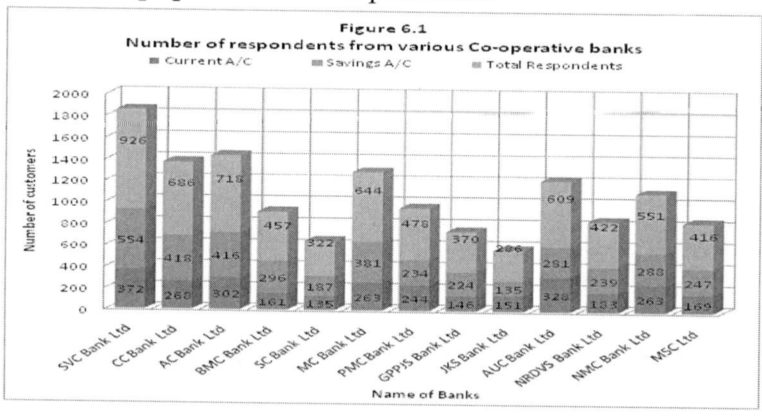

Figure 6.1
Number of respondents from various Co-operative banks

6.2.2 Distribution of Sample respondents by Gender (Male/ Female):

Sex can play an important role in socio-economic activities of individual. When we differentiate the sample in different sex groups, we find the participation of male and female account-holders who are using or not using the technological services.

From the total number of respondents, 50.4 per cent (3469) males and 49.6 per cent (3416) females indicating that the number of male customers using e-banking services are little more than female customers.

Table 6.2

Distribution of Sample Customers by Gender

Sr. No	Name of Banks	Number of Customers by Gender		
		Males	Females	Total
1	SVC Bank Ltd	484	442	926
2	CC Bank Ltd	353	333	686
3	AC Bank Ltd	359	359	718
4	BMC Bank Ltd	223	234	457
5	SC Bank Ltd	156	166	322
6	MC Bank Ltd	322	322	644
7	PMC Bank Ltd	250	228	478
8	GPPJS Bank Ltd	198	172	370
9	JKS Bank Ltd	125	161	286
10	AUC Bank Ltd	295	314	609
11	NRDVS Bank Ltd	224	198	422
12	NMC Bank Ltd	262	289	551
13	MSC Ltd	218	198	416
Total Respondents		3469 (50.4)	3416 (49.6)	6885 (100)

Source: Primary data

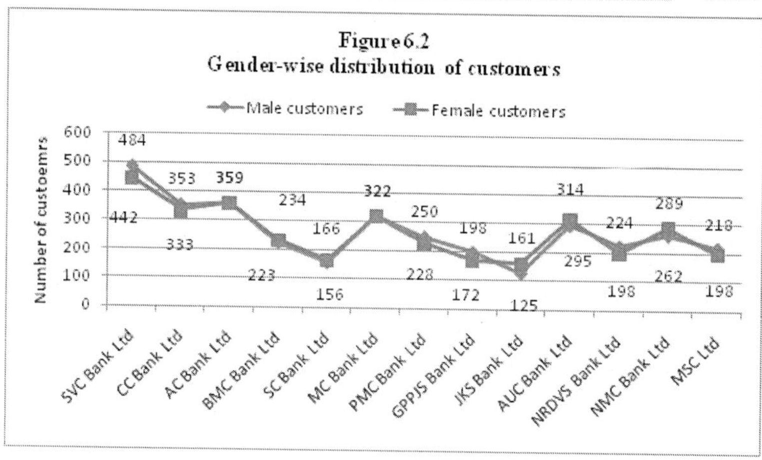

It means both the males and females have equal attitude in opening their account into banks and for using techno-based services provided by banks. In a little span it will happen that the number of male and female customers will be equal.

6.2.3 Distribution of Customers by Age groups

Customers' age is an important factor in utilization of e-banking services provided by banks. Young customers are more enthusiastic in utilizing computerized banking services than the older customers. This tendency among the bank customers has been tested in Table 6.3 given below:

Table 6.3

Distribution of Sample Customers by Age Groups

Sr. No	Name of Banks	Customers by Age groups				Total
		18-25	26-45	46-60	60+	
1	SVC Bank Ltd	31	499	313	83	926
2	CC Bank Ltd	26	447	177	36	686
3	AC Bank Ltd	68	442	203	5	718
4	BMC Bank Ltd	26	281	145	5	457

5	SC Bank Ltd	10	234	78	0	322
6	MC Bank Ltd	21	416	186	21	644
7	PMC Bank Ltd	10	208	229	31	478
8	GPPJS Bank Ltd	26	224	99	21	370
9	JKS Bank Ltd	5	151	104	26	286
10	AUC Bank Ltd	0	265	308	36	609
11	NRDVS Bank Ltd	16	187	203	16	422
12	NMC Bank Ltd	36	250	218	47	551
13	MSC Ltd	6	223	155	32	416
Total Respondents		281 (4.1)	3827 (55.6)	2418 (35.1)	359 (5.2)	6885 (100)

Source: Primary data

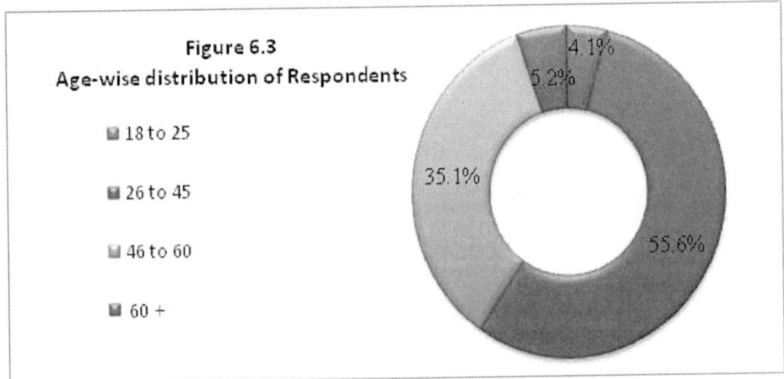

The distribution according to the age group of respondents shows that 55.6 per cent (3827) respondents are from the age group of 26 years to 45 years, followed by 35.1 per cent (2418) respondents from the age group of 46 to 60 years. There are only 5.2 per cent (359) respondents from the age group of above 60, followed by 4.1 per cent (281) customers from the age group of 18 to 25 years. It shows that the customers from the younger group are more and the adoption level of younger customers is also more among the all categories.

6.2.4 Distribution of Customers by Levels of Education

Well educated persons are more likely to use e-banking services than ill-educated or illiterate persons. Educational qualifications of customers show the developing attitude, which is useful for accepting the new avenues introduced in banking sector.

Table 6.4

Distribution of Sample Customers by Levels of Education

Sr. No	Name of Banks	Customers by Level of Education					Total
		SSC	HSC	Diploma	Graduate	PG & +	
1	SVC Bank Ltd	244	161	21	198	302	926
2	CC Bank Ltd	181	109	16	156	224	686
3	AC Bank Ltd	182	120	16	166	234	718
4	BMC Bank Ltd	120	67	16	88	166	457
5	SC Bank Ltd	78	46	5	68	125	322
6	MC Bank Ltd	161	94	19	146	224	644
7	PMC Bank Ltd	125	73	5	104	171	478
8	GPPJS Bank Ltd	99	52	10	83	126	370
9	JKS Bank Ltd	73	47	5	73	88	286
10	AUC Bank Ltd	151	99	16	130	213	609
11	NRDVS Bank Ltd	109	73	17	88	135	422
12	NMC Bank Ltd	146	88	5	125	187	551
13	MSC Ltd	83	68	21	83	161	416
Total Respondents		1752 (25.5)	1097 (15.9)	172 (2.5)	1508 (21.9)	2356 (34.2)	6885 (100)

Source: Primary data

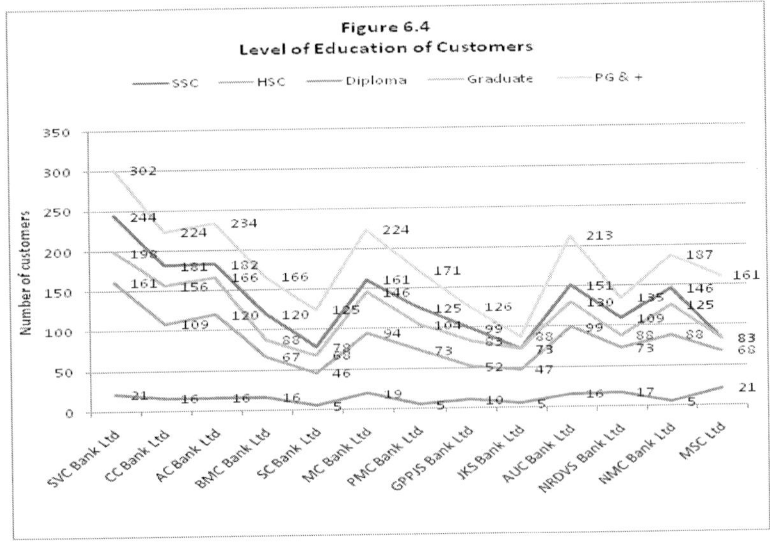

Figure 6.4
Level of Education of Customers

Table 6.4 shows educational qualification of customers. It observed that 34.2 per cent (2356) respondents have completed post-graduation and more than it. There are only 25.5 per cent (1752) respondents from the education taken till SSC, followed by 21.9 per cent (1508) customers who are graduates. 15.9 per cent (1097) customers are educated till HSC and remaining 2.5 per cent (172) customers are Diploma holders. It shows that the number of customers from the well-educated category is using e-banking services in large quantity.

6.2.5 Distribution of Customers by Occupations

Occupation of the bank customer is an important parameter in determining the frequency of bank transactions by him. A Businessman or a factory owner needs to undergo large number of bank transactions than a service person or a farmer. Table 6.5 gives classification of sample bank customers by their occupations.

Table 6.5

Distribution of Sample Customers by Occupations

Sr. No	Name of Banks	Number of Customers by Occupations				Total
		Farmers	Business	Private Service	Public Service	
1	SVC Bank Ltd	125	250	166	385	926
2	CC Bank Ltd	88	182	135	281	686
3	AC Bank Ltd	94	187	130	307	718
4	BMC Bank Ltd	52	130	88	187	457
5	SC Bank Ltd	42	83	62	135	322
6	MC Bank Ltd	83	172	120	269	644
7	PMC Bank Ltd	57	135	99	187	478
8	GPPJS Bank Ltd	52	94	63	161	370
9	JKS Bank Ltd	31	83	63	109	286
10	AUC Bank Ltd	83	161	114	251	609
11	NRDVS Bank Ltd	53	109	83	177	422
12	NMC Bank Ltd	77	151	99	224	551
13	MSC Ltd	47	114	83	172	416
Total Respondents		884 (12.8)	1851 (26.9)	1305 (19.0)	2845 (41.3)	6885 (100)

Source: Primary data

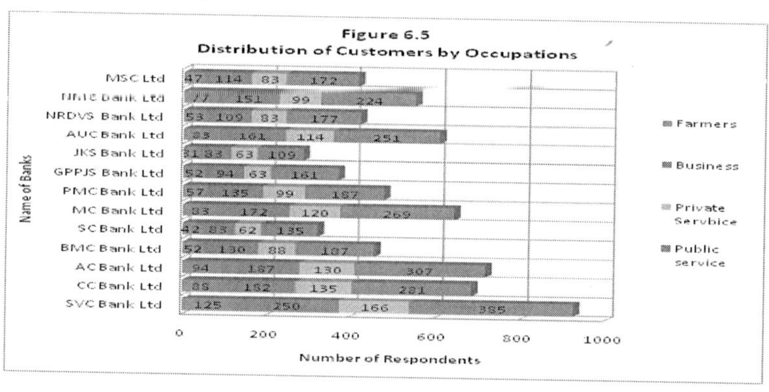

Among this occupational category, 41.3 per cent (2845) customers are from public sector services followed by Business category with 26.9 per cent (1851). The customers from public sector and from Businessmen have greater positive approach at banking sector. The number of farmers and employees from private sector are 12.8 per cent (884) and 19 per cent (1305) respectively, which shows normal positive approach at banking sector. It indicates that the numbers of public sector employees are comparatively more in opening their account into banks but it doesn't mean that they are frequent users of techno-based e-banking services.

6.2.6 Distribution of Customers by the size of their Income

Income is one of the most important factors which working as an indicator of Economic background of customers which are doing their transactions with the help of banks and are using e-banking services provided by banks. Distribution of customers as per their personal income is key factor for indicating his standard of living.

Table 6.6

Distribution of Customers by Size of their Annual Income

Sr. No	Name of Banks	Annual Income of Customers			Total
		Upto Rs. 3 Lakh	Rs. 3.1 Lakh to Rs. 5 Lakh	Rs. 5.1 Lakh +	
1	SVC Bank Ltd	250	510	166	926
2	CC Bank Ltd	260	270	156	686
3	AC Bank Ltd	229	322	167	718
4	BMC Bank Ltd	207	177	73	457
5	SC Bank Ltd	88	151	83	322
6	MC Bank Ltd	229	281	134	644
7	PMC Bank Ltd	130	218	130	478
8	GPPJS Bank Ltd	42	224	104	370

9	JKS Bank Ltd	47	156	83	286
10	AUC Bank Ltd	120	328	161	609
11	NRDVS Bank Ltd	78	224	120	422
12	NMC Bank Ltd	94	322	135	551
13	MSC Ltd	218	166	32	416
Total Respondents		1992 (28.9)	3349 (48.6)	1544 (22.4)	6885 (100)

Source: Primary data

Table 6.6 indicates that 48.6 per cent (3349) customers are having annual income of their Rs. 3.1 lakh to 5 lakh, followed by 28.9 per cent (1992) customers whose annual family income is up to Rs. 3 Lakh and 22.4 per cent (1544) customers have their annual family income above Rs. 5.1 lakh. It shows that majority of the customers are from the income group of Rs.3.1 lakh to 5 lakh.

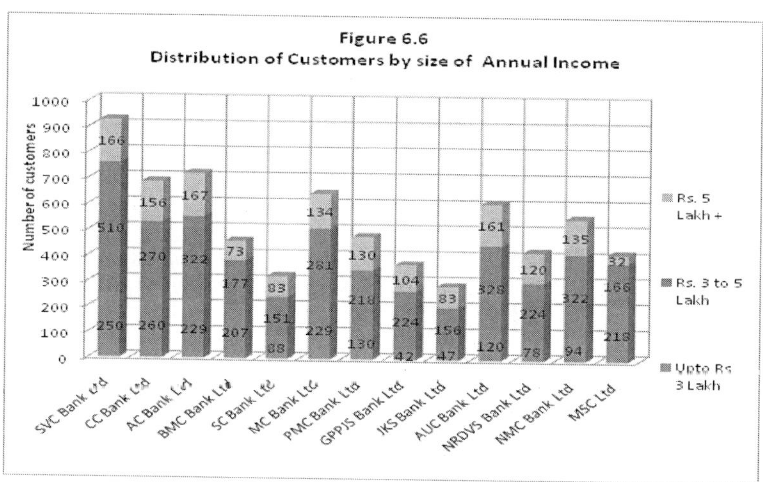

6.3 Sources of Savings by Sectors

Various investment sources are available in the market which is used for the purpose of investment. Banking sector is one of the most preferential sectors among all the other sectors available in the market.

6.3.1 Preferences of sectors for saving and Investment

Attitude of customers towards investments is most important factor. Investment in proper sector improves the confidence level of customers for making transactions. Thus it becomes necessary to study the preference of customers for investment and saving purpose.

Table 6.7

Sectors Preferred by the Customers for Safe Saving and Investment

Sr. No	Name of Banks	Preferred sector for saving-investment				Total
		Public sector	Private Sector	Cooperative Sector	All or any	
1	SVC Bank Ltd	172	93	229	432	926
2	CC Bank Ltd	99	83	192	312	686
3	AC Bank Ltd	244	42	109	323	718
4	BMC Bank Ltd	52	68	146	191	457
5	SC Bank Ltd	109	42	83	88	322
6	MC Bank Ltd	26	130	68	420	644
7	PMC Bank Ltd	52	68	151	207	478
8	GPPJS Bank Ltd	114	36	62	158	370
9	JKS Bank Ltd	26	42	57	161	286
10	AUC Bank Ltd	166	62	159	222	609
11	NRDVS Bank Ltd	31	62	111	218	422
12	NMC Bank Ltd	151	47	125	228	551
13	MSC Ltd	42	31	26	317	416
Total Respondents		1284 (18.6)	806 (11.7)	1518 (22.1)	3277 (47.6)	6885 (100)

Source: Primary data

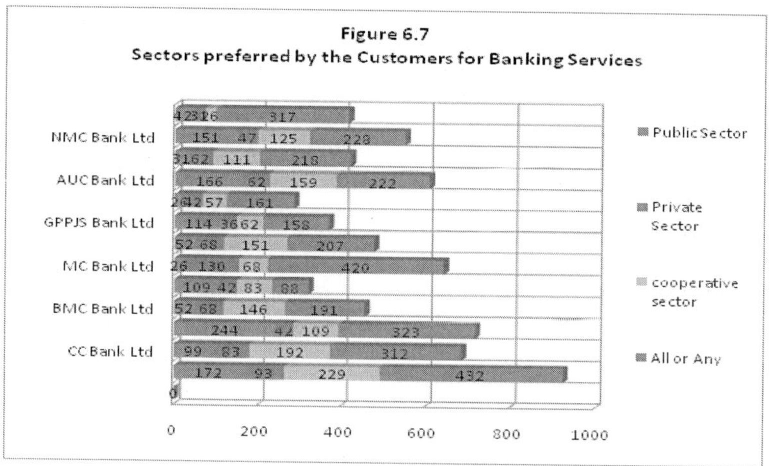

Figure 6.7
Sectors preferred by the Customers for Banking Services

Table 6.7 indicates that highest number of 22.1 per cent (1518) customers prefer for cooperative sector, followed by 18.6 per cent (1284) customers who prefer to public sector banks for investment purpose. 11.7 per cent (806) customers prefer their investment in private sector. However, as many as 47.6 per cent (3277) customers do not have any preference for a typical type of Bank. They choose any of the three categories or all of those for investment purposes.

6.3.2 Points of consideration while opening an Account with Bank

Saving is the important part for the development of the people and thus they prefer banking sector for savings being an important financial sector. For this purpose customers have their own account with the bank. While opening an account in to the bank, customers focus on various important issues such as security, relations, available facilities in the banks etc. Thus it becomes necessary to study these issues in the view of customers.

Table 6.8

Factors Considered by the Customers while Opening an Account with the Bank

Sr. No	Name of Banks	Preferred sector for saving-investment				Total
		Security	Relation	Available facilities	All the three	
1	SVC Bank Ltd	256	365	191	152	926
2	CC Bank Ltd	183	130	146	276	686
3	AC Bank Ltd	68	192	310	218	718
4	BMC Bank Ltd	151	166	207	166	457
5	SC Bank Ltd	62	99	158	88	322
6	MC Bank Ltd	159	52	222	328	644
7	PMC Bank Ltd	111	73	218	250	478
8	GPPJS Bank Ltd	115	130	128	133	370
9	JKS Bank Ltd	26	107	117	139	286
10	AUC Bank Ltd	187	130	150	144	609
11	NRDVS Bank Ltd	161	73	182	103	422
12	NMC Bank Ltd	109	140	187	213	551
13	MSC Ltd	151	135	130	198	416
Total Respondents		1739 (25.3)	1792 (26)	2346 (34.1)	2408 (35)	6885 (100)

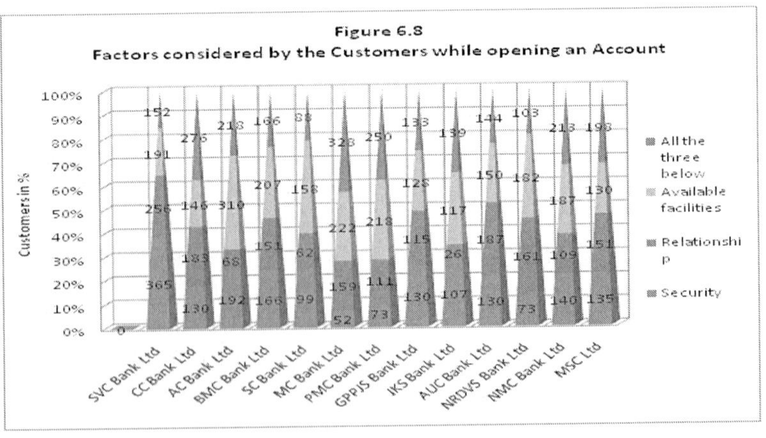

Figure 6.8
Factors considered by the Customers while opening an Account

all the three considerations; security, relation and available facility in to the bank while opening an account, followed by 34.1 per cent (2346) customers who prefer available facility in the bank as a top most important reason for opening an account. 26 per cent (1792) customers are interested in keeping their relations with bank employees and 25.3 per cent (1739) customers prefer services of any bank for security provided by those. Among the three major considerations, relationship is considered as least important by majority of customers.

6.3.3 Bank preferred for using e-banking services

Customers prefer e-banking services rather than traditional banking system. These services have features of time saving, cost reduction, anytime anywhere banking and many more, but with these services customers also prefer reliability, flexibility, trust, fluent services and availability of more services into bank. To use these services, customers have many options such as Public sector, Private sector and Cooperative sector. To know the response of customers, it is necessary to study preference of customers at particular banking sector.

Table 6.9

Bank Preferred for Using E-Banking Services

Sr. No	Name of Banks	Preferred Sector for Using E-Banking Services				Total
		Public Sector	Private Sootor	Cooperative Sector	All or any	
1	SVC Bank Ltd	489	354	166	125	926
2	CC Bank Ltd	328	281	83	109	686
3	AC Bank Ltd	369	307	94	125	718
4	BMC Bank Ltd	213	244	135	120	457
5	SC Bank Ltd	208	161	42	99	322
6	MC Bank Ltd	255	291	109	192	644

7	PMC Bank Ltd	265	250	47	88	478
8	GPPJS Bank Ltd	192	218	52	94	370
9	JKS Bank Ltd	140	161	114	62	286
10	AUC Bank Ltd	296	338	94	62	609
11	NRDVS Bank Ltd	302	255	130	203	422
12	NMC Bank Ltd	281	322	68	83	551
13	MSC Ltd	322	276	88	62	416
Total Respondents		3660 (53.2)	3458 (50.2)	1222 (17.7)	1424 (20.7)	6885 (100)

Source: Primary data

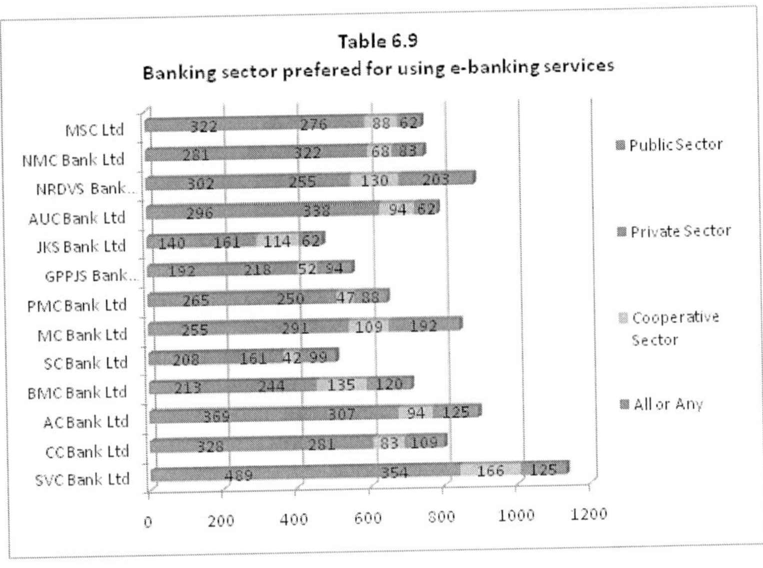

Table 6.9 indicates that 20.7 per cent (1424) customers prefer all the three sectors for the purpose of investment. 53.2 per cent (3660) customers who prefer Public sector banks as a top most important reason of nationalized bank. 50.2 per cent (3458) customers are interested in using e-banking services of Private sector banks and 17.7 per cent (1222) customers prefer cooperative banks for using e-banking services.

6.3.4 Causes for using e-banking services in non-cooperative sector

Customers need efficiency in using e-banking services and efficiency improve the satisfaction level of customers. Customers prefer non-cooperative banking sector rather than cooperative sector due to lack of number of branches, inter-bank connectivity, availability of services and reliability. For the progress of cooperative banks it is necessary to study the particular cause of neglecting the cooperative banking sector.

Table 6.10

Causes for Using E-Banking Services in non-Cooperative Sector

Name of Banks	Causes for using e-banking services in non-cooperative sector				Total
	Number of branches	Inter-bank connectivity	Availability of services	Reliability	
SVC Bank Ltd	328	270	400	250	926
CC Bank Ltd	369	281	322	484	686
AC Bank Ltd	265	250	333	369	718
BMC Bank Ltd	255	276	224	265	457
SC Bank Ltd	182	218	281	234	322
MC Bank Ltd	400	322	296	395	644
PMC Bank Ltd	322	302	276	255	478
GPPJS Bank Ltd	255	161	198	255	370
JKS Bank Ltd	239	213	114	177	286
AUC Bank Ltd	281	192	317	354	609
NRDVS Bank Ltd	255	208	109	218	422
NMC Bank Ltd	198	140	151	244	551
MSC Ltd	244	276	172	234	416
Total Respondents	3593 (52.2)	3109 (45.2)	3193 (46.4)	3734 (54.2)	6885 (100)

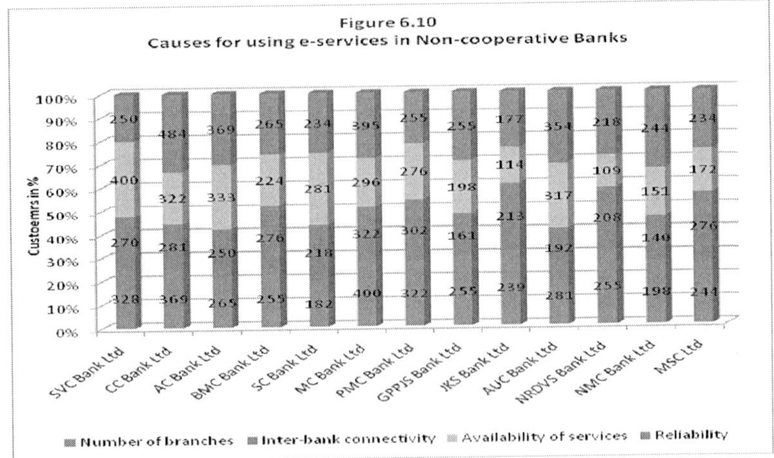

Table 6.10 indicates that 54.2 per cent (3734) customers prefer non-cooperative banks due to its reliability, followed by 52.2 per cent (3593) customers who prefer number of branches of banks. 46.4 per cent (3193) customers prefer to availability of services and 45.2 per cent (3109) customers prefer inter-bank connectivity.

6.3.5 Perception of Customers on use of e-banking services

E-banking services are provided by banks to its customers. Most of the banks are providing these services for smooth transactions and cost controlling, but all the customers are not using of these services. Thus it becomes necessary to study the perception of customer and to find out causes of not using e-banking services.

Table 6.11

Perception of Customers

Name of Banks	Whether the Customers are Aware of...					
	Information about e-banking	Ease in using e-banking services	Know-ledge for Use of cards	Theft/ mis-use of cards	trust on Techno-based services	Total
SVC Bank Ltd	634	738	733	738	879	926
CC Bank Ltd	322	593	536	645	515	686
AC Bank Ltd	504	629	588	624	400	718
BMC Bank Ltd	380	395	354	416	224	457
SC Bank Ltd	156	291	239	291	182	322
MC Bank Ltd	400	452	525	588	260	644
PMC Bank Ltd	270	437	390	442	437	478
GPPJS Bank Ltd	286	333	276	338	312	370
JKS Bank Ltd	203	244	244	255	31	286
AUC Bank Ltd	463	567	484	562	338	609
NRDVS Bank Ltd	302	348	348	359	94	422
NMC Bank Ltd	395	437	458	510	468	551
MSC Ltd	282	235	337	399	389	416
Total Respondents	4597 (66.8)	5699 (82.8)	5512 (80.1)	6167 (89.6)	4529 (65.8)	6885 (100)

Source: Primary data

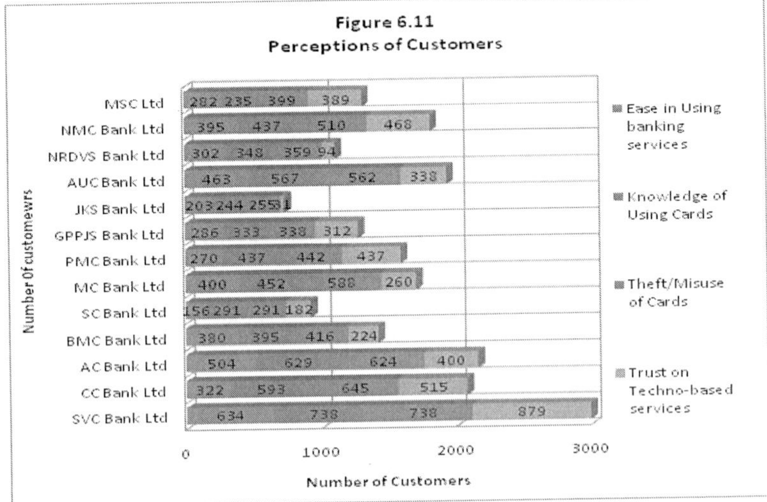

Table 6.11 indicates that out of 6885 sample customers, 66.8 per cent (4597) customers have proper information about e-banking services and others have no proper information regarding e-banking services and they are not using these services. In all, 1096 sample customers 82.8 per cent (5699) experienced that e-banking services are comparatively easy to use than manual/traditional transaction system. Further 80.1 per cent (5512) customers, using debit/credit cards have little more knowledge about these instruments and thus they are using it. Another 89.6 per cent (6167) customers are suspicious about theft/mis-use of cards and so they are avoiding these services. Only 65.8 per cent (4529) customers believed on techno-based online services through internet service providers and techniques, thus they are enjoying e-banking services.

6.3.6 Customers' feedback on Reliability of e-transactions

Reliability of customers about e-transaction plays an important role in showing the confidence of customers about e-banking services. Customers prefer to those banks whose services are more reliable and which provides better services to the customers. Thus to study the reliability about e-banking services is important.

Table 6.12

Customers' Feedback on Reliability of E-Transactions

Name of Banks	The extent to which the e-transactions are reliable				Total
	Fully	Partially	In Exceptional cases only	Not at all	
SVC Bank Ltd	193	297	245	191	926
CC Bank Ltd	146	213	182	145	686
AC Bank Ltd	156	243	172	147	718
BMC Bank Ltd	83	151	114	109	457
SC Bank Ltd	62	88	83	89	322
MC Bank Ltd	125	208	172	139	644
PMC Bank Ltd	135	135	94	114	478
GPPJS Bank Ltd	88	109	88	85	370
JKS Bank Ltd	57	73	88	68	286
AUC Bank Ltd	146	182	151	130	609
NRDVS Bank Ltd	83	120	120	99	422
NMC Bank Ltd	125	177	140	109	551
MSC Ltd	83	131	114	88	416
Total Respondents	1482 (21.5)	2127 (30.9)	1763 (25.6)	1513 (22.0)	6885 (100)

Source: Primary data

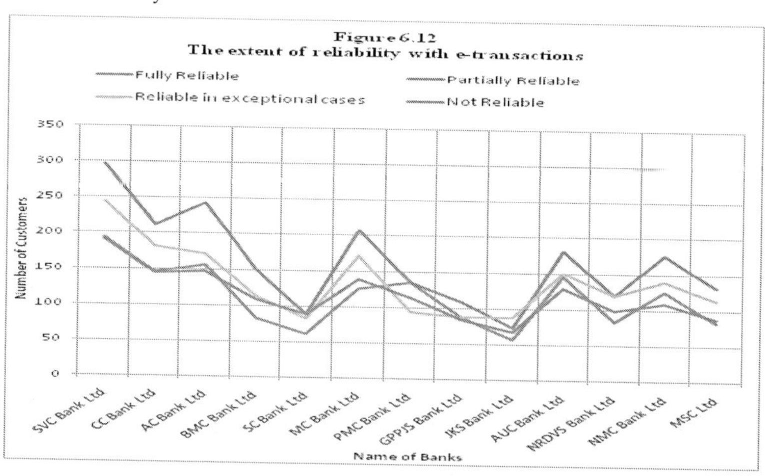

followed by 25.6 per cent (1763) customers who viewed that these services are reliable in exceptional cases only. 22.0 per cent (1513) customers are declared that these services are not reliable in any way and only 21.5 per cent (1482) customers are indicated that these services are fully reliable.

6.3.7 Number of Customers Using E-banking services

E-banking services are customer oriented. Feedback of customers indicates its utility. Maximum numbers of customers' indicate positive perception towards particular e-banking services, easiness and importance of e-banking services.

Table 6.13 indicate that out of 6885 sample customer, 67.1 per cent (5548) customers are using ATM services, phone banking services and mobile banking services of the banks, followed by 23.5 per cent (1778) customers who are using debit/credit card services.

Table 6.13

Number of Customers Using E-banking Services

Name of Banks	Number of Customers Using E-banking services							
	ATM	Debit Credit Cards	Phone Banking	Mobile Banking	RTGS EFT	Online Bill Payment	Internet Banking	Total Customers
SVC Bank Ltd	926	161	926	926	317	99	140	926
CC Bank Ltd	452	130	452	452	281	83	120	686
AC Bank Ltd	577	218	577	577	135	88	57	718
BMC Bank Ltd	385	192	385	385	182	73	78	457
SC Bank Ltd	265	177	265	265	94	68	42	322
MC Bank Ltd	588	109	588	588	135	94	57	644
PMC Bank Ltd	224	120	224	224	109	88	99	478
GPPJS Bank Ltd	296	130	296	296	99	78	94	370
JKS Bank Ltd	203	57	203	203	57	83	78	286

AUC Bank Ltd	504	109	504	504	78	62	88	609
NRDVS Bank Ltd	374	125	374	374	125	73	140	422
NMC Bank Ltd	385	120	385	385	151	83	99	551
MSC Ltd	369	130	369	369	68	78	83	416
Total Respondents	5548 (67.1)	1778 (23.5)	5548 (67.1)	5548 (67.1)	1830 (22)	1050 (15.3)	1175 (17.1)	6885 (100)

Source: Primary data

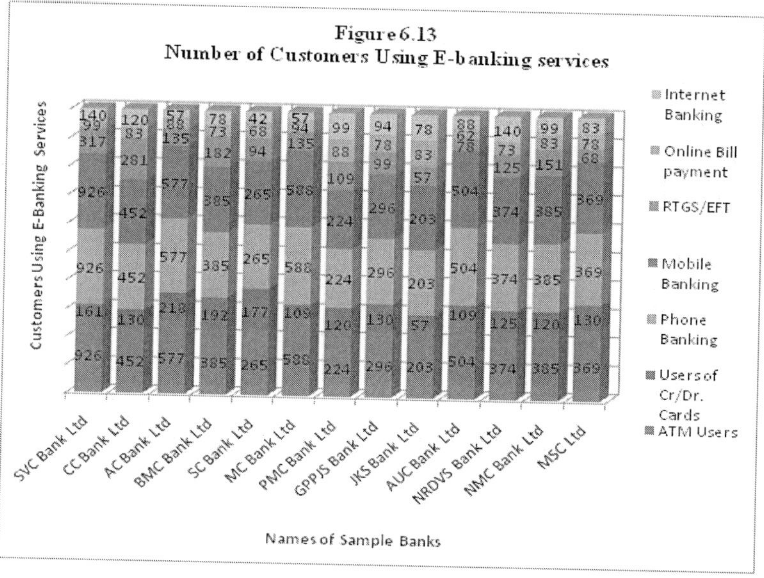

Figure 6.13
Number of Customers Using E-banking services

22.0 per cent (1830) customers are using e-banking services only for the purpose of RTGS/EFT, followed by 17.1 per cent (1175) Internet Banking users. There are only 15.3 per cent (1050) customers who are using e-banking services only for the purpose of online payment of bills.

6.3.8 Customers feeling Safety in Use of E-banking services

Customers want safely for their investments. Banks are preferred for investment due to its feature of safety. The factors which are safe for use and for investment are preferred by customers. Thus it is necessary to study feelings of customers about safety of e-banking services.

Table 6.14

Customers Feeling Safety in Use of E-Banking Services

Name of Banks	Customers feeling Safety in Use of E-banking services							Total Customers
	ATM	Debit Credit Cards	Phone Banking	Mobile Banking	RTGS EFT	Online Bill Payment	Internet Banking	
SVC Bank Ltd	770	146	21	21	161	140	333	926
CC Bank Ltd	499	36	47	36	161	296	166	686
AC Bank Ltd	582	104	42	52	213	322	286	718
BMC Bank Ltd	374	62	36	36	68	218	192	457
SC Bank Ltd	302	5	36	47	57	57	83	322
MC Bank Ltd	515	88	16	5	135	120	229	644
PMC Bank Ltd	343	21	31	68	104	229	83	478
GPPJS Bank Ltd	296	68	36	42	125	198	182	370
JKS Bank Ltd	192	57	47	16	57	156	125	286
AUC Bank Ltd	468	104	10	42	198	234	135	609
NRDVS Bank Ltd	359	47	5	26	125	218	114	422
NMC Bank Ltd	458	73	10	31	161	265	125	551
MSC Ltd	312	104	10	16	156	125	52	416
Total Respondents	5470 (79.5)	915 (13.3)	348 (5.1)	437 (6.3)	1721 (25.0)	2579 (37.5)	2106 (30.6)	6885 (100)

Source: Primary data

Table 6.14 indicates that out of 6885 sample customers, 79.5 per cent (5470) customers feel safety while using ATM services, followed by 37.5 per cent (2579) customers using online system for payment of bills. 30.6 per cent (2106) Internet banking users feel safety, followed by 25.0 per cent (1721) customers of RTGS/EFT. Only 13.3 per cent (915) Debit/Credit card holders feel safety, followed by 6.3 per cent (437) mobile banking users. Only 5.1 per cent (348) Phone banking service users feel safety while using the services.

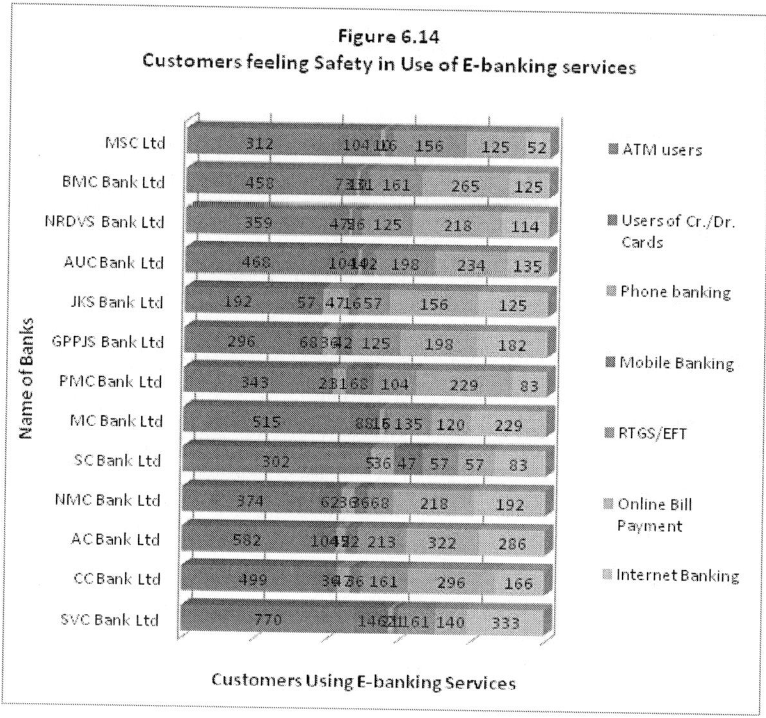

Figure 6.14
Customers feeling Safety in Use of E-banking services

6.3.9 Frequency of Using the E-Banking Services

Frequency of use of e-banking services indicates its importance to the customers that they are using e-banking services frequently. Some customers use these services daily, twice in a week, weekly or according to their need. Frequency also shows positive perception of customers towards e-banking services. 'Practice makes man perfect', with this statement, frequently use of services helps to control problems raised while using these services. Thus it is necessary to study frequency of customers using e-banking services.

Table 6.15

Frequency of Using the E-Banking Services

Name of Banks	frequency of using the e-banking services				Total Customers
	Daily	Twice in a week	Weekly	Anytime	
SVC Bank Ltd	192	244	296	194	926
CC Bank Ltd	146	182	209	149	686
AC Bank Ltd	156	172	239	151	718
BMC Bank Ltd	83	120	146	108	457
SC Bank Ltd	62	83	88	89	322
MC Bank Ltd	125	172	208	139	644
PMC Bank Ltd	135	94	135	114	478
GPPJS Bank Ltd	88	88	109	85	370
JKS Bank Ltd	42	88	88	68	286
AUC Bank Ltd	146	151	182	130	609
NRDVS Bank Ltd	83	120	120	99	422
NMC Bank Ltd	125	140	177	109	551
MSC Ltd	83	114	130	89	416
Total Respondents	1466 (21.3)	1768 (25.7)	2127 (30.9)	1524 (22.1)	6885 (100)

Source: Primary data

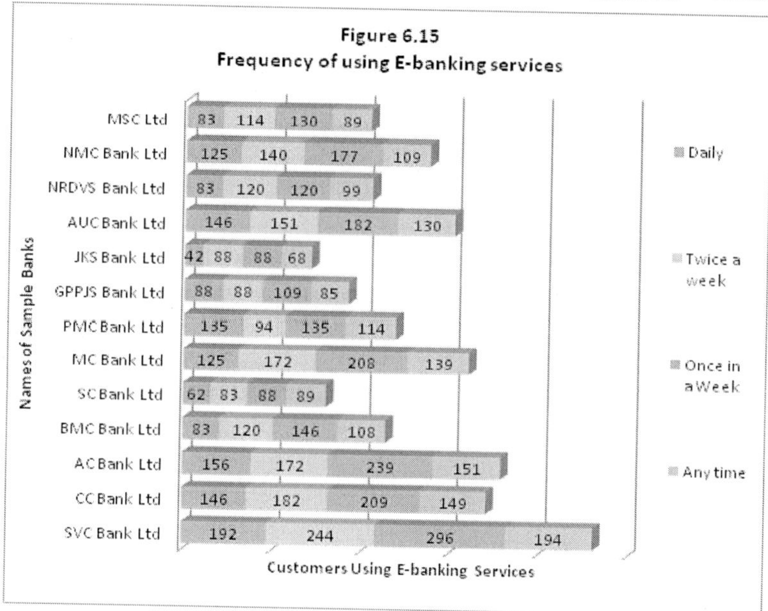

Table 6.15 indicates that, out of 6885 sample customers, 30.9 per cent (2127) customers are using e-banking services weekly, followed by 25.7 per cent (1768) customers which are using these services twice in a week. 21.3 per cent (1466) customers are using these services anytime as per their need, and there are only 21.3 per cent (1524) customers which are using these services daily.

6.4 Customers enjoying Benefits of e-banking services

Customers use only those facilities which give them financial, physical, psychological, or other type of benefits. Banks are providing various services but all the customers are not using these services. Only those customers, who are enjoying benefits of e-banking services, are using it. Generally the benefits while using e-banking services are anytime anywhere banking, 24*7 facility, cashless transactions, high transaction frequency, quick transactions, SMS alerts, etc. Thus to know the most benefited services, it is necessary to study that how many customers are enjoying the benefits of e-banking services and from which services.

Table 6.16

Number of Customers Enjoying Benefits of E-Eanking Services

Name of Banks	Customers enjoying Benefits of e-banking services						
	Anytime any where	24*7 facility	Cashless transactions	High Transaction frequency	Quick transaction	SMS alerts	Total Customers
SVC Bank Ltd	827	244	296	177	333	848	926
CC Bank Ltd	525	57	182	78	312	525	686
AC Bank Ltd	614	120	244	78	348	504	718
BMC Bank Ltd	406	83	125	62	250	395	458
SC Bank Ltd	307	47	125	57	130	276	322
MC Bank Ltd	530	114	172	68	161	619	645
PMC Bank Ltd	348	31	99	47	244	411	478
GPPJS Bank Ltd	307	78	135	52	198	328	369
JKS Bank Ltd	213	62	88	31	187	218	286
AUC Bank Ltd	489	114	218	42	234	541	608
NRDVS Bank Ltd	374	52	151	36	224	312	421
NMC Bank Ltd	484	83	203	57	276	489	551
MSC Ltd	291	104	187	26	140	348	416
Total Respondents	5715 (83.0)	1191 (17.3)	2226 (32.3)	811 (11.8)	3037 (44.1)	5814 (84.4)	6885 (100)

Source: Primary data

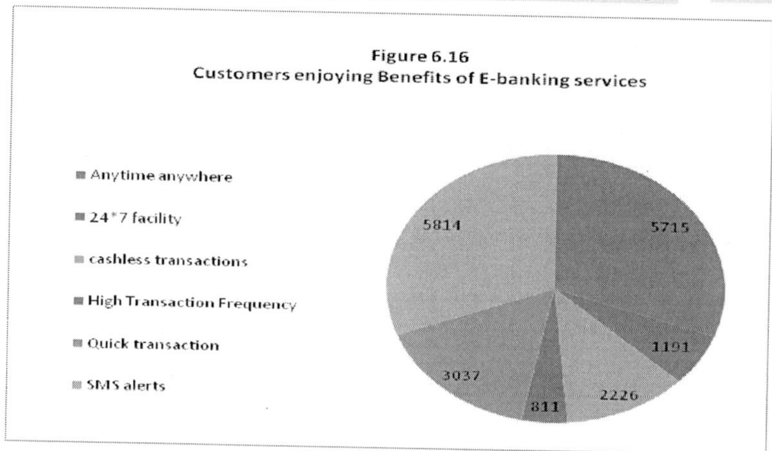

Figure 6.16
Customers enjoying Benefits of E-banking services

Table 6.16 indicates that 84.4 per cent (5814) customers enjoying benefits of SMS alerts, followed by 83.0 per cent (5715) customers take benefits of anytime anywhere services. 44.1 per cent (3037) customers are doing quick transactions, followed by 32.3 per cent (2226) customers. 17.3 per cent (1191) customers get 24*7 days facility, and only 11.8 per cent (811) customers have high transaction frequency.

6.4.1 Customers satisfaction with e-banking services

Customers use techno-based services for their mind satisfaction only and mind satisfaction have achieved by using the prompt services rendered by banks which helps to fulfill their needs of customers. The customers which are completing their basic needs are with the help of services are fully satisfied; the customers' whose needs are sometimes fulfilled are partially satisfied and the customers whose needs are completed their needs by facing majority of problems are satisfied in exceptional cases only and the customers who are facing problems are not satisfied with e-banking services. Thus it is necessary to study the satisfaction level of customers.

Table 6.17

Customers' Satisfaction with E-Banking Services

Name of Banks	Satisfaction with e-banking services				Total
	Fully	Partially	Rarely	Not at all	
SVC Bank Ltd	244	260	224	198	926
CC Bank Ltd	150	182	208	146	686
AC Bank Ltd	151	172	239	156	718
BMC Bank Ltd	109	114	146	88	457
SC Bank Ltd	89	83	88	62	322
MC Bank Ltd	82	172	213	177	644
PMC Bank Ltd	114	94	135	135	478
GPPJS Bank Ltd	85	88	109	88	370
JKS Bank Ltd	68	88	88	42	286
AUC Bank Ltd	130	151	182	146	609
NRDVS Bank Ltd	99	120	120	83	422
NMC Bank Ltd	109	140	177	125	551
MSC Ltd	88	114	130	84	416
Total Respondents	1518 (22.1)	1778 (25.8)	2059 (29.9)	1530 (22.2)	6885 (100)

Source: Primary data

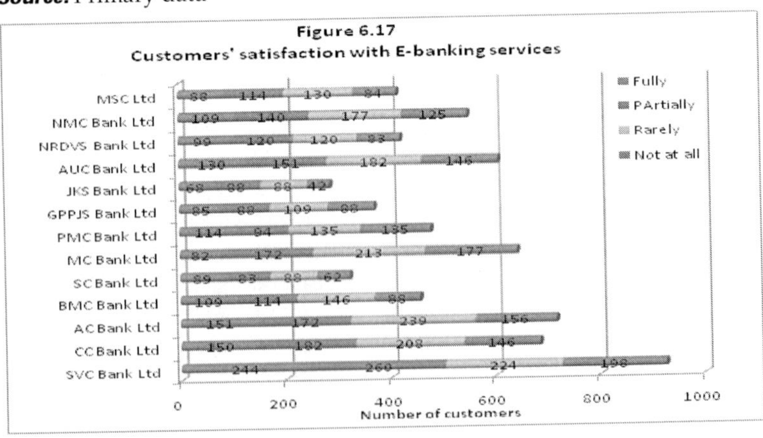

Figure 6.17

Customers' satisfaction with E-banking services

Table 6.17 indicates the satisfaction of customers using e-banking services, where 29.9 per cent (2059) customers are satisfied in exceptional cases only, followed by 25.8 per cent (1778) customers who are partially satisfied. 22.2 per cent (1530) customers are not satisfied with e-banking technological services. There are only 22.1 per cent (1518) customers who are fully satisfied with the e-banking services of banks and they are enjoying the benefits of these services.

6.4.2 Security while Performing E-transactions Through Website

Security is the key factor of the progress of e-banking services provided to customers and also key factor of banks. Customers are giving preference to the e-banking services for economical convenience and due to larger security. Some banks provide information to the customers as per their need regarding the security policy of banks due to which customers trust on them, but all the customers are not interested for taking any information from banks but they give preference to their experience. Due to which customers have suspect for security of their deposits. Thus it is necessary to study the knowledge of security while performing e-transactions through website.

Table 6.18

Security while Performing E-transactions Through Website

Name of Banks	Security while performing e-transactions through Net				Total
	Fully	Partially	Rarely	Not at all	
SVC Bank Ltd	244	260	244	178	926
CC Bank Ltd	156	213	198	119	686
AC Bank Ltd	192	203	172	151	718
BMC Bank Ltd	99	120	151	87	457
SC Bank Ltd	47	130	83	62	322

MC Bank Ltd	182	218	140	104	644
PMC Bank Ltd	99	120	151	108	478
GPPJS Bank Ltd	73	125	104	68	370
JKS Bank Ltd	73	109	68	36	286
AUC Bank Ltd	156	177	151	125	609
NRDVS Bank Ltd	99	114	111	98	422
NMC Bank Ltd	161	146	130	114	551
MSC Ltd	83	109	138	86	416
Total Respondents	1664 (24.2)	2044 (29.7)	1841 (26.7)	1336 (19.4)	6885 (100)

Source: Primary data

Table 6.18 indicates security while performing e-transactions through website, where 29.7 per cent (2044) customers are partially secured while performing e-transactions through website, followed by 26.7 per cent (1841) customers who think that e-transactions are secured in exceptional cases. 24.2 per cent (1664) customers pointed that e-transactions performing through websites are fully secured, followed by 19.4 per cent (1336) customers who think that e-transactions are not secured.

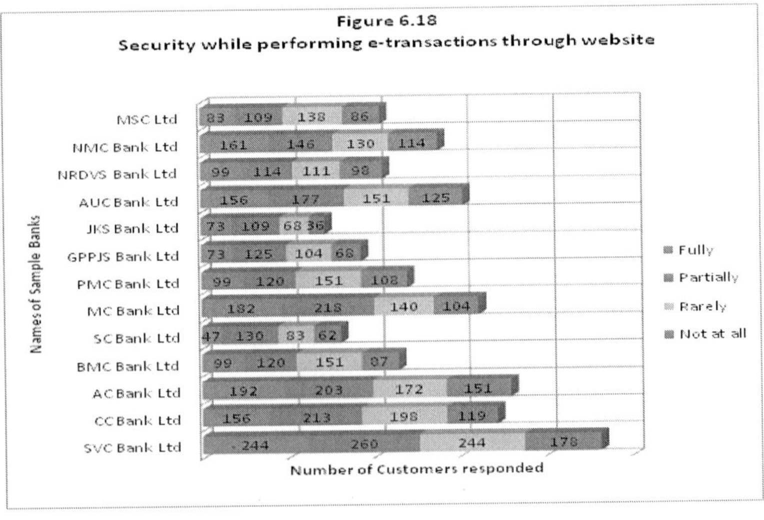

6.4.3 Level of satisfaction: information available on bank website

Customers use e-banking services for mind satisfaction only and mind satisfaction have achieved by using the prompt services rendered by banks which helps to fulfill the needs of customers. The customers' needs are often completed with the help of information available on bank website and enjoying greater benefits of such information are fully satisfied; The customers' needs are completed partially with the help of information available on bank website and enjoying partial benefits of such information are partially satisfied; The customers' needs are often completed by facing various problems with the help of information available on bank website and enjoying benefits of such information only in some cases are satisfied in some extent; the customers who are not at all satisfied with the information provided by banks on bank website are not satisfied. Thus it is necessary to study the satisfaction level of customers regarding the availability of information on banks website.

Table 6.19

Satisfaction From Information Available on Bank Website

Name of Banks	Satisfaction about information available on website				Total
	Fully	Partially	In Exceptional cases only	Not at all	
SVC Bank Ltd	270	291	198	167	926
CC Bank Ltd	291	254	83	58	686
AC Bank Ltd	265	343	62	48	718
BMC Bank Ltd	224	161	42	30	457
SC Bank Ltd	130	156	21	15	322
MC Bank Ltd	260	312	42	30	644

PMC Bank Ltd	175	219	42	42	478
GPPJS Bank Ltd	198	135	21	16	370
JKS Bank Ltd	104	125	31	26	286
AUC Bank Ltd	218	303	52	36	609
NRDVS Bank Ltd	182	178	36	26	422
NMC Bank Ltd	215	274	36	26	551
MSC Ltd	146	213	31	26	416
Total Respondents	2678 (38.9)	2964 (43.1)	697 (10.1)	546 (7.9)	6885 (100)

Source: Primary data

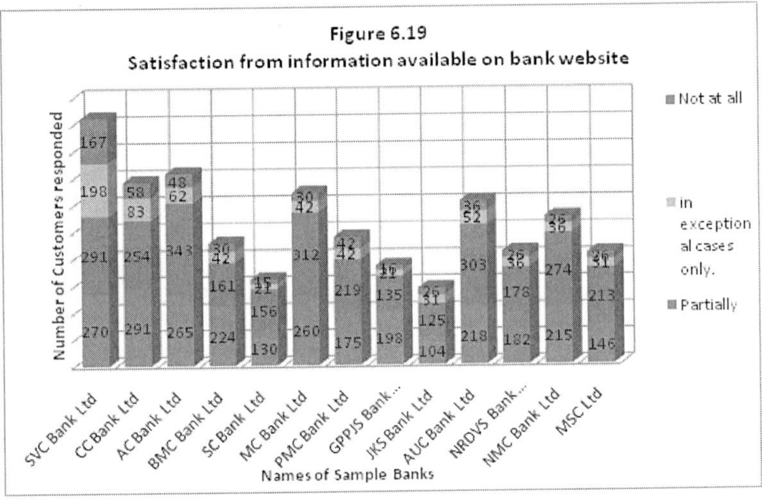

Figure 6.19
Satisfaction from information available on bank website

Table 6.19 indicates the satisfaction of customers with regards to the information available on website of banks with respect to the e-banking services, where 43.1 per cent (2964) customers are partially satisfied, followed by 38.9 per cent (2678) customers who are fully satisfied. 10.1 per cent (697) customers are satisfied in exceptional cases only. 7.9 per cent (546) customers are not satisfied with the information available on website of banks regarding e-banking services.

6.4.4 Expectation of Customers about e-banking services from banks

Customers are the key factors of e-banking services. Though the banks are providing these services, customers should have to use it. E-banking services are benefited to the customers as well as to the bankers.

These services are provided by banks thus for improvement in the quality of services it is necessary to study the expectations of customers. These expectations are classified as; more efficient services, maximum cooperation for solving e-problems, maximum availability of e-services and all these.

Table 6.20

Expectation of Customers About E-Banking Services from Banks

Name of Banks	Expectation About E-Banking s Ervices from Banks				Total
	More efficient services	Maximum co-operation for solving e-problems	Maximum availability of e-services	All the above	
SVC Bank Ltd	151	182	302	291	926
CC Bank Ltd	58	88	244	296	686
AC Bank Ltd	57	78	318	265	718
BMC Bank Ltd	36	57	177	187	457
SC Bank Ltd	21	26	145	130	322
MC Bank Ltd	31	42	295	276	644
PMC Bank Ltd	36	52	203	187	478
GPPJS Bank Ltd	21	36	136	177	370
JKS Bank Ltd	21	26	119	120	286
AUC Bank Ltd	47	68	281	213	609
NRDVS Bank Ltd	31	47	162	182	422
NMC Bank Ltd	21	36	270	224	551
MSC Ltd	31	47	177	161	416
Total Respondents	562 (8.2)	785 (11.4)	2829 (41.1)	2709 (39.4)	6885 (100)

Source: Primary data

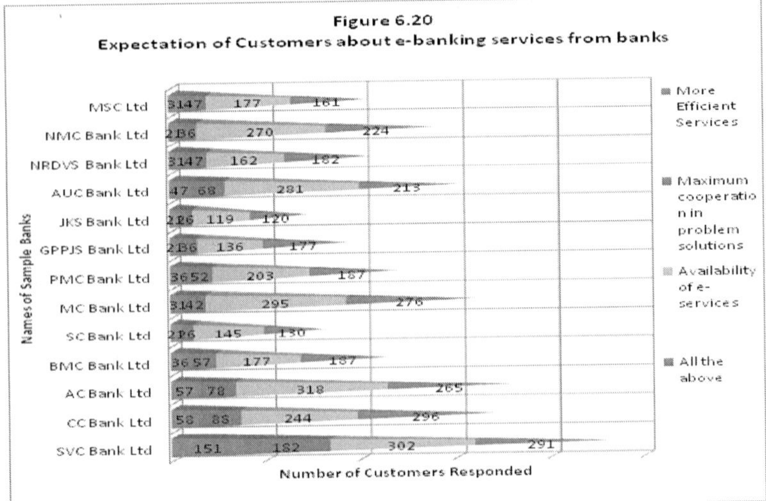

Table 6.20 shows expectation of Customers about e-banking services from banks. 41.1 per cent (2829) customers want availability of maximum number of e-banking services, followed by 39.4 per cent (2709) customers who have all expectations from the banks. 11.4 per cent (785) customers want maximum cooperation from bank employees for solving the problems raised while performing e-banking services followed by 8.2 per cent (562) customers who need more efficient services.

6.4.5 Problems Encountered while Performing E-Banking Transactions

Identification of problems is one of the most important factors that anyone can try to solve it. Because of proper treatment, it is necessary to find out problems face by customers. The problems which may face by customers are classified into four categories, such as technological/ operational problems, socio-cultural problems, managerial problems, transactional problems etc.

Table 6.21

Problems Encountered by Customers while Performing E-Banking Transactions

Name of Banks	Problems encounter by customers				Total
	Technological problems	Socio-cultural problems	Managerial problems	Transactional problems	
SVC Bank Ltd	848	182	281	109	926
CC Bank Ltd	634	156	270	140	686
AC Bank Ltd	650	244	234	130	718
BMC Bank Ltd	426	140	156	83	457
SC Bank Ltd	291	99	99	52	322
MC Bank Ltd	598	203	224	120	644
PMC Bank Ltd	458	88	172	83	478
GPPJS Bank Ltd	244	104	78	47	370
JKS Bank Ltd	364	88	146	83	286
AUC Bank Ltd	582	104	213	99	609
NRDVS Bank Ltd	374	99	172	78	422
NMC Bank Ltd	515	161	177	94	551
MSC Ltd	364	114	109	47	416
Total Respondents	6349 (92.2)	1784 (25.9)	2330 (33.8)	1165 (16.9)	6885 (100)

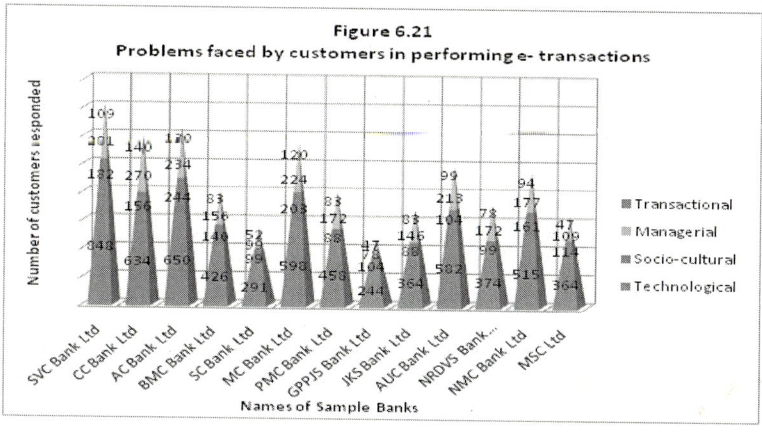

Figure 6.21
Problems faced by customers in performing e- transactions

Table 6.21 indicates, problems encounter by customers while performing e-banking transactions. Out of 6885 sample customers, 92.2 per cent (6349) customers are facing the problem of technological/operational followed by 33.8 per cent (2330) customers facing the managerial problem. 25.9 per cent (1784) customers are facing socio-cultural problems whereas 16.9 per cent (1165) customers are facing the problem of Transactions.

6.4.6 Solution on problem encounter

After identification of problem, it is necessary to solve it as early as possible. Customers prefer only those services on which the solutions are taken earlier. Some bank solves problems immediately some banks solve it within two days, some solve within a week and some banks solve these problems within a quarter.

Table 6.22

Time Required for Solution on Problems Encountered

Name of Banks		Time required for Solution on problem encountered			Total
	Instantly	Within 2 days	Within a week	Within a quarter	
SVC Bank Ltd	250	264	220	192	926
CC Bank Ltd	156	182	166	182	686
AC Bank Ltd	192	203	177	146	718
BMC Bank Ltd	98	130	151	78	457
SC Bank Ltd	68	67	109	78	322
MC Bank Ltd	156	171	187	130	644
PMC Bank Ltd	146	145	104	83	478
GPPJS Bank Ltd	88	88	116	78	370
JKS Bank Ltd	52	83	94	57	286
AUC Bank Ltd	125	140	204	140	609

NRDVS Bank Ltd	114	121	109	78	422
NMC Bank Ltd	161	161	120	109	551
MSC Ltd	88	104	136	88	416
Total Respondents	1694 (24.6)	1859 (27.0)	1893 (27.4)	1439 (20.9)	6885 (100)

Source: Primary data

Table 6.22 indicates the duration of solution on the problems raised to the customers while performing e-banking services. 27.4 per cent (1893) customers reported that e-banking problems are solved within a week, followed by 27.0 per cent (1859) customers who defined that the e-banking problems are solved within 2 days from the day of complaint registered. Whereas 24.6 per cent (1694) customers pointed that the problems are solved instantly when the problems are registered, followed by 20.9 per cent (1439) customers who opinioned that the problems are solved within a quarter.

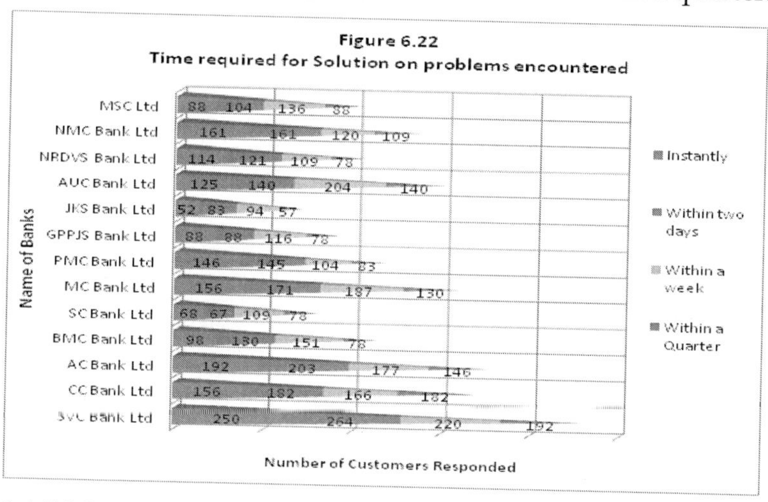

Figure 6.22
Time required for Solution on problems encountered

6.4.7 Necessity and Availability to customers

For smooth conduct of e-banking transactions and improving the level of satisfaction of customers, it is necessary to make availability of various factors which are needed to the customers. These necessity and availability may be from bank or from customers, such as proper guidelines or suggestions provided to the customers or not, customers need training for improving the level of satisfaction or not whether the accurate and detailed information is provided to the customers or not and whether the customers have their own laptop, computers or android mobile phone with internet connection.

71.1 per cent (4893) customers need proper guidelines and suggestions as per their requirements from bank employees when they are in problems. 57.5 per cent (3957) customers need training regarding proper use of e-banking services and improve their awareness.

Table 6.23

Necessity and Availability to Customers

Name of Banks	Necessity to customers		Availability to customers		Total
	Guidelines suggestions from Banks	Training to e-banking users	Accurate and detailed information	Owned PC laptop	
SVC Bank Ltd	671	530	411	463	926
CC Bank Ltd	468	359	400	380	686
AC Bank Ltd	536	416	390	385	718
BMC Bank Ltd	307	276	250	213	457
SC Bank Ltd	218	203	198	203	322
MC Bank Ltd	458	359	348	333	644
PMC Bank Ltd	359	296	281	234	478
GPPJS Bank Ltd	270	203	224	213	370
JKS Bank Ltd	182	166	182	146	286
AUC Bank Ltd	426	359	317	312	609
NRDVS Bank Ltd	296	234	224	213	422
NMC Bank Ltd	411	328	317	276	551
MSC Ltd	291	229	234	203	416
Total Respondents	4893 (71.1)	3957 (57.5)	3775 (54.8)	3572 (51.9)	6885 (100)

Source: Primary data

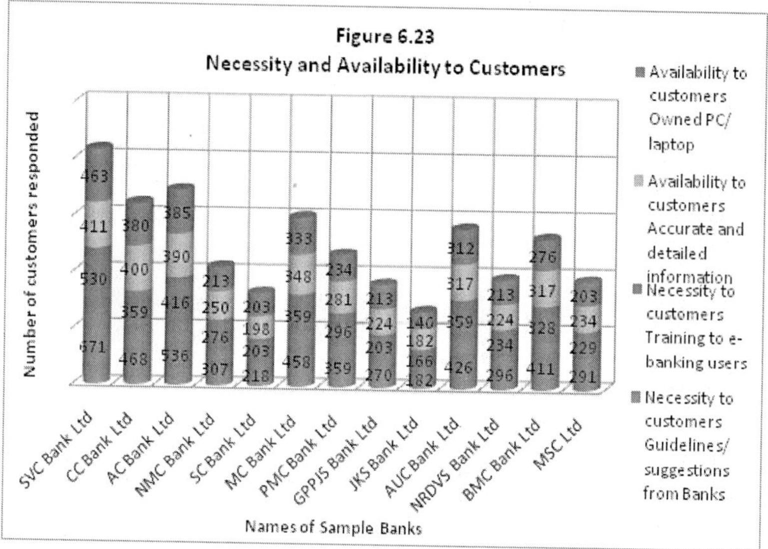

54.8 per cent (3775) customers get accurate and detailed information from the banks on their accounts, 51.9 per cent (3572) customers have laptop/computer/android mobile phones for getting the information available through internet.

6.4.8 Service charges Charged by customers

Banks have adopted policy of techno-based services which is by product of IT sector. These techno-based services are cheaper than traditional/manual system. Banks are charging fees from customers for providing these services. Banks are providing various types of e-banking services freely i.e. SMS Alert, Phone Banking, Mobile Banking, Internet Banking etc and other services are provided with charges. The charges charged by banks are classified into four categories such as; quite reasonable, little more than reasonable, much higher than reasonable, exorbitant.

Table 6.24

Service charges Charged to customers

Name of Banks	Service charges Charged to customers				Total
	Quite reasonable	Little more than reasonable	Much higher than reasonable	Exorbitant	
SVC Bank Ltd	156	182	302	286	926
CC Bank Ltd	78	109	213	286	686
AC Bank Ltd	120	130	239	229	718
BMC Bank Ltd	31	52	166	208	457
SC Bank Ltd	31	42	125	124	322
MC Bank Ltd	68	94	250	232	644
PMC Bank Ltd	83	99	161	135	478
GPPJS Bank Ltd	36	42	135	157	370
JKS Bank Ltd	31	47	83	125	286
AUC Bank Ltd	36	57	276	240	609
NRDVS Bank Ltd	62	83	135	142	422
NMC Bank Ltd	94	109	187	161	551
MSC Ltd	42	47	130	197	416
Total Respondents	868 (12.6)	1093 (15.9)	2402 (34.9)	2522 (36.6)	6885 (100)

Source: Primary data

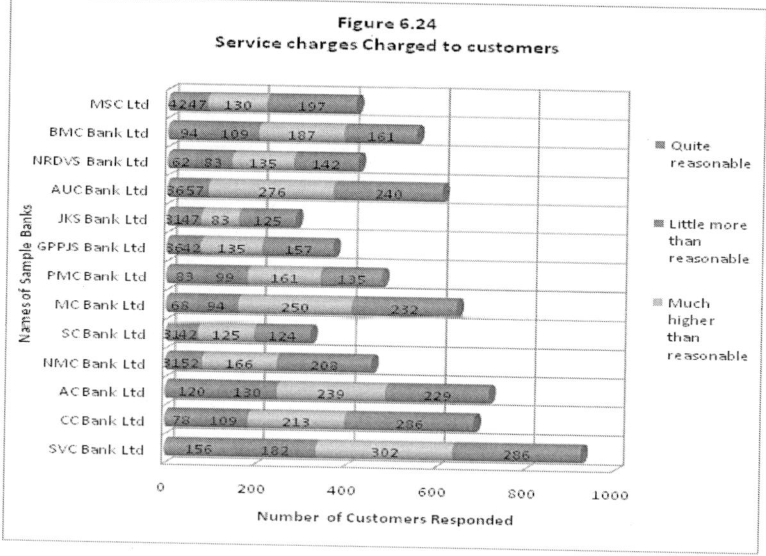

Figure 6.24
Service charges Charged to customers

Table 6.24 indicates that out of 6885 sample customers, 36.6 per cent (2522) customers replied that the banks charges are exorbitant, followed by 34.9 per cent (2402) customers who replied that the services charges are much higher than reasonable. Whereas 15.9 per cent (1093) customers opinioned that the charges are little more than reasonable, and 12.6 per cent (868) customers opinioned that the bank charges are quite reasonable.

6.4.9 Satisfaction level of customers on current infrastructure facilities

Infrastructural facilities play an important role in the progress of e-banking services as well as banking sector. Quality of infrastructural facility indicates quality of services and satisfaction of customers is also depended on the quality of services. The satisfaction level of customers regarding infrastructural facilities are classified into four categories as; fully satisfied, partially satisfied, and satisfied in exceptional cases and not satisfied. Thus it becomes necessary to study satisfaction level of customers regarding infrastructural facilities provided by banks.

Table 6.25

Satisfaction of customers From Current Infrastructure Facilities

Name of Banks	Satisfaction about infrastructure facility				Total
	Fully	Partially	Rarely	Not at all	
SVC Bank Ltd	250	312	192	172	926
CC Bank Ltd	302	239	83	62	686
AC Bank Ltd	213	187	177	141	718
BMC Bank Ltd	146	224	42	45	457
SC Bank Ltd	166	73	47	36	322
MC Bank Ltd	229	234	104	77	644
PMC Bank Ltd	125	140	109	104	478
GPPJS Bank Ltd	125	140	57	48	370
JKS Bank Ltd	99	88	57	42	286
AUC Bank Ltd	156	156	161	136	609
NRDVS Bank Ltd	109	120	104	89	422
NMC Bank Ltd	166	182	115	88	551
MSC Ltd	114	125	88	89	416
Total Respondents	2200 (31.9)	2220 (32.3)	1336 (19.4)	1129 (16.4)	6885 (100)

Source: Primary data

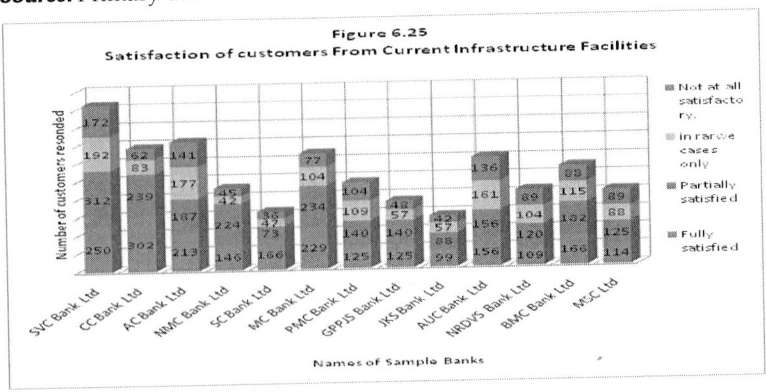

Figure 6.25
Satisfaction of customers From Current Infrastructure Facilities

to the infrastructural facilities provided to the customers by the banks with respect to the e-banking services, where 31.9 per cent (2200) customers are fully satisfied, followed by 32.3 per cent (2220) customers who are partially satisfied. 19.4 per cent (1336) customers are satisfied in exceptional cases only. 16.4 per cent (1129) customers are not satisfied with the information available on website of banks regarding e-banking services.

6.4.10 Purpose of using e-banking services

When there is need, there is use and so when the bank customers are in need, they do use e-banking services. Customers are using e-banking services for various purposes such as withdrawal of cash, cash deposits, online payments of bills, inquiry about availability of balance on account, transfer of money for various purposes and for other purposes also. Thus it is necessary to study the need/ purpose of customers for using e-banking services.

Table 6.26

Purpose of Using E-Banking Services

Name of Banks	Purpose of using e-banking services						Total
	Cash withdrawal	Cash deposits	Online bill payments	Balance enquiry	Money transfer	others	
SVC Bank Ltd	790	156	250	276	125	73	926
CC Bank Ltd	546	120	62	291	88	16	686
AC Bank Ltd	666	146	213	286	125	78	718
BMC Bank Ltd	437	83	130	208	73	47	457
SC Bank Ltd	296	57	88	120	47	62	322
MC Bank Ltd	577	140	172	239	88	52	644
PMC Bank Ltd	442	88	130	187	68	42	478
GPPJS Bank Ltd	244	83	68	73	31	26	370
JKS Bank Ltd	322	130	109	120	68	42	286

AUC Bank Ltd	520	62	172	218	83	47	609
NRDVS Bank Ltd	307	36	120	213	47	42	422
NMC Bank Ltd	484	130	151	161	83	57	551
MSC Ltd	338	31	120	166	47	26	416
Total Respondents	5970 (86.7)	1264 (18.4)	1784 (25.9)	2558 (37.2)	972 (14.1)	608 (8.8)	6885 (100)

Source: Primary data

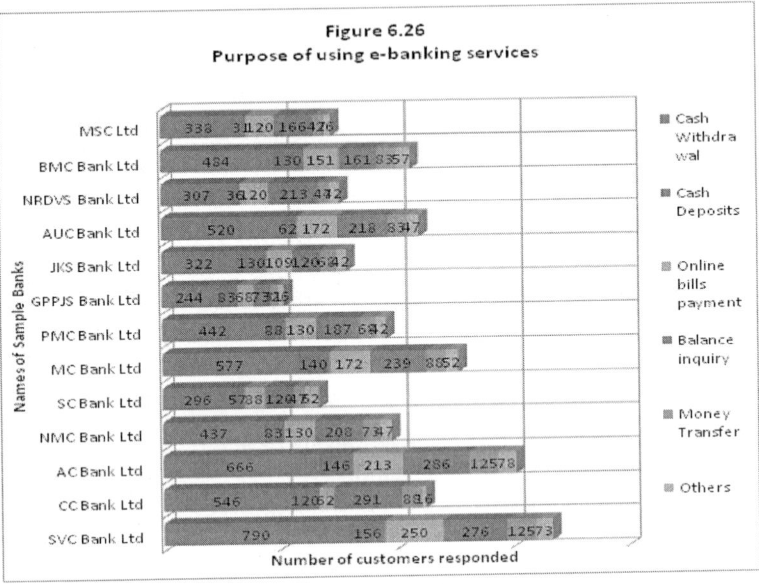

Figure 6.26
Purpose of using e-banking services

Table 6.26 indicates that 86.7 per cent (5970) customers are using e-banking services for the purpose of withdrawal of cash, followed by 37.2 per cent (2558) customers who are using e-banking services for the purpose of balance inquiry. 25.9 per cent (1784) customers are making payment through online process, followed by 18.4 per cent (1264) customers who deposit their cash through e-banking system. 14.1 per cent (972) customers are using these services for transfer of money from one account to others' account. Only 8.8 per cent (608) customers are using these services for other purposes.

6.4.11 Perception of customers on usage of e-banking services

Perception of customers' about e-banking services plays an important role for progress of techno-based services. Thus it becomes necessary to study perception of customers through availability of regular records, avoid of direct contact with employees/banks and their trust (on employee of banks/ machinery)

Table 6.27

Perception of Customers on Usage of E-Banking Services

Name of Banks	Perception of customers				Total
	Regular records	Avoid direct contact	Trust Employees	Machine	
SVC Bank Ltd	192	411	863	63	926
CC Bank Ltd	536	281	665	21	686
AC Bank Ltd	588	322	671	47	718
BMC Bank Ltd	354	192	457	0	457
SC Bank Ltd	239	120	302	20	322
MC Bank Ltd	525	312	614	30	644
PMC Bank Ltd	390	198	442	36	478
GPPJS Bank Ltd	276	146	349	21	370
JKS Bank Ltd	244	130	270	16	286
AUC Bank Ltd	481	260	562	47	609
NRDVS Bank Ltd	348	187	400	22	422
NMC Bank Ltd	458	250	525	26	551
MSC Ltd	338	172	380	36	416
Total Respondents	4971 (72.2)	2980 (43.3)	6500 (94.4)	385 (5.6)	6885 (100)

Source: Primary data

High perception indicates rapid progress and vice-versa. The perception of customers regarding availability of regular records, opinion about direct contact and their trust on employees or on machinery plays an important role in evaluating the perception of customers towards e-banking services.

Table 6.27 indicates that 72.2 per cent (4971) customers are getting regular records of their account transactions and others are not receiving the regular records.

43.3 per cent (2980) customers think that the adoption and use of e-banking services is the way of avoiding the customers from banks.

Table 6.27 indicates that out of 6885 sample customers, 94.4 per cent (6500) customers have trust on bank employees whereas 5.6 per cent (385) customers believe on the technological device.

6.5 Summing Up

The researcher has studied all the three cooperative banks and found that the progress of these cooperative banks is comparatively slow than other banking sector and the cause may that cooperative banks are services oriented and also managed and controlled according to the cooperative sector law. But after introduction of new economic reforms in banking sector, maximum numbers of banks are providing techno-based services to their customers. Due to features of 24*7 services, quick access, online shopping, cashless transactions customers are giving their preference to the banks which are providing various types of techno-based services. Nearby all the branches of banks are providing techno-based services to its customers. Banks are facing various problems in providing these services but they are in developing stage, and a few of them are developed and competing with other banks also. Customers' loyalty is depends on the availability of services, quality of services and the satisfaction achieved from transactions made with the help of e-banking technology.

Though the structure of cooperative banks is spread in all over India; its administration and management system is decentralized and the purpose of establishment of banks is also different (based on the needs of local persons/ members). Thus the network of branches is found limited. Techno-based services are provided to the bank customers but these services are available for the current account holders and saving account holders only and it is realized that the number of saving account holders are more than the number of current account holders. The numbers of female users are nearby equal to the male users and the preference of younger customers is more than the customers from other age groups; well educated customers have positive attitude at e-banking services thus their numbers are more.

The customers working in public sectors units are comparatively more because the salary is credited through banks and thus it becomes necessary to open an account into public sector banks. 47.6 per cent customers prefer public sector, private sector and co-operative sector for investment. 22.1per cent customers prefer for cooperative sector, customers prefer security, relation and available facility in to the bank and are also interested in keeping their relations with bank employees. Many customers experienced that e-banking services are comparatively easy to use than manual/traditional transaction system and they believe on techno-based services provided with the help of internet services providers and techniques, they experience that these services are fully reliable and so they are using e-banking services frequently and also take benefits of anytime anywhere services.

Today customers need more efficient services (without any interruption) and if any problem occurred they need instant solution on their problems. Customers have trust on employees and not on machines so banks have to keep and to raise their relations with customers by providing more efficient and more valuable services.

Findings and Recommendations

7.1 Introduction

Whether the bank unit is large, medium or small, as an impact of globalization, it is necessary to provide various techno-based services to their customers. These techno-based services play an important role in the financial inclusion of banks. This study attempted to examine the impact of behavioral, perceptual and attitudinal factors of bank manager and bank employees on the adoption and usage of techno-based e-banking services provided by Co-operative banks in Nasik District. This research work was conducted to focus on the current and prompt technological revolution controlling the whole banking sector on state, national and on international levels and also to examine the perception of bank customers and bank employees on the adoption and its usage such as ATMs, Debit/Credit Cards, Phone Banking, Mobile Banking, Internet Banking, Online payment of Bills, RTGS/EFT, etc. This research study also focuses on those factors which are reflecting the progress of Co-operative banks as compared to the other banking sectors such as adoption level of techno-based services (extent of adoption of technology), perception of customers regarding quality of services, satisfaction level of customers, etc.

A random sample of 9916 individual customers and 13 managers of (20 per cent) sample banks were selected and the questionnaire method was used to understand the behaviour of bank managers and perception of bank customers. But only 6885 questionnaires were prompt and thus selected for the study. The sample covered 2985 customers from current account and 3900 customers from saving account in which 3469 are male customers and 3416 are female customers. The result included adoption levels, perception about service quality, Customers' satisfaction and usage pattern. Three hypotheses were proposed for the research work and all of them were tested using appropriate logical and tabular method.

The ratio of literate and younger's is greater than the other customers. It was observed that saving behaviour of the individuals of public sector employees is more and the attitude of female customers is also growing at investment, it showed changing dynamics of the saving behaviour of female customers. For the entire research work, two different questionnaires for bank managers and for customers were framed in such a manner that it would reveal the following-

1. Which types of e-banking services are provided by banks to their customers?
2. What is the satisfaction level of customers while using e-banking services?
3. What is the current financial position of banks for providing technical infrastructure facilities?
4. Which types of problems faced by bank employees and by customers while using techno-based E-Banking services?
5. Which types of special facilities are available in bank for disabled and illiterate customers?
6. What benefits do the banks gain from providing E-Banking services?
7. Overall utility of bank employee's performance for bank customers towards e-banking services.

The present study work entitled "A study of E-banking services provided by Co-operative Banks in Nasik District" is aimed at finding the quality of techno-based services, its impact on financial position of banks, progress of cooperative banks, perception and satisfaction of customers and of bank employees from these services.

7.2 Summary of Work Done

Title of this research project is "A study of E-banking services provided by Co-operative Banks in Nasik District" and it is presented in seven chapters as detailed below:

Chapter 1: Introduction and Research Design

Chapter 1 covers the introduction to the topic under study and the theoretical framework of the topic under research. It includes an Introduction to Co-operation, Development of Co-operative Banks and Evolution of E-banking services in banking sector. This chapter ends with a narration of research methodology in the conduct of this research.

Chapter 2: Review of Literature

Chapter 2 contains the theoretical and conceptual aspects of related literature of e-banking technology adopted by banks and impact of e-banking technology on banking sector, competitive strategy of banks, advantages and disadvantages, etc.

Chapter 3: Socio-Economic profile of Nasik District

Chapter 3 deal with the role of banking sector in the economic development of Maharashtra and also covers the ratio of banking sector in the development of Nashik district.

Chapter 4: E-banking: A Theoretical framework

Chapter 4 is devoted to the theoretisation of the research topic related with working definitions and the progress of banking sector after introduction of New Economic Reform Policy 1991.

Chapter 5: Business Analysis of Banks

Chapter 5 presents Analysis of Business of Sample Banks.

Chapter 6: Management of Customers' services with E-banking Services

Chapter 6 is an in-depth study of Management of Customers Services with E-banking services.

Chapter 7: Findings and Suggestions

This chapter devoted to; findings of the work with reference to objectives set in advance, testing of hypotheses and suggestions with regard to changes needed in the development of techno-based e-banking services. The next part of this chapter follows findings on Bank Managers and Bank Customers with their perception, attitude, awareness, problems, remedies and satisfaction which are discussed in detail.

7.3 Findings-

In the findings, Researcher has focused on findings related to the branches of Nasik District. The findings are related to the perception of bank employees, various types of e-banking services provided by banks, quality of e-banking services, problems faced by bank employees and by customers while using e-banking services, quality improvement programs organized by banks, facilities available for illiterate and differently enabled customers, impact of e-banking services on the business of banks etc.

7.3.1 Findings on the feedback of Bank Managers

1. As per the report of Rural Bank Association of Nasik District, there are 49 registered Co-operative banks but a very few banks have their branches elsewhere. As an impact of globalization, many banks have established their branches elsewhere. There are 64 cooperative banks which have their branches in Nashik District and have adopted e-banking technology. For this reason, the researcher has based her sample selection on the basis of 20 per cent banks from total number of banks which are providing e-banking services to their customers.

2. Among these 13 sample Co-operative Banks, only 2 branches, one each of NMC and another is GPPJS bank which are rural in nature and maximum number of branches of these banks are in rural areas. But all the remaining 11 branches are urban in nature. The banks having multi-branches and providing maximum types of e-banking services are selected. All the 13 branches in the sample Co-operative banks are mainly concentrated in urban areas and less in rural areas.
3. Adoption of e-banking technology Without adoption of e-banking services, it is impossible to survive in banking sector and thus Co-operative banks have also adopted the e-banking technology and are providing these services to their customers. Cooperative banks have adopted these services one by one from 21st century and today all cooperative banks are providing all types of e-banking services through all the branches. (Table 5.1)
4. Branch expansion of banks There are only 46.15 per cent (6 banks) banks which have their network in all over the nation. Only 38.46 per cent (5) banks have their network in Maharashtra and there are only 15.38 per cent (2 banks) banks which are working only in Nashik district. From all the branches of cooperative banks, 25 per cent branches are in other states whereas remaining 75 per cent branches are in Maharashtra and only 15.5 per cent are in Nasik District. It indicated that the geographical scope of Co operative banks is growing /developing. (Table 5.2)
5. Gender wise classification of Branch managers The ratio of male managers are 76.92 per cent (10), and the female Managers are 23.1 per cent (3). It is clear that the numbers of female managers are increasing but maximum numbers of branches are dominated by male Managers. (Table 5.3)

6. Educational qualifications only 23.1 per cent (3) post-graduates managers and 53.84 per cent (7) graduates, followed by 15.38 per cent diploma holders (2). Among the graduates, 15.38 per cent (2) are holding GDC&A diploma. It indicated that the educational qualifications of the branch managers of Co-operative banks are very high and so are ready for accepting new technology in banking. (Table 5.3)

7. Age wise classification of managers It indicated that in the Co-operative banks there is a maximum number of Managers (46.15 per cent) are in the senior age groups of 36-50 and 51-60 age groups constituting 6 each, followed by one managers from Co-operative bank which is in the age group of 26-50 years. It indicated that the branch managers from Co-operative banks are more senior and the reason may be that the vacancies in the Co-operative banks are filled on promotion base. This may also the reason of low level of adoption of new trends in banking sectors. (Table 5.3)

8. Distribution of E-banking services in the group of e-banking services it observed that all Co-operative banks are providing all types of e-banking services through their branches.

9. Number of E-banking services users In Co-operative banks, preferential services are ATM, Phone Banking and Mobile Banking and Internet banking services because except ATMs service other services are providing in free of cost and also provided to all the customers. Cent per cent customers from all the banks are using ATM, Phone Banking and Mobile Banking and Internet banking services. 64.42 per cent Customers are using Debit/Credit Cards followed by 9.38 per cent customers who are using service of online bill payment. (Table 5.4)

10. Number of branches providing e-banking services 84.61 per cent Branches of Co-operative banks (11)

are providing all types of e-services through their branches, whereas another 7.69 per cent branch each (1 each) of GPPJS (46 branches) and JKS (09 branches) bank ltd are providing these services through more than 50 per cent services and in less than 50 per cent branches respectively. (Table 5.5)

11. Number of ATM centers in sample branches There are 1298 ATM centers of Co-operative banks out of which 94.53 per cent (1227 centers) ATMs are located in urban area and remaining 5.47 per cent (71 centers) are in rural area. It showed that the network of e-banking is spread in urban area and very less in rural areas and cooperative banks are keener in providing liberal services to urban community rather than rural. (Table 5.6)

12. Time required for solving problems of customers, 4 branches (30.8 per cent) are capable of solving the problems of ATMs instantly. 3 Branches each (23.1 per cent) resolve the problems within 3 days, within a week and are unable to solve the problems due to absence of technical staff respectively. (Table 5.7)

13. Availability of 24*7*365 days helpline facility 53.8 per cent (7) branches of cooperative banks, provide 24*7*365 helpline assistance but the remaining 46.2 per cent branches (6) provide helpline assistance only during office hours. (Table 5.8)

14. Availability of information and guidelines regarding use of e-banking services 69.2 per cent branches of Co-operative bank (9) have their information or guidelines for using e-banking on website and 30.8 per cent branches (4) have not yet developed their website or have not given any information or guidelines for using e-banking services. (Table 5.9)

15. Awareness of customers about transactional security 53.8 per cent branches of Co-operative banks (7) customers are fully aware about their transaction security. Customers of remaining 46.2 per cent

branches (6) are less aware about their transaction security or have less knowledge about their transactions. Thus their frequency for using these services is also comparatively less and they prefer for manual transactions. Banks need to organize training programs and have to introduce new policies for improving the awareness of customers. (Table 5.10)

16. Training programs for customers, Only 53.84 per cent branches of Co-operative banks (7) banks have prepared Demo Videos, but remaining 46.15 per cent branches (6) did nothing to motivate the customers. (Table 5.11)

17. Means of Motivation As per table 5.11 all the branches of Co-operative banks are making face to face communication with the customers to motivate them for using e-banking services by giving advertisement, by publishing advantages of these services in pamphlets', reports, newspapers, booklets or in journals also.

18. Satisfaction from technical support As per table 5.12, Managers of 15.4 per cent branches of Co-operative Banks (2) expressed very high satisfaction whereas another 38.5 per cent branch managers (5) expressed high satisfaction, followed by 23.1 per cent branch managers each (3) agreed to moderate satisfaction and low satisfaction respectively about technical service providers.

19. Special assistance to physically enabled customers It is revealed that only 30.76 per cent (4) branches of Co-operative banks, namely; SVC Bank and Cosmos Cooperative Bank, Saraswat Cooperative bank and MSC bank limited, none of the remaining 69.23 per cent (9) branches of Co-operative banks provide any special assistance to physically disabled persons.

20. Special assistance to illiterate customers The facility for illiterate customers is available in all the branches

of Co-operative and other branches of Nashik District. In case the illiterate customer is found incapable of grasping the message, any person on the nearby counter advises such customer with utmost care in any of the branch offices. Therefore, helping an illiterate customer is not at all a serious problem in the area under study.

21. Use of cookie software Cookie is one of the software which helps to the bankers in identifying their customers. As this it helps to the customers in identifying their number of transactions made during a particular period. However, identifying a customer at the bank is not so difficult problem thus no any bank is using this software.

22. Growth in deposits This is a clear indication from table 5.13 that the progress in the growth of deposits is slowest among 69.23 per cent Co-operative banks as compared to other banks. In other words, depositors feel less safe with their deposits in Co-operative Banks as compared to other banks. Less flexibility of operations may be a cause of neglecting cooperative banks for deposits.

23. Advances provided to customers The growth trend clearly indicate, that the advances of Co-operative banks grown fastest during these 5 years from 100 to 195.4, This is an indicator of credit deposit ratio being highest in case of Co-operative bank branches. (Table 5.14)

24. Reserves available in banks Table 5.16 indicate that provision for reserves made and accumulated by the Co-operative banks is growing fastest in case of Co-operative banks from 100 in 2008-09 to 183.7 in 2012-13. The reason may be that the 25 per cent amount should be reserved per year from profit.

25. Profits and losses Table 5.17 clearly show that all the banks are making profits during the period under review. The branches of Co-operative banks have

made 99.2 per cent gain. And 15.38 per cent banks have their profit more than 100 per cent and no any bank was suffered in loss during last five years. Perhaps it is the result of adoption of e-banking technology.

26. Net Performing Assets (NPA) As per table 5.19, NPAs of all banks are declining at a much faster rate during recent times. SVC bank is top most efficient in bringing down NPAs to zero in 2009-10 and maintaining the same at zero till the end of 2012-13. NMC could reduce its NPAs from 2.1 per cent in 2008-09 to 1.7 per cent in 2009-10 and further to 1.1 per cent in 2010-11. NMC has brought her NPAs to zero since 2011-12 onwards. Remaining 84.61 per cent Co-operative Banks are gradually bringing down their NPAs but could not reduce it to zero even in 2012-13.

27. Problems faced by managers Most severe problem faced by 92.3 per cent (12) managers of Co-operative banks is technological, followed by socio-cultural problems faced by 61.5 per cent (8) managers, Transactional problems faced by 53.8 per cent (7) managers and the least 38.5 who managers had Managerial problems in providing e-services to their customers.

7.3.2 Findings on Data Analysis of customers

1. Number of account holders Table 6.1 showed the number of current and saving account holders and it is realized that the number of saving account holders (3900) are more than the number of current account holders (2985).

2. Gender wise distribution of customers indicated that 50.4 per cent (3469) males and 49.6 per cent (3416) females are using e-banking services and the number of male customers using e-banking services are little more than female customers. It is a welcome feature

of positive social change in Indian society that offers equal participation of women along males in economic activities. (Table 6.2)

3. Age-wise distribution of sample customers Table 6.3 indicated that 55.6 per cent (3827) respondents are from the age group of 26 years to 45 years and 4.1 per cent (281) customers from the age group of 18 to 25 years. It shows that the numbers of customers from the age group of 26 to 45 years are relatively more than the customers from other age groups. (Table 6.3)

4. Level of education of customers It observed that there is majority of educated customers which are using techno-based services. 34.2 per cent (2356) customers are post graduate and 25.5 per cent (1752) customers have their education till 10th (SSC). 21.9 per cent (1508) customers are graduates and 15.9 per cent (1097) customers are 12th (HSC). There are only 2.5 per cent diploma holders. It indicated that most of the customers are well educated. (Table 6.4)

5. Distribution of customers by their occupation It noted that the numbers of public sector employees are comparatively more in opening their account into banks and are using techno-based e-banking services that the 41.3 per cent (2845) customers are from public services followed by businessmen with 26.9 per cent (1851). The customers from public sector and from businessmen have greater positive approach towards banking sector. The number of farmers and employees from private sector are 12.8 per cent and 19 per cent respectively, (Table 6.6)

6. Annual Income Table 6.6 indicates that 48.6 per cent (3349) customers are having annual income of their Rs. 3.1 lakh to 5 lakh, followed by 28.9 per cent (1992) customers whose annual family income is up to Rs. 3 Lakh and 22.4 per cent (1544) customers have their annual family income above Rs. 5.1 lakh. It shows

that majority of the customers are from the income group of Rs.3.1 lakh to 5 lakh and thus they need banking facility for the purpose of security for their income/investment.

7. Preferences of sectors for saving and investment It is observed that 47.6 per cent (3277) customers prefer all three sectors for investment. 22.1 per cent (1518) customers prefer for Co-operative sector, followed by 18.6 per cent (1284) customers who prefer to PSB for investment purpose. Only 11.7 per cent customers prefer their investment in private sector. It indicated that customers' preference is not guided by ownership pattern of banks but by personal convenience of customers. (Table 6.7)

8. Factors considered by customers while opening an account into banks It noted that 35 per cent (2408) customers prefer security, relation and available facility in to the bank while opening an account, and 34.1 per cent (2346) customers who prefer available facility in the bank as a top most important reason for opening an account. Compared with other factors, relationship is considered as least important by majority of customers. (Table 6.8)

9. Factors considered by customers for using e-banking services Table 6.9 indicates that, Most of the customers prefer Public (53.2 per cent) or Private (50.2 per cent) sector bank for using e-banking services. A very few customers (17.7 per cent) prefer cooperative banks for using e-banking services and 20.7 per cent (1424) customers prefer all or any sector for this purpose. (Table 6.9)

10. Preference of customers towards banking sector As per table 6.10, the customers prefer to non-cooperative banks due to the causes of reliability (54.2 per cent), maximum number of branches (52.2 per cent), availability of services (46.4 per cent) and inter-bank connectivity (45.2 per cent) of these banks. It noted that reliability is the most important factor in the views of customers.

11. Perception of customers at e-banking services As per table 6.11, 66.8 per cent (4597) customers have proper information, 82.8 per cent (5699) experienced that e-banking services are comparatively easy to use than manual/traditional transaction system. Further 80.1 per cent (5512) customers, using debit/credit cards have little more knowledge about these instruments and thus they are using it. Another 89.6 per cent (6167) customers are suspicious about theft/mis-use of cards and so they are avoiding these services. Only 65.8 per cent customers believed on techno-based services provided with the help of internet services providers and techniques, thus they are enjoying e-banking services.

12. Feedback of customers' on reliability of e-transactions it noted that 30.9 per cent (2127) customers feel that e-transactions are partially reliable followed by 25.6 per cent (1763) customers which opined that these services are reliable in exceptional cases only. 22.0 per cent (1513) customers declared that these services are not reliable in any way and only 21.5 per cent (1482) customers opined that these services are fully reliable. It resulted that around 80 per cent customers feel that these transactions are not dependable. (Table 6.12)

13. Number of customers using e-banking services it observed that 67.1 per cent (5548) customers are using ATM services, phone banking services and mobile banking services of the banks, and 23.5 per cent (1778) customers are using debit/credit card services. 22.0 per cent (1830) customers are using e-banking services only for the purpose of RTGS/EFT, followed by 17.1 per cent Internet Banking users. 15.3 per cent customers are using e-banking services only for the purpose of online payment of bills. It is cleared that least of e-banking services such as ATMs, Phone banking and Mobile banking services are preferred by most of the customers. (Table 6.13)

14. Feelings of safety in use of e-banking services 79.5 per cent (5470) customers feel safety while using ATM services. Only 5.1 per cent Phone banking service users feel safety while using the services. It observed that use of ATM services is safer than the others and so the preference of customers is comparatively more for this service. (Table 6.14)

15. Frequency of using e-banking services it observed that 30.9 per cent (2127) customers are using e-banking services weekly, and 25.7 per cent (1768) customers are using these services twice in a week. 21.3 per cent (1466) customers are using these services anytime as per their need, and there are only 21.3 per cent (1524) customers which are using these services daily. (Table 6.15)

16. Number of customers using e-banking services 84.4 per cent (5814) customers enjoying benefits of SMS alerts, and 32.3 per cent customers. 17.3 per cent (1191) customers get 24*7 days facility, and only 11.8 per cent (811) customers have high transaction frequency. It noted that maximum number of customers using SMS service due to availability of quick transactional records and also provided free of cost. (Table 6.16)

17. Satisfaction of customers with e-banking services As per table 6.17, 29.9 per cent customers are satisfied in exceptional cases only, followed by 25.8 per cent customers who are partially satisfied. 22.2 per cent customers are not satisfied with e-banking/ technological services. There are only 22.1 per cent customers who are fully satisfied with the e-banking services of banks and they are enjoying the benefits of these services.

18. Feelings of security while performing e-transactions through website It opined that 29.7 per cent (2044) customers are partially secured while performing e-transactions through website, and 26.7 per cent

(1841) customers think that e-transactions are secured in exceptional cases. 24.2 per cent (1664) customers experienced that e-transactions performing through websites are fully secured, followed by 19.4 per cent (1336) customers who think that e-transactions are not secured in any way. Due to this experience customers neglected Internet banking services. (Table 6.18)

19. Satisfaction of customers regarding available information It noted that 43.1 per cent (2964) customers are partially satisfied, and 38.9 per cent customers are fully satisfied. 10.1 per cent (697) customers are partially satisfied. 7.9 per cent (546) customers are not satisfied with the information available on website of banks regarding e-banking services. Majority of customers are satisfied with the available information and thus they are using e-banking services. (Table 6.19)

20. Expectations of customers about e-banking services provided by banks It indicated that 41.1 per cent customers wanted availability of maximum number of e-banking services, and 39.4 per cent customers who have all expectations from the banks. 11.4 per cent customers wanted maximum cooperation from bank employees for solving the problems raised while performing e-banking services followed by 8.2 per cent customers who needed more efficient services. And due to more efficient services number of customers will be attract at e-banking services. (Table 6.20)

21. Problems encountered to the customers while performing e-banking transactions It observed that 92.2 per cent (6349) customers are facing the problem of technological/operational followed by 33.8 per cent (2330) customers facing the managerial problem. 25.9 per cent (1784) customers are facing socio-cultural problems thus they neglected e-banking services. (Table 6.21)

22. Solution on problems encountered by customers while using e-banking transactions 27.4 per cent (1893) customers reported that e-banking problems are solved within a week, and 27.0 per cent (1859) customers defined that the e-banking problems are solved within 2 days from the day of complaint registered. Whereas 24.6 per cent (1694) customers pointed that the problems are solved instantly when the problems are registered, followed by 20.9 per cent (1439) customers who opined that the problems are solved within a quarter. (Table 6.22)

23. Necessity and availability of various facilities to the customers It indicated that

    a) 71.1 per cent (4893) customers get proper suggestions and guidelines as their requirements from the banks.

    b) 57.5 per cent (3957) customers need proper training from the banks for improving their satisfaction by fulfilling their expectations.

    c) 54.8 per cent (3775) customers get accurate and detailed information from the banks on their accounts as their requirements.

    d) 51.9 per cent (3572) customers have laptop/computer/android mobile phones for getting the information available through internet. (Table 6.23)

24. Service charges charged by banks from customers 36.6 per cent (2522) customers replied that the banks charges are exorbitant, followed by 34.9 per cent (2402) customers who replied that the services charges are much higher than reasonable. Whereas 15.9 per cent (1093) customers opined that the charges are little more than reasonable, and 12.6 per cent (868) customers opined that the bank charges are quite reasonable. (Table 6.24)

25. Satisfaction of customers regarding availability of infrastructural facilities Table 6.25 indicated that 31.9

per cent (2200) customers are fully satisfied, and 32.3 per cent (2220) customers are partially satisfied but 16.4 per cent (1129) customers are not satisfied with regards to the infrastructural facilities provided to the customers by the banks respect to the e-banking services.

26. Purpose of using e-banking services 86.7 per cent (5970) customers are using e-banking services for the purpose of withdrawal of cash, and 37.2 per cent (2558) customers are using e-banking services for the purpose of balance inquiry. 14.1 per cent customers are using these services for transfer of money from one account to others' account. Only 8.8 per cent customers are using these services for other purposes. It indicated that majority of customers prefer these services for cash withdrawal and for balance enquiry. (Table 6.26)
27. Perception of customers on usage of e-banking services It is observed that

    a) 72.2 per cent (4971) customers are getting regular records of their account transactions and remaining is not.

    b) 43.3 per cent (2980) customers think that the adoption and use of e-banking services is the way of avoiding interface with the customers by banks.

    c) 94.4 per cent (6500) customers have trust on bank employees whereas 5.6 per cent (385) customers believe on the technological machines. (Table 6.27)

7.4 Testing of Hypotheses

Researcher has tested following statements of hypotheses through the study at hand:

1 H_1: "E-banking Services in Co-operative banks:

a. E-banking services in cooperative banks are slowly developing.

It is evidenced from the researcher's finding revealed from Table 5.1 that the span of adapting e-banking services of the sample branches of cooperative banks from 2002 to 2012 during this period, gradually all the cooperative banks have adopted provision of e-banking services one by one. Except 30.76 per cent branches, all the remaining 69.23 per cent (09) banks have adopted this technology in the first decade of 21st century.

Table 5.5 indicated that a few banks (15.38 per cent) are not providing e-banking services through their all branches and they are in developing process. However, the process of expansion of these services is very slow. Thus this statement of hypothesis is accepted.

b. E-banking services in cooperative banks are slowly accepted by customers."

From the table 6.10, it is revealed that (54.2 per cent) most of the customers prefer non-cooperative banks for e-banking purpose.

Table 6.11 showed perception of customers and it revealed that a very few (average 22.8 per cent) customers have negative perception for using e-banking services.

As per table 6.12, 22.0 per cent (1513) customers revealed that these services are not reliable.

As per table 6.13, 67.1 per cent (5548) customers are using ATMs services, Phone banking and Mobile banking services and a few customers are using other services.

Table 6.14 indicated that a few (79.5 per cent) customers feel safety in using these services.

As per table 6.16 all the customers of banks are not enjoying the benefits of e-banking services. This proves our statement of hypothesis. So this statement of hypotheses is also accepted.

2 H_2: E-banking services have positive impact on the development (business) of cooperative banks.

Table 5.14 indicated that the progress in the growth of deposits is slowest among 69.23 per cent Co-operative banks

As per Table 5.15 the advances of Co-operative banks have grown fastest during these 5 years from 100 to 195.4 per cent. This is an indicator of credit deposit ratio being highest in case of Co-operative bank branches. ()

Table 5.17 indicated that provision for reserves made and accumulated by the Co-operative banks is growing fastest in case of Co-operative banks from 100 in 2008-09 to 183.7 in 2012-13.

Table 5.18 clearly showed that all the banks are making profits during the period under review. The branches of Co-operative banks have made 99.2 per cent gain. And 15.38 per cent banks have their profit more than 100 per cent

As per table 5.20, NPAs of all banks are declining at a much faster rate during recent times. 84.61 per cent Co-operative Banks are gradually bringing down their NPAs but could not reduce it to zero. This proves our statement of hypothesis. So this statement of hypotheses is also accepted.

3 H_3: Customers in need of e-banking services prefer Public and Private sector banks rather than cooperative banks

From the table 6.9, just 17.7 per cent customers (1222) exclusively relay on services of cooperative banks remaining 82.3 per cent (5663) customers depend either on Public sector, Private sector or a combination of all the three types of banks. This proves our statement of hypothesis. So this statement of hypotheses is also accepted.

7.5 Recommendations

1. All types of Cooperative banks have to adopt new technology and to provide maximum types of e-

banking services to their customers; it means banks have to shift themselves from brick banking to click banking.

2. Awareness regarding use of e-banking services should be created among the bank customers by organizing seminars, workshops, training programs, etc.
3. Bank customers should shift from traditional banking to e-banking.
4. Banks should provide ATM at more places.
5. E-banking services should be provided either free of cost or at less cost and the amount would be involved in other banking transactions.
6. Banks have to adopt cookies software for controlling frauds.
7. The bank should plan to introduce new schemes for attracting new customers and satisfying the present ones.
8. Customers think that e-banking is not trustful so Banks have to improve reliability among customers regarding the events of frauds in e-banking services. Thus Banks should improve their services in terms of processing time.
9. Unfortunately, due to a policy of "profits for the company but losses to be borne by the government" has made a number of these operations inefficient. Thus government has to provide financial assistance only to those banks which have adopted modern technology.
10. Management make greater impact on the development of banking sector thus dormant membership and lack of active participation of members in the management of Co-operatives banks is important.
11. Government has to appoint administrators/special committee for the development of cooperative banks.

12. Lack of mobilization of internal resources and over-dependence on Government assistance is also a cause of less development of banks instead this lack of professional management is also a cause of less development.
13. Bureaucratic control and interference in the management, political interference and over-polarization have proved harmful to the development of cooperative bank. Thus it has to remove or to liberalize.
14. Government of India and RBI, both have to lead for the development of cooperative banks by introducing new policies/development schemes.
15. Financial inclusion policies and other development policies should be similar for cooperative banks and other banks.
16. All cooperative banks have to develop inclusive fiscal policy which will useful for all banks.
17. Banks have to appoint skillful and trustful person as a Planning and Development Officer and also have to appoint proper technical staff to handle e-banking system.
18. Registrar of cooperative banks has to appoint an auditor for regular auditing purpose and for controlling mal-practices.
19. Total automation should be made in all cooperative banks and GoI/RBI has to finance for this purpose to cooperative banks.
20. Rural development is the base of cooperative sector thus banks have to focus on the development of rural area by establishing new branches in rural areas.
21. To enhance the transparency and security, alerts should be provided to customers for each type of e-services while doing any type of banking transactions. Alerts should be provided through mail, SMS or post and this service should be free of cost at the initiative of banks itself.

7.6 Areas for further research

Following are some topics on which the researcher herself would have loved to work, but she couldn't because of the limitation of time. However, young researchers who wish to try their work in the new era of modern banking, they may choose any one or a part of the topics suggested below:

1) Similar research study could be done out regarding the adoption of technology based banking services in Metro-Politian cities, urban areas, semi-urban areas and in rural areas also.
2) In the globalised era, banks are looking at the financial inclusion through various factors and thus there is scope for further study on the financial inclusion in various types of banks through e-banking services.
3) Further study may take place on the theme of impact of technology based banking services on the priority sectors or on the corporate sector.
4) Progress or growth of banking sector through technology based banking services could be a research topic for further study.
5) All the techniques which are used in the study could be utilized to capture the attitude of customers on various issues of e-banking services and to insights into the adoption of technology solutions in other sectors such as retailing, insurance services, transports, communication, travelling, and tourism and so on.

7.7 Summing Up

From this research work it is fond that all types of banks are providing techno-based e-banking services to their customers such as ATMs, Debit/Credit Cards, Phone banking, Mobile banking, Internet banking, RTGS/EFT, Online bill payment facility, etc. Though these services are emerged in foreign/ developed nations; now-a-days these services are also adopted by developing nations and undeveloped nations. In India, these services are provided by all types of public sector banks and private sector banks. Later on many units of Co-operative banks are also providing techno-based e-banking services to their customers.

From the category of e-banking services, ATMs are widely adopted by the customers of all banks and other services are not merely adopted by the customers. Customers prefer personal contact, personal relationships and personal satisfaction from the banks. Instead this mutual trust between bank employees and customers also play an important role in the development of banking sector. Credibility of bank services are also plays an important role in the development of banking services.

LIST OF ABBREVIATIONS

AC	-	Ahmednagar Cooperative Bank Ltd
AIFI	-	All India Financial Institution
AML	-	Anti-Money Laundering
ANBC	-	Adjusted Net Bank Credit
ATM	-	Automated Teller Machine
AUC	-	Abhyuday Urban Cooperative Bank Ltd
BCBS	-	Basel Committee on Banking Supervision
BFS	-	Board for Financial Supervision
BMC	-	Bombay Merchantile Cooperative Bank Ltd
BO	-	Banking Ombudsman
BOI	-	Bank of India
BPR	-	Business Process Re-engineering
BPSS	-	Board for Regulation and Supervision of Payment and Settlement Systems
BR Act	-	Banking Regulations Act
CBS	-	Core Banking Solutions
CC	-	Cosmos Cooperative Bank Ltd
CCB	-	Committee of the Central Board

CCIL	-	Clearing Corporation of India Ltd.
CD	-	Certificate of Deposits
CDS	-	Current Daily Status
CPC	-	Cheque Processing Centre
CPSS	-	Committee on Payment and Settlement Systems
CR	-	Contingency Reserve
CRA	-	Credit Rating Agency
CRAR	-	Capital to Risk weighted Assets Ratio
CRR	-	Cash Reserve Ratio
CSDs	-	Central Securities Depositories
CTS	-	Cheque Truncation System
DBT	-	Direct Benefit Transfer
DCCBs	-	District Central Co-operative Banks
EBT	-	Electronic Benefit Transfer
ECCS	-	Express Cheque Clearing Systems
ECS	-	Electronic Clearing Service
FDI	-	Foreign Direct Investment
FI	-	Financial Inclusion
FII	-	Foreign Institutional Investor
GCC	-	General Credit Card
GDP	-	Gross Domestic Product
GDR	-	Global Depositary Receipt
GoI	-	Government of India
GPPJS	-	Gopinath Patil Parsik Janata Sahakari Bank Ltd

IB	-	Internet Banking
IBA	-	Indian Banks' Association
ICT	-	Information and Communication Technology
IDRBT	-	Institute for Development and Research in Banking Technology
IFC	-	Indian Financial Code
IFSC	-	Indian Financial Security code
IS	-	Information System
IT	-	Information Technology
ITes	-	Information Technology-enabled services
JKS	-	Jankalyan Sahakari Bank Ltd
KYC	-	Know Your Customer
LAB	-	Local Area Bank
LBS	-	Lead Bank Scheme
LLP	-	Limited Liability Partnership
LTD	-	Long Term Deposits
LTV	-	Loan to Value
MB	-	Mobile banking
MC	-	Mahanagar Cooperative Bank Ltd
MICR	-	Magnetic Ink Character Recognition
MSC	-	Maharashtra State Cooperative Bank Ltd
NABARD	-	National Bank for Agriculture and Rural Development
NACH	-	National Automated Clearing House
NBFC	-	Non-Banking Financial Company

NBFI	-	Non-bank Financial Institution
NEFT	-	National Electronic Fund Transfer
NHB	-	National Housing Bank
NMC	-	Nashik Merchant Cooperative Bank Ltd
NPA	-	Non Performing Asset
NRDVS	-	Nashik Road Deolali Vyapari Sahakari Ltd
NSE	-	National Stock Exchange
PC	-	Personal Computer
PIN	-	Personal Identification Number
PIN	-	Personal Identification Number
PMC	-	Punjab & Maharashtra Cooperative Bank Ltd
PPP	-	Public Private Partnership
PSB	-	Public Sector Banks
PSEs	-	Public Sector Enterprises
PSL	-	Priority Sector Lending
RBI	-	Reserve Bank of India
RBI	-	Reserve Bank of India
RRB	-	Regional Rural Bank
RTGS	-	Real Time Gross Settlement
RTI Act	-	Right to Information Act
SAA	-	Swap Amortization Account
SBI	-	State Bank of India
SC	-	Saraswat Cooperative Bank Ltd
SCB	-	Scheduled Commercial Bank
SEBI	-	Securities Exchange Board of India

SHGs	-	Self-Help Groups
SMS	-	Short Messaging Service
SSTs	-	Self-Service Technologies
SVC	-	Shamrao Vitthal Cooperative Bank Ltd
SWIFT	-	Society for World Wide Inter-Bank Financial Tele-Communication
SWIFT	-	Society for Worldwide Inter-bank
TB	-	Tele banking/Telephone banking
TEBSS	-	Technology-Enabled Self-Services
UCBs	-	Urban Cooperative Banks
UIDAI	-	Unique Identification Authority of India
WAP	-	Wireless Application Protocol

Bibliography

1. Books

Mathur B.S., (2005), *'Co-operation in India'*, Sahitya Bhavan, Agra, Pp-73

Gokhale S.D. (2009), *'Problems & Prospectus of Rural Development in Maharashtra'*, Shrividya Prakashan, Pune, Pp-46-48

Sangale B.R., Sangale G.T., Kayandepatil, Pawar N.C., *'Indian Banking System'*, Chaitanya Publication, Nagpur, Pp-6.16-6.22

Kunjukunju Benson, *'Commercial Banks in India: Growth, Challenges & Strategies'*, First Edition 2008, New Century Publications, New Delhi, Pp-184-89

Bhagwati, Jagdish (1993), *'Banking for Rural Development'*, Clarendon Press, Oxford Publication

Datta, Sundaram (2012), 63rd Edition, *'Indian Economy'*, S. Chand Publication, New Delhi, Pp-593-597

Tripathy S.N. (2000), *'Cooperative: Growth and New Dimensions'*, Discovery Publishing House, New Delhi

Seetaraman S.P., Mohanan N., (1986), *'Framework for studying Cooperative Organisation'*, Oxford & IB Publishing Company, New Delhi

Dwiwedi Shyam Mohan & Mishra Hridya Narayan, Ranjana Patel, *'Service Sector in India: Growth Potential'*, Service Sector in India- Editorial, Adhyayan Publications, Pune, Pp-46-51

Rabindra Kumar Mishra, (2013) *'New Avenues in Banking sector'*, Economic Development in India, AVON publication, New Delhi, 1st Edition,: Pp-60

Poonia, M.S., *'Development Banking in India'*, Pratiksha publication, Jaipur (2013), Pp-91

Rangarajan C., *'Know Your Banking,'* RBI press, Mumbai, Pp-14-15

Swami.R, Gupta B.L., *'Rural Development & Cooperation in India'*, Indus Valley Publications, New Delhi, Pp-17-21

Kohok M. A. (1993), Financial Services in India, *'Credit Cards'*, First Edition, Digvijay Publication, Nashik, Pp-257-261

Jhingan M.L., Cooperative Banks in India, *'Money, Banking, International Trade and Public Finance'*, 7th Edition, 2008, Vrinda Publications, pp-605-606

Ahluwalia Rupali (2008), Service Sector in India, *'Banking Services-Vision and Prospects'*, Adhyayan publication, New Delhi, editorial, , pp-70-72

Bhaskaran R. (Chief Executive Officer-RBI-2011), Know Your Banking, *'Electronic Banking'*, Pp-111

Padhye, Kishor C. and Mishra Rakesh Roshan (2013), A to Z banking and finance, Himalaya Publishing House, First Edition, 2013, Pp. 15

Mishra Rabindrakumar, Economic Development in India, AVON Publication, New Delhi, 1st Edition, 2013, Pp-110

S.S. Sisodia (1995), Cooperative Banks in India, New century Publication, New Delhi, First Edition, Pp-42-43

Avadhani V.A. (2008), Marketing of Financial Services, Himalaya Publications House, Mumbai, Pp-642-649

Mishra & Puri (2013), Indian Economy, Himalaya Publishing House, Pp-745

Chakrabarti Rajesh (2009), *'The Financial Sector in India-Emerging Issues'*, Oxford Publications, Pp-154-177

Sundaram V. (2009), *'Banking Development'*, Alfa Publication, New Delhi, Pp-27-33

Kaptan S.S., (2005), New Concepts in Banking, Sarup & Sons Publications, New Delhi, Pp-47

Sarma Naina (2007), Banking and Social Change in India: The early Decades, Aalekh Publishers, Jaipur

Amit Barak (2010), Cooperative banks in India, New century Publication, New Delhi, First Edition, Pp-42-43

Sriram Revathy 2013, Core Banking Solution: Evaluation of Security and Controls, PHI Learning Private Limited, New Delhi,

Morvanchikar R.S. (1993), 'History of Maharashtra', First Edition, Pratima Publications, Pune, Pp-172

Pragati for NET/SET, Paper 2 & 3, *'E-banking'*, Pragati Publications, Pune, Pp-7.51

Rodrigues C.P., Joshi S.V, Khan Azhar, *'Indian Banking System,'* Excellent Publishing House, New Delhi, pp-207-213

Vashistha,v.k (1997), *'Indian Economy and Regional development'*, Pratiksha Publications, Jaipur, pp-207

P.C. Pardeshi, 'Public Sector', Business Finance, First Edition, June 2003, Nirali Publication,

Avadhani, V.A. (2010), 'Marketing of Financial Services' Himalaya Publications House, New Delhi, Pp-642-649

Deshpande V.S. (2013), Developmental Strategies in India, Editorial, 'Status of Human Development', , Vidya Prakashan, Nagpur, pp-123-124

Agrawal Meenu, *'Regional Rural Banks in India'*, First Edition 2009, New Century Publications, New Delhi

2. Journals/Articles

Yashwantha Dongre (2011), *'Rural reconstruction through co-operative resurgence'*, Editorial, G.V. Joshi, P.A. Rego, Sinam M., 'Banking for Rural Development in India', Bangalore University, Published by Macdonald & Evans, Pp-147-156

Trehan, Ruchi, Soni Niti & Sharma Arti, *'Indian Banking moving towards better Tomorrow'*, Editorial, R.K. Uppal, Innovations in Banking, Mahamaya Publications, page-48

Kulwant Singh Pathania and Mamta Sharma, *'Adoption of Banking Technologies'*, Indian Journal of Commerce, July-Sept., 2010, Vol. 63, Number. 3.

Editorial, *'Risk/Opportunities in E-banking services'*, IRJCM, ISSN-2277-5838, Vol-1, No-1, Feb., 2014, Pp-110-113

Ashwinikumar Bhalla, *'Financial services,'* editorial: R.K. Uppal, Indian Banking Industry in 2020, Mahamaya Publishing house,Pp-266-276

Pravinkumar Tayal & Sugan C. Jain, *'Financial Reporting of Banking Companies in India- an Evolutionary stage'*, Editorial- Dangwal R.C.& Kashmir Singh, New trends in Finance, Pp-255

Kundi and Shah, 2009, *'Indian Banking in Globalised Era'*, Indian banking moving towards better tomorrow, Editorial, R.K.Uppal ,Pp-5

Ganesan, S., (2009), E-banking: Opportunities and Challenges, Editorial-R.K. Uppal, 'Mahamaya Publications, New Delhi, Pp-37

Uppal R.K., Jatana Rimpi, (2009), Editorial, 'E-banking: Opportunities and Challenges', Mahamaya Publications, New Delhi, Pp-6

Maheshwari V. & Govindrajan K. (2009), *'Modern Banking Technologies'*, Southern Economist, Vol-48, No-16, Dec., 2009

Acharya & Shankar, 'Macro *Economic Management in the 90s'*, Economic & Political Weekly, 2002, Vol-37, No-16, Pp-15-38

S. Sanmuga Pria, (2009), E-banking: opportunities and challenges, Editorial R.K.Uppal and Rimpi Jatana, Mahamaya Publishing House, New Delhi, First Edition, Pp-49-53

Joshi Shrinivas, Banking Sector Towards Global Competition, Yojana, March-2009, Pp-26 -29

Puja Arora, (2009), E-banking: Opportunities and Challenges, Editorial R.K.Uppal and Rimpi Jatana, Mahamaya Publishing House, New Delhi

Keyur Nayak (2009), Retail Banking In India, *'Indian Banking Sector: Its Efficiency'*, New Delhi, Editorial R.K. Uppal, Pp-270-283

Biswas Nigamananda, *'Biometric ATM: Boon to Indian Rural Bank Customers'*, Southern Economist, ISSN-0038-4046, Vol-48, No-19, Feb-2010, Pp-29

Kaur Gian, (2011), New Trends in Finance, *'Risk, Efficiency & Return of PSBs and Private Banks in India'*, Editorial, Pravin Kumar Toyal, Sugan Jain, RBSA Publishers, Pp-256-272

H. Rajeshwari, (2011) Banking sector reform in India: A critical evaluation, Editorial: R.K.Uppal, editorial, Adhyayan publication, pp- 87-99

Gupta, O.P. and Poonam Nagpal (2011), Banking Sector Reform, '*Banking Sector Reform in India in the Phase of Globalisation*', Uppal, R.K. editorial, Mahamaya Publishing House, New Delhi, Pp- 76-86

V.S. Deshpande (2013), Developmental Strategies in India, *Status of Human Development*', Editorial-Vidya Prakashan, Nagpur, Pp-123

Chetia Dilip Kumar, Indian Journal of Commerce, '*Banking Infrastructure in North-East India*', Vol-61, No-03, July-Sept-2008, Pp-49

Goyal Ritu & Kaur Rajinder, Indian Journal of Commerce, '*Performance of New Private Sector Banks in India*', Vol-61, No-03, July-Sept-2008, Pp-1-5

Ram Mohan T.T., Indian Journal of Commerce, '*Performance and Development of Indian Banking*', Vol-63, No-01, Jan-March-2010, Pp-21-25

Syal Ginni & Gulati Sonu (2011), Indian Banking Industry in 2020, Editor-R.K.Uppal, an article on '*Indian Banking: Role of Financial Growth*', Mahamaya Publishing House, New Delhi.

Gandatra Navdeepkumar & Rama (2011), 'Banking Sector Reforms: A fresh Outlook', Editor-R.K.Uppal, an article on '*Competition in Indian Banking Sector-Issues and Strategies in Global Scenario*', Mahamaya Publishing House, New Delhi, Pp-125-128

Kumar Navdeep (2011), Indian Banking Industry in 2020, Editor-R.K.Uppal, an article on '*FDI in Indian Banking Sector*', Mahamaya Publishing House, New Delhi, Pp-158-167

John H. Dunning, Elsevier, '*Trade And Foreign Direct Investment*', Reserve Bank of India, Occasional Papers, Globalization, Vol-20, No-2, Monsoon-1999, Pp-339-340

Herbst '*Trade And Foreign Direct Investment*', RBI, Occasional Papers, Globalization, Vol-20, No-2, Monsoon-2001, Pp-207-208

Bhasin T.M., 2001, '*E-Commerce in Indian Banking*', IBA Bulletin, Vol-XXIII, No. 4-5

Reddy Y.V., '*Asian Perspective on Growth: Outlook for India*', RBI Bulletin-2006, Pp-11

Uppal R.K. and Kaur Rimpi (2007), Indian banking in globalised Era, Editorial-Mahamaya Publishing House, pp-2

Janardhanan V.K., '*Relevance of Service Sector Growth in India*', Southern Economist, Vol-47, No-14, Nov., 2008

Sharma Arti & Kaur Navneet (2009), Indian Banking sector: Its Efficiency, '*Indian Banking Challenges in Liberalized Era*', New Century Publication, New Delhi, Pp-195-206

Bimal Anjum, Sofat Rajni, Sridhar Rajan (2011), 'Indian banking industry in 2020, '*Impact of Globalization on Indian Banking*', Editorial: R.K.Uppal, Mahamaya Publishing House, Pp-247

Bhalla Ashwani Kumar (2011), Indian Banking Industry in 2020, '*Indian Financial Services*', R.K.Uppal, Editorial, ,Mahamaya Publishing House, Page No. 266-276

Prakash Garewal & Nandini Garewal (2013), Banking sector Reform: A fresh Outlook, Editor-R.K. Uppal, Adhyayan publication, Pp- 76-86

Takle Dinkar, '*Challenges in Banking Sector After Globalization*', Arthasanvad, July-Sept., 2014, Vol-38, No-2, Pp-204-209

Ruchi Trehan, Niti Soni, Arti Verma, Indian Banking Moving towards Better Tomorrow, '*Innovations in Banking*', R.K. Uppal, Editorial, Mahamaya publishing house, New Delhi, 2009, pp-43-47

R.K.Uppal (2012), editorial, Indian Banking Industry in 2020, '*Globalization*', Mahamaya Publishing house, Pp-19

Uppal R.K & Rimpi Kaur (2007), 'Indian Banking in Globalised Era: Moving Towards Better Tomorrow', Editoriral, Mahamaya Publishing House, New Delhi, Pp-01

Jayalakshmi. S. and Asok. A., '*WTO and Indian banking sector: An Overview*', Southern Economist, vol-47, No-15, Dec., 2008

Patel Ranjana (2009), Service Sector in India, '*Service Sector in India: Growth & Potential*', Editor-Shyam Mohan Dwivedi & Hridyanarayan Mishra, Adhyayan Publications, Jaipur, Pp-46-51

Maheswari V. & Govingrajan K. (2009), '*Modern Banking Technologies*', Southern Economist, Vol-48, No-16, Dec., 2009

Selvaraju R. & Vasanthi G., *Marketing Mix Strategy of Banking Services*, Southern Economist, Vol-47, No-20, Feb-2009

Shyam Mohan Dwivedi & Hridyanarayan Mishra (2011), Service Sector in India, '*Role of IT & Internet in Service Sector*', Editor-Shyam Mohan Dwivedi & Hridyanarayan Mishra, Adhyayan Publications, Jaipur, Pp-127-133

Gurpreet Kaur, Niti Soni, Arti Verma (2011), Indian Banking Moving Towards Better Tomorrow, '*Banking with Technology*', Editorial, R.K. Uppal, Mahamaya Publishing House, New Delhi, 2009, Pp-54

R.P. Gupta (2003), 'Dynamics of Banking Technology', Journal of Internet Banking and Commerce, Vol-3, No-2, June 2003,

Goyal B.B. & Kumar Nitesh (2007), Indian Banking Industry in 2020, '*Globalisation: a Paradigm Shift in Indian Banking System*', Mahamaya Publishing House, New Delhi, Editor-R.K. Uppal, Pp-138

Ashwini Gupta (2009), Editorial R.K.Uppal and Rimpi Jatana, E-Banking: Opportunities and Challenges, New Century Publication, New Delhi, Pp-

Rainy Sofat, Amarpreet Singh and Inderpreet Kaur(2009), Indian Banking Moving Towards Better Tomorrow, '*Indian Banking Challenges in Liberalized Era*', Editorial, R.K. Uppal, Pp-175-194

Sathiya & Jay kumar (2009), '*E-banking services*', Southern Economist, Vol-48, No-8, August-2009

S. Valli Devasena and M. Gurupandi (2010), '*Service Quality Analysis of Banks*', Indian Journal of Commerce, Vol-63, No-01, Jan-March-2010, Pp-21-25

Niti Soni, Arti Verma, '*Innovations in banking*', Indian Banking: Moving Towards Better Tomorrow, Editorial, R.K.Uppal, RuchiTrehan, , Mahamaya Publication, New Delhi, pp-51

Pravinkumar Goyal & Sugan C. Jain, '*Financial Reporting of Banking Companies in India- an Evolutionary stage*', Editorial- Dangwal R.C.& Kashmira Singh, New trends in Finance, , Page no. 255

Karunaiathal, '*Performance of Private Sector Banks in Erode District*', Banking, Micro Finance and SHGs (Self Help Groups) in India, New Century Publication, First Edition, July 2009, New Delhi.

Kaur Rimpi, Soni Niti, '*Banking in Globalized Era*', editorial: R.K.Uppal, Indian banking industry in 2020, Mahamaya Publishing house, pp-:111-114

Navdeep Kumar, '*FDI in Indian Banking Sector*', editorial: R.K.Uppal, Indian Banking Industry in 2020, Mahamaya Publishing house, pp-158-167

Nigamananda Biswas: Southern Economist, Banking sector in India: Challenges ahead, Vol. 48, No- 14, Nov.-2009

Gupta, O.P. and Poonam Nagpal, Role of IT and Internet in service sector, Uppal, R.K. editorial, Adhyayan publication, pp- 32-36

Editorial: G.V.Joshi, P.A.Rego, Sinam M., 'Banking for rural development in India', Bangalore University, pp-147-156

Indian banking moving towards better tomorrow, R.K. Uppal, Editorial, Innovations in

Prakash Garewal and Nandini Garewal, Banking sector Reform: A fresh outlook (2013) , R.K. Uppal, editorial, Adhyayan publication, pp- 76-86

Indian banking moving towards better tomorrow2011, R.K.Uppal, Editorial, banking with technology, gurpreetkaur, nitisoni, artiverma, Mahamaya publishing house, New Delhi, 2009, pp-54-55

Indian banking Industry in 2020, R.K.Uppal, Editorial, Financial services, Ashwani Kumar Bhalla, ,Mahamaya Publishing House, Page No. 266-276

Arti Sharma, Navgeet Kaur, Indian banking sector: its efficiency, Indian banking moving towards better tomorrow, editorial R.K.Uppal, pp-195-206

Kumbhar V.M., Arthasanvad, Dec., 2008, Vol-32, No-3, Pp-214-222

JIBC, Editorial, December 2009, Vol. 14, No. 3, Pp-2

3. Newspapers /News channels

M. Narendra, MD, BOI, Chennai, Chairmen's speech, on 8/06/2013, published in The Economic times on 1st July, 2014

Iyer V.R., BOI, Chairperson's speech, '*17th Annual General Meeting of shareholders at Mumbai*', 29th June 2013, published in The Economic times on 1st July, 2013

Bhatt Sanjeev (1988), '*Bank Marketing*', An article in The Economic Times, dated 1st Sept., 1988

Jack Ewing, New York Times News Service, '*Bank Resists Pressure to Scale Back Global Ambition*', The Economics Times, Page 7, Dated 31st May., 1992

Bhagwat Ashwini, An article on '*Security of Cards*', in Daily Loksatta, dated 19th Nov., 2011, Pp-6

Ashish Thakur, '*Development-Qualitative or Quatitative*', Loksatta-Arthbramha, No-2, 2015-16, Pp-74

Vasant Desai, An Article in Daily Sakal, '*Central Banking & Economic Development*', dated 24th July, 2006

Thakur Vishwas, (Chairman-Vishwas Cooperative Bank limited, Nashik), an article, '*Dynamic changes in banking sector*', in Daily Deshdoot, supplement of Banking Special, dated 20th Feb., 2015, Pp-1

ABP News, 27th August, 2015, Time 7.35Pm

Daily Lokmat, dated 28th August, 2015

The Economic Times, '*Technology, Not Coercion for Banks*', 27th June 2013, Pp-10

4. Ph.D. Thesis

Vijay Maruti Kumbhar, 'An empirical study of Alternative Banking and its impact on customers' satisfaction: a case study of Public and Private sector banks in Satara city', a thesis submitted to Shivaji University, Kolhapur for the degree of Ph.D. in economics, December 2010

Joshua a. J., 'Adoption of Technology-Enabled Banking Self-services: Antecedents and Consequences', Thesis submitted to Cochin University of Science and Technology, for the award of the degree of Doctor of philosophy, Kochi-682 022, Kerala, *August 2009*

Buracom Khemanij (2003), The Relationship between Service Quality and Customer satisfaction in the Formation of Customer Loyalty: Theoretical Adaptation and Practical Implications for Management, Ph. D. thesis submitted to International Graduate School of Management Faculty of Business and Management, University of South Australia, Sept, 2003

Fang He, (2009), Decision Factors For The Adoption Of E-Finance And Other E-Commerce Activities, A Dissertation Submitted in Partial Fulfillment of the Requirements for the Doctor of Philosophy in Business Administration, Department of Management In the Graduate School Southern Illinois University Carbondale May, 2009

Nair. Raman V., (2003), Marketing of Financial Services by Commercial Banks in Kerala; A Case Study of &ate Bank of Travancore, Ph. D. Thesis submitted to Faculty of Management Studies, Mahatma Gandhi University , Kottayam (Kerala),

Nam Sungjip (2008), The Impact of Culture on the Framework of Customer Value, Customer Satisfaction and Customer Loyalty, Submitted in partial fulfillment of the Requirements For the degree of Doctorate of Business Administration, Golden Gate University, 2008

George,J G. (2009), Assessing SERVQUAL and the Automotive Service Quality Model: A Comparative Study, Dissertation Submitted to North Central University Graduate Faculty of the School of Business and Technology Management in Partial Fulfillment of the Requirements for the Degree of Ph.D., 2009

Khanh Van La (2005), Customer Loyalty in Web-based Retailing, A thesis submitted in fulfilment of the requirements for the degree of Doctor of Philosophy, School of Management, RMIT University

Ching-Wen Hsu (2007), The Relationship Among Service Quality, Customer Satisfaction and Behavioral Intension: A Empirical Study of Online Shopping, Master Thesis Submitted to National Change Kung University, January 2007,

5. Reports

Economic Survey, 2013-14, Technological Banks in India, '*Financial Intermediation and Markets*', Pp-110-111

Bimil Jalan, '*Strengthening Indian Banking and Finance; Progress and Prospects*', Bank Economist Conference, Mumbai, RBI Bulletin, 2002

Reports of RBI on Basel Policy

Reports of RBI on Small banks

RBI (1998), '*Report of the Committee on Banking Sector Reform*', Narsimhan Committee, Mumbai.

Rangarajan C., (1997), Governor's Speech, RBI Bulleting, Pp-51

Report on Trend and Progress of Banking in India, 2008-2009, Pp-124

Basel Committee on Banking Supervision, (2010), '*Principles for enhancing Corporate Governance*', Basel: Bank of International Settlements.

State Planning Commission, 12th Plan Vol. II Pp-11

RBI Report on payment and settlement system, Sept., 2012

Economic Survey of Maharashtra, 2013-14

Report on Banking Ombudsman Scheme of India, 2013-14

HRD-Maharashtra 2006-07

Statistical Data of Nashik District 2012-13

Report on Nashik District Census 1991 to 2011

Education Department, Nasik District, 2013-14

Nashik District Census Report-2011, page 54

Nasik District Gazetter, 2014

C. Rangrajan, 'RBI-Reports on Trends and Progress of Banking in India, 2013

Kelkar Kaustubh, An article in Daily Lokmat dated 16th Sept., 2010

Editorial, '*Co-operative banking in India,*' The Economic Times, 24th March, 2011 Pp-6

6. Websites

Aggarwal, 2002, E-Banking for Comprehensive Democracy; An Indian Discernment, www.JIBC.Com/e-banking 2002

www.internetworldstats.com

www.rbi.org.in

www.spc.tn.gov.in/tenthplan

www.cooperative_banking.com

www.spc.tn.gov.in/tenthplan

Http://Www.Mit.Gov.In/Eg/Home.Asp MIT 2003, Official Website of MIT, GoI,

www.cooperatives-nashik.ac.in

http://www.nashik.nic.in

www.nashikdistrictgazetter.com

www.planningcommission.nic.in

www.banking_ombudsman.com